"Jesus was a game-changer ~~...~~ rs, but the lines connecting his death ~~and resurrection to~~ ~~...~~ :s, and forms of belonging were anything but sharp, straight, or self-evident. The New Testament documents their attempts at drawing those lines in real time and in response to unforeseen challenges. Spencer is the consummate eavesdropper on their conversations, providing commentary that enables readers to hear more clearly voices that have been muffled or distorted in the intervening centuries."

—**Patrick Gray**, Rhodes College

"Taking seriously the different genres and the occasional nature of the New Testament writings, Spencer brings the debates of these authors and their communities alive for contemporary readers. With his characteristic engaging style, Spencer takes readers on a journey into the diverse world of the earliest Jesus-followers and helps us see the ways in which their debates, questions, and emotions are not so different from our own."

—**Alicia D. Myers**, Campbell University Divinity School

"Studying the New Testament can feel like an excursion in a strange land. Spencer provides an accessible and clarifying guide to the ideas that shaped and were reshaped by the New Testament. Most helpfully, these ideas are not simple binaries but complex tensions befitting the difficult and vital work the earliest followers of Jesus took up. This book is an ideal companion for those students seeking to understand anew both the historical significance and the contemporary significance of these important texts."

—**Eric D. Barreto**, Princeton Theological Seminary

"My students, especially students who are part of faith communities, tend to struggle with the humanness of the New Testament books. Spencer's *Seven Challenges* offers these students an invitation to grapple with the historical and cultural situatedness of the New Testament, understand why different books give different perspectives on key questions, and appreciate the New Testament as a record of the experiences of first-century Christians. This book will be an excellent resource for anyone who has wondered how to read the New Testament in its ancient context and how to hear its messages in our modern context."

—**Caryn A. Reeder**, Westmont College

"With engaging and accessible style, Spencer provides an excellent introduction to seven interrelated challenges that have confronted Christians over the centuries. Through bringing New Testament texts into conversation with each other and with an eye to the cognitive and emotional upheaval early Christians likely experienced, Spencer provides an honest account of tensions within Christianity. This book does not seek to resolve these tensions but allows early Christian faith, love, and hope to speak into them."

—**Katherine M. Hockey**, University of Aberdeen

"A creative and enlightening strategy for explaining some key trajectories in biblical thought. By treating the New Testament books as works-in-progress, Spencer explores how different authors deal with the 'big ideas' that engaged many people at the time. These authors do so in diverse and potentially contradictory ways that, Spencer demonstrates, contribute to the richness of Christian thought. This is a book that illuminates important aspects of what the New Testament authors wanted to convey while at the same time expanding our appreciation for the relevance of scriptural witness."

—**Mark Allan Powell**, Trinity Lutheran Seminary (retired)

"Various dimensions of New Testament faith in Jesus as Messiah, Lord, and Savior are in creative tension—such as the tension between the new and the old, between the cross as victory and as humiliation, between wholeness in Christ and ongoing suffering, and between the hope of Jesus's imminent return and the reality of the delay of the *parousia*. In this wonderfully readable book, Scott Spencer shows how the New Testament is shaped by and responds to seven creative and productive tensions. In the process, he expertly illuminates the big ideas of New Testament faith. Highly recommended!"

—**Paul Trebilco**, University of Otago, Dunedin, New Zealand

SEVEN CHALLENGES THAT SHAPED the NEW TESTAMENT

SEVEN CHALLENGES THAT SHAPED the NEW TESTAMENT

UNDERSTANDING the INHERENT TENSIONS of EARLY CHRISTIAN FAITH

F. SCOTT SPENCER

Baker Academic
a division of Baker Publishing Group
Grand Rapids, Michigan

© 2024 by F. Scott Spencer

Published by Baker Academic
a division of Baker Publishing Group
Grand Rapids, Michigan
BakerAcademic.com

Printed in the United States of America

Library of Congress Cataloging-in-Publication Data
Names: Spencer, F. Scott (Franklin Scott), author.
Title: Seven challenges that shaped the New Testament : understanding the inherent tensions of early
    Christian faith / F. Scott Spencer.
Description: Grand Rapids, Michigan : Baker Academic, a division of Baker Publishing Group, [2024] |
    Includes bibliographical references and index.
Identifiers: LCCN 2023044327 | ISBN 9781540966346 (paperback) | ISBN 9781540967862 (casebound)
    | ISBN 9781493446384 (ebook) | ISBN 9781493446391 (pdf)
Subjects: LCSH: Jesus Christ—Person and office—Biblical teaching | Bible. Gospels. | Bible. New
    Testament.
Classification: LCC BT203 .S5163 2024 | DDC 232—dc23/eng/20231130
LC record available at https://lccn.loc.gov/2023044327

Cover design by David Carlson, Studio Gearbox

Baker Publishing Group publications use paper produced from sustainable forestry practices and postconsumer waste whenever possible.

24   25   26   27   28   29   30   7   6   5   4   3   2   1

In memory of
Professor James ("Jimmy") D. G. Dunn

CONTENTS

Acknowledgments

While pursuing a second master's degree in theological studies in the early 1980s, I ran across a book by a rising British New Testament scholar named James D. G. Dunn, who had recently been appointed Professor of Divinity at Durham University in England. (He later became the Lightfoot Professor of Divinity there.) That book was titled *Unity and Diversity in the New Testament: An Inquiry into the Character of Earliest Christianity* and was published in 1977. It would not turn out to be Dunn's most celebrated work over the course of his long and distinguished career, which he actively pursued beyond his formal retirement up to his death in 2020 at the age of eighty. He became best known for his studies of Paul, especially what he called the "New Perspective." But *Unity and Diversity in the New Testament* had the most influence on my life.

It led me across the pond to pursue my doctorate at Durham University under Dunn's supervision. But more than that, it opened my eyes to the rich diversity of the New Testament writings. From my religious background, I had the unity part down pat: one Bible, one truth, one faith, one Lord. But my perspective was rather flat and formulaic. Worse, it was rigid and reductionist, preventing me from appreciating the luscious variety and thick texture of early Christian faith as it unfolds in the twenty-seven books of the New Testament.

My picture of Jesus was too thin and one-dimensional; it boiled down the multifaceted perspectives of a lively corpus of writings into a simple snapshot or a short Wikipedia profile (though Wikipedia wasn't around in the 1980s). Dunn's work helped me begin to flesh out my emaciated image of Jesus, more specifically to see how the various New Testament writers were working out—*writing out*—their dawning understandings of Jesus in dynamic, distinctive ways. I came to see the New Testament as a work in progress—or rather work*s* in progress.

To this day, I'm still working my way through these marvelous foundational works, to say nothing of working out my own fragile faith in conversation with these sacred texts. I have a long way to go and long ago gave up on finding all the answers. But I journey in hope with the New Testament writers as faithful pioneers in and through *their* struggles and challenges to "know Christ and the power of his resurrection and the sharing of his sufferings" (Phil. 3:10).

I dedicate this book to my Doktorvater, Jimmy Dunn (everyone called him Jimmy), in memory of him and his monumental (for me) *Unity and Diversity in the New Testament*. My exploration of seven challenges and tensions that shaped the New Testament writings is more modest than Jimmy's project and takes a somewhat different approach, as I explain in the preface. But Jimmy would have been fine with that. Though a strong defender of his viewpoints, he never forced me or anyone else into his mold. He (together with his wife, Meta) was unfailingly gracious to me and my family and supportive of my research interests, even when they weren't exactly his cup of tea.

Speaking of family, I couldn't make it without mine. My wife, Janet, and I married in our teens and will be celebrating our golden anniversary right about the time this book comes out in 2024. What a journey we've shared in all areas of life, including academic life. She was the real driving force in getting us to England for postgraduate study. As we were both trying to produce doctoral dissertations, our first daughter, Lauren, was born in Durham, England. Our second daughter, Meredith, came along as we were beginning our teaching careers in North Carolina. Both daughters have since married wonderful men and built their own successful lives. Granddaughter Madeline (Maddie) popped into our lives to steal the show in 2022. She will soon share the spotlight with a little brother, due to make his debut between the time I'm penning these words and the time of their publication. One of these due dates is markedly more important than the other. As much as I appreciate the love, joy, and support my family members provide me, I also appreciate how they help me keep my work in perspective. I, like many authors, may occasionally refer to a book I'm writing as my "baby." I, like many authors, exaggerate my own importance.

I'm grateful, too, for the amazing staff at Baker Academic. It's been a pleasure to work again with senior acquisitions editor Bryan Dyer and associate editor Melisa Blok, both consummate professionals. I'm also indebted this time around to Dustyn Keepers for her stellar help with images and illustrations and to Nate

Johnson for his sharp editorial comments. I also commend the valuable work of Baker's top-notch production and marketing team.

Finally, a couple of nuts-and-bolts matters. Sources in footnotes are cited in abbreviated form; full bibliographic information is provided at the back of the book. Unless otherwise noted, I quote from the New Revised Standard Version (NRSV) of the Bible.

Preface

What and What Not to Expect from This Book

I know what you're thinking about a book brazenly titled *Seven Challenges That Shaped the New Testament*. In her typically incisive way, my wife raised the issue from the outset of the project: "Why [my love] are you claiming *seven* formative challenges, *these seven* in particular? Did the happy septet just happen to work out?" She knows full well seven's honored place as the biblical number of complete perfection, but she wasn't buying my proposed book as the "perfect" distillation of factors that shaped the New Testament writings. As well she shouldn't!

There's nothing magical about "*Seven* Challenges," though I confess I like the number's biblical resonance and nice association with Warren Carter's stellar *Seven Events That Shaped the New Testament World*, which got me thinking about a companion work concentrating more on ideas than events. But I don't take the number that seriously. I love the cheeky tweak in the neuropsychologist Lisa Feldman Barrett's book *Seven and a Half Lessons about the Brain* (it has nothing to do with the Bible). *Seven and a half*—wish I'd thought of that!

I do not claim that the seven challenges I discuss cover all elements that shaped the New Testament or even that these are necessarily the *top* seven. I easily imagine my scholar friends saying, "You missed or slighted a very important issue." Or "You're making too much of challenge 3 or 5." I'd be happy if readers took the book seriously enough to debate it. I offer a suggestive rather than definitive set of challenges. But I do contend that the seven areas I address—historical, moral, political, material, social, perceptual, and temporal—are significant enough to demand attention.

Though I focus on important "big ideas," that is no guarantee that I've un-packed them adequately. Again, there's room for debate. I make no claim to ex-haustive coverage in this modest-sized volume designed for introductory college and seminary courses and a general readership. Though not a huge corpus, the New Testament comprises a library of twenty-seven writings. That's been plenty to keep scholars, preachers, teachers, and Christian readers going for centuries, with no end in sight (though biblical literacy is in sharp decline). I offer a sam-pling of New Testament texts to illustrate the challenges I propose. But I try to present a substantial sampler (more like a two-pound box of chocolates than a matchbox teaser) representing the major New Testament genres—narrative, letter, apocalypse—and all New Testament books. Yet I do not give them equal treatment (the books vary in size) and may well overplay some texts and under-play others.[1]

My main purpose is to *expose tensions* within and among New Testament writ-ings on critical matters related to believing in and following Jesus as Lord and Messiah/Christ (Acts 2:36). These writings became the foundational scriptures for the emerging "Christian" religion in its Jewish matrix. The works themselves evidence the forming/shaping process of Christ-centered faith and practice a generation or two after Jesus's death. The world-shattering events of Jesus's career took time for New Testament writers to sort out. Indeed, to a great extent they *wrote out* their questions and concerns in the books (*biblia*) that came to make up the New Testament canon.

Given their "occasional" nature—having been composed for particular audi-ences at particular times, not for everyone everywhere for all time[2]—the New Testament writings address issues, big and small, from various angles. While cohering around the core confession "Jesus is Lord" (1 Cor. 12:3), these writ-ings apply and adapt this confession in distinctive, diverse ways, as delineated in James D. G. Dunn's stimulating study *Unity and Diversity in the New Testament.*[3] Dunn takes a genealogical approach, tracing developments from the historical

1. A possible student assignment could be to evaluate my treatment of, say, Paul's approach to one or more "challenges" in 1 Corinthians. Is it a "fair" treatment or not? How does it fit with Paul's perspectives in other letters or with other New Testament approaches to the problem?

2. The New Testament letters and the book of Revelation (which includes embedded letters to seven congregations) are the most obviously "occasional" correspondences. Yet we may also presume target audiences for the Gospel and Acts narratives. This is not to deny that all these writings circulated beyond their original recipients. But the writers had no idea that their documents would later be considered sacred Scripture on par with the Hebrew Bible/Old Testament.

3. See my acknowledgments for further discussion of Dunn's volume, which was published in three editions (1977–2006) and is still in print.

Jesus to early second-century Christianity. Though I take account of evolving understandings about Christ in the New Testament, I'm less confident about plotting precise historical trajectories. Ideas are as likely to ebb and eddy as flow forward. Plus, dating ancient New Testament documents is no exact science, especially since no original "autographs" have survived. My approach, then, is more canonical and genre-based than genealogical. I aim to expose nuances, variations, and tensions within and among different New Testament documents. Accordingly, I read the New Testament less as a strict evolution and resolution of doctrines than an ongoing negotiation of tensions between basic tenets and apparent countervailing realities.

Does this swirl of ideas not then lead to convolution? Not at all. The New Testament writers were eternal optimists, not cynical nihilists. But they were also realists, not fantasists. They believed with all their hearts and minds that Jesus was God's hope for the world while acknowledging that the ongoing world in which they lived—even after Jesus's resurrection and ascension—was still in bad shape. They continued to suffer and struggle, sometimes *because of* their faith. And they were not afraid or ashamed to confess their consternation—but not at the expense of their tenacious hope! "Hoping against hope" at times (Rom. 4:18), yes, but never giving up hope.

Still, another concern arises: Is "tension" not just a waffle way of saying "contradiction" without offending New Testament devotees? Partly, perhaps (to waffle further). But "tension" implies stretching without breaking, whereas "contradiction" makes a clean break between opposing ideas. Again, the New Testament writers remain intent on keeping the faith, not breaking it, however much it might be stretched and however many might defect (see challenge 2). They vigorously argue their views against their opponents with intellectual and rhetorical sophistication that reflects well-reasoned, deeply felt beliefs. Among other tools, they trade in the noble theological and philosophical tradition of paradox (see challenge 3), which attempts to hold apparent contradictory notions together—*in tension*!

For our part, it may be useful to relax and even revel a bit in this tension. Two modern thinkers from different backgrounds and perspectives speak to this. First, the nineteenth-century New England transcendentalist Ralph Waldo Emerson:

> A foolish consistency is the hobgoblin of little minds, adored by little statesmen and philosophers and divines. With consistency a great soul has simply nothing to do. He may as well concern himself with his shadow on the wall. Speak what you think now in hard words, and tomorrow speak what tomorrow thinks in hard words

again, *though it contradict everything you said to-day.*—"Ah, so you shall be sure to be misunderstood."—Is it so bad, then, to be misunderstood? Pythagoras was misunderstood, and Socrates, and Jesus, and Luther, and Copernicus, and Galileo, and Newton, and every pure and wise spirit that ever took flesh. To be great is to be misunderstood.[4]

I will have more to say about "shadows on the wall" (on Plato's cave wall, that is) in challenge 6. Suffice it to say now that Jesus, Paul, and company were no shadow boxers. Moreover, they had no interest in "foolish" games, consistent or otherwise. Paul's supposed playing the "fool" in his Corinthian correspondence is pure sarcasm against his truly foolish rivals, as he sees them (1 Cor. 1:18–30; 2 Cor. 11:16–29). And though they sought to reveal and clarify the truth, Jesus and the New Testament writers were under no illusions about always being understood. Misunderstanding was part of the deal, which frustrated them but did not defeat them. "Do you not yet understand?" (Mark 8:21) was almost a mantra for Jesus concerning his disciples. In Emerson's terms, misunderstanding was part of the price of Jesus's greatness.

Second, consider the twentieth-century Algerian-French existentialist Albert Camus: "But it is bad to stop, hard to be satisfied with a single way of seeing, to go without contradiction, perhaps the most subtle of all spiritual forces. The preceding merely defines a way of thinking. But the point is to live."[5] The incalculable global impact of Jesus and those who wrote about him in the New Testament attests to their status as substantial (not subtle!) "spiritual forces." More importantly, their multifocal "way of seeing" through the Christ-lens is for the sake of ethics, not optics. "The point is to *live*" a loving, joyful, hopeful, fruitful life, whatever the circumstances. Paul sums it up well: "For to me, living is Christ" (Phil. 1:21; cf. 4:10–14).

---

4. Emerson, "Self-Reliance" (emphasis added).
5. Camus, *Myth*, 65.

Abbreviations

General

BCE	before the Common Era	lit.	literally
CE	Common Era	n.	note
cf.	confer, compare	rev.	revised
ed(s).	editor(s), edition	vol.	volume
e.g.	*exempli gratia*, for example	vv.	verses
et al.	*et alia*, and others		

Bible Versions

CEB	Common English Bible	NIV	New International Version
KJV	King James Version	NLT	New Living Translation
LXX	Septuagint/Greek Old Testament	NRSV	New Revised Standard Version
NAB	New American Bible	NRSVue	New Revised Standard Version,
NASB	New American Standard Bible		updated edition
NETS	New English Translation of the Septuagint	RSV	Revised Standard Version

Old Testament

Gen.	Genesis	1 Kings	1 Kings
Exod.	Exodus	2 Kings	2 Kings
Lev.	Leviticus	1 Chron.	1 Chronicles
Num.	Numbers	2 Chron.	2 Chronicles
Deut.	Deuteronomy	Ezra	Ezra
Josh.	Joshua	Neh.	Nehemiah
Judg.	Judges	Esther	Esther
Ruth	Ruth	Job	Job
1 Sam.	1 Samuel	Ps(s).	Psalm(s)
2 Sam.	2 Samuel	Prov.	Proverbs

Eccles.	Ecclesiastes	Obad.	Obadiah
Song	Song of Songs	Jon.	Jonah
Isa.	Isaiah	Mic.	Micah
Jer.	Jeremiah	Nah.	Nahum
Lam.	Lamentations	Hab.	Habakkuk
Ezek.	Ezekiel	Zeph.	Zephaniah
Dan.	Daniel	Hag.	Haggai
Hosea	Hosea	Zech.	Zechariah
Joel	Joel	Mal.	Malachi
Amos	Amos		

New Testament

Matt.	Matthew	1 Tim.	1 Timothy
Mark	Mark	2 Tim.	2 Timothy
Luke	Luke	Titus	Titus
John	John	Philem.	Philemon
Acts	Acts	Heb.	Hebrews
Rom.	Romans	James	James
1 Cor.	1 Corinthians	1 Pet.	1 Peter
2 Cor.	2 Corinthians	2 Pet.	2 Peter
Gal.	Galatians	1 John	1 John
Eph.	Ephesians	2 John	2 John
Phil.	Philippians	3 John	3 John
Col.	Colossians	Jude	Jude
1 Thess.	1 Thessalonians	Rev.	Revelation
2 Thess.	2 Thessalonians		

Old Testament Apocrypha / Deuterocanonical Books

| 1 En. | 1 Enoch | Sir. (Ecclus.) | Sirach (Ecclesiasticus) |
| 1–4 Macc. | 1–4 Maccabees | Wis. | Wisdom (of Solomon) |

Dead Sea Scrolls

| 1QpHab | Pesher Habakkuk |

Secondary Sources

BDAG	Bauer, W., F. W. Danker, W. F. Arndt, and F. W. Gingrich. *Greek-English Lexicon of the New Testament and Other Early Christian Literature*. 3rd ed. Chicago: University of Chicago Press, 2000	*EuroJTh*	*European Journal of Theology*
		HTR	*Harvard Theological Review*
		JSNT	*Journal for the Study of the New Testament*
		NTL	New Testament Library
BTB	*Biblical Theology Bulletin*	*NTS*	*New Testament Studies*
CBQ	*Catholic Biblical Quarterly*	*Rev&Exp*	*Review & Expositor*

Prologue

Creative Tensions of Mind and Heart

The New Testament comprises a collection of twenty-seven documents written across several decades by multiple authors in different styles and genres. The contents of these "books" reflect a wide array of religious themes, concepts, and issues. Yet these writings also fit, more or less, under the big umbrella of "one body and one Spirit, . . . one Lord, one faith, one baptism" (Eph. 4:4–6; see also Heb. 6:1–2). They all bear witness to robust faith in Jesus as Lord, Messiah/Christ, and Savior. The authors all write primarily to strengthen the faith of fellow believers (confirmation) and secondarily to persuade religious seekers to follow Christ (evangelism).[1]

Although New Testament faith includes elements of spiritual and mystical encounter with Christ, it does not float in celestial cloud-space. Religious experience is forged in the social and historical events of its era—events large and small, momentous and momentary. The New Testament testifies to faith on the edge: the cutting edge of new perspectives and directives in light of the complex Christ-event; the jagged edge of defining and refining Christ-centered faith in the face of disputes and disappointments.

As Warren Carter's *Seven Events That Shaped the New Testament World* unpacks major formative events, this book centers on unraveling seven "big ideas"[2]

---

1. The expressed purpose for writing the Fourth Gospel may be read either "so that you may *come to* believe that Jesus is the Messiah, the Son of God" or "so that you may continue to believe that Jesus is the Messiah, the Son of God" (John 20:31).

2. Wiggins and McTighe, *Understanding by Design*, 5, 40–44, 65–78.

or tenets of faith in Jesus Christ that shaped the New Testament writings in the crucible of challenging events. Great crises birth great literature, like the war epics of Homer and Tolstoy or incisive novels responding to 9/11.[3] Likewise, the New Testament reflects not only peculiar habits and opinions of Jesus and his followers before and after his death but sweeping *worldviews* on matters of historical, moral, political, material, social, perceptual, and temporal importance.

Windows and Mirrors

In seeking to understand the worldviews of New Testament writings shaped by events on multiple levels—global, national, congregational, familial, individual—we face a first-order challenge: documents that are not primarily philosophical treatises, constitutional articles, or educational manuals but, rather, occasional narratives, letters, and vision-reports addressed to selected audiences about whom we have limited knowledge. In reading the New Testament today, we should humbly confess that our understanding is always partial and provisional; as Paul says, "We see through a glass darkly" (1 Cor. 13:12 KJV), or more accurately, "We see in a mirror, dimly. . . . [We] know only in part" (NRSV).

Whichever reading metaphor we choose—treating the text as a window through which we discover background information or as a mirror from which we see reflected images—we are confronted with an inconvenient truth. Windows provide limited viewpoints, and mirrors skew our perspectives with even slight shifts in angles. Further, if we are preoccupied with the world behind the text (looking through a window) and the world before the text (looking in a mirror), we can miss much of the text itself. Still, these limitations do not completely wreck the prospect of interpreting the intertwining historical, sociocultural, and ideological worlds within New Testament texts in creative tension with worlds outside the texts. As with any thoughtful literary product, the New Testament both shapes and is shaped by its environment.

A better picture of perceptive reading involves not peering through the foggy text-window to conjure some outlying mystery or preening before the text-mirror to confirm our preconceived notions but, rather, stepping *through the looking-glass* like Alice, entering the multifaceted text-worlds and engaging them in all their resonances and dissonances. Worldviews within and between eras inevitably collide and collude in various ways. We should thus expect to encounter

---

3. Among the works referenced in Haubner, "11 Novels about 9/11," see Hamid, *Reluctant Fundamentalist*; and Foer, *Extremely Loud and Incredibly Close*.

ideological ("big idea") tensions negotiated within and among the New Testament writings, not to mention strange notions challenging our customary vantage points.[4]

We might even claim that the authenticity of New Testament documents demands such tensions. The ancient legend of seventy scribes translating the Hebrew Bible into Greek, each independently producing an *identical* translation in a separate room, makes for a nice *incredible* story.[5] And so it would be if the four canonical Gospels were carbon-copy reports of Jesus's life or if Paul's letters to different congregations were the same basic newsletter with only the addresses changed. The

Pencil sketch from *Alice through the Looking-Glass* by Lewis Carroll

distinct textures of the New Testament texts attest to their realistic grappling with the challenges that dynamic faith in Christ confronted in real-world situations.

Sample Case: Blessed Are the Poor

Jesus's most famous "sermon" appears in two forms: Matthew's "Sermon on the Mount" (Matt. 5–7) and Luke's "Sermon on the Plain" (Luke 6:17–49). These are not transcripts of synagogue sermons but rather collections of Jesus's public teachings. Yet they have spawned countless sermons and lessons throughout Christian history, even as they influenced other New Testament writings, such as the letter of James, which is traditionally attributed to Jesus's brother.[6]

Both "sermon" versions open with Jesus's beatitudes regarding those who experience "blessed" or "happy" lives. The first statement spotlights "the poor": "Blessed are the poor in spirit, for theirs is the kingdom of heaven" (Matt. 5:3);

4. Lewis Carroll's "looking-glass" metaphor applies broadly to that which appears strange, dissonant, or topsy-turvy from the familiar order of things. For a political application of "a through-the-looking-glass feeling," see Applebaum, *Twilight of Democracy*, 138–39.

5. Carter, *Seven Events*, 24–34.

6. Hartin, *James*, 81–88; L. Johnson, *Writings of the New Testament*, 452–53.

"Blessed are you who are poor, for yours is the kingdom of God" (Luke 6:20). Notice that Matthew's Jesus qualifies the blessed poor in "spiritual" terms. Luke's Jesus counterpoints the benediction on the poor with a "woe to the rich" and speaks more directly to both groups ("you/your," 6:24). Further, different language characterizes the divine realms that the poor inherit and inhabit: Matthew uses "kingdom of *heaven*" while Luke uses "kingdom of *God*." However we interpret these distinctives (substantive, subtle, stylistic?), we must acknowledge *creative tensions* between these Gospel versions of Jesus's first beatitude.

Yet Matthew and Luke both select this saying of Jesus among many others and set it at the head of key teaching units. Why? The Gospel authors adapted and arranged traditions about Jesus into their own "orderly account[s]" (Luke 1:1, 3), just as preachers and teachers explain and apply Gospel texts in creative ways relevant to their audiences. The reported words of Jesus are living words that are not simply to be read and recited but to be reflected on and refitted to new contexts or "situations in life"[7]—including *poverty*. Matthew's "spiritualized" beatitude does not preclude a concern for "real" poverty, as evidenced later in Jesus's summary of his mission ("the poor have good news brought to them," Matt. 11:5; cf. Luke 7:22) and in his stunning call to an otherwise commendable rich man to sell all possessions "and give the money to the poor" (Matt. 19:23; cf. Luke 18:22).

We may assume, then, that poor-rich polarity was one challenge that shaped Matthew's and Luke's Gospels. This premise fits the broad profile of first-century Mediterranean society and New Testament congregations. The Greco-Roman world was highly stratified in a pyramid structure, with the top 1 percent perched at the peak and the bulk of the rest (90 percent) packed into the bottom levels under bare-bones conditions.[8] The early Christ communities, clustered mainly in urban centers, were similarly stratified. As Paul pegged believers in Corinth, "Not many of you were wise by human standards, not many were powerful, not many were of noble birth" (1 Cor. 1:26). While "not many" were well-bred and well-heeled, a privileged few *were*, which made for communal tensions, even in the core Christian practice of the Lord's Supper (11:17–34). James's advice also suggests underlying socioeconomic divisions: "Brothers and sisters who are poor should find satisfaction in their high status. Those who are wealthy should find satisfaction in their low status, because they will die off like wildflowers" (James 1:9–10 CEB; cf. 2:1–7; 5:1–6).

<hr>

7. German *Sitz im Leben* ("setting/situation in life"), a key feature of twentieth-century New Testament study known as "form criticism." See H. Carey, "Traditio-Historical Criticism."

8. See Downs, "Economics," 156–60; Friesen, "Poverty," 337–48.

Because the plight of the poor mattered so much to New Testament writers and affected so many, it was bound to generate impassioned responses. Think of the raging debates in our era about welfare programs, economic inequalities, and personal responsibilities—ranging from global UN assemblies to local school boards—fueled by religious and political beliefs. There's little new under the sun. Is poverty primarily a "spiritual" and "moral" problem or a "social" and "material" one? Do we side with Matthew's or Luke's Jesus—or are we missing the point(s)? At any rate, we can be sure "the poor" didn't randomly show up as character extras in the Gospel narratives; on a critical level, they shaped the Christ-centered message.

In sum, the literary products of Matthew, Luke, and other New Testament books allow us to infer formative situations that the Christ story challenges from various perspectives. In turn, however, continuing crises—like unmitigated suffering of the poor, including poor believers in Christ—also challenge the story's validity. How do the words, deeds, experiences, and events involving Jesus the Christ stand the test of time and withstand the pressure of persisting problems? The New Testament writings aim to negotiate these challenges and respond to them as much as reflect them.

To help us understand how persisting challenges shaped New Testament thought, we will consider two patterns of human experience—*cognitive dissonance* and *emotional upheaval*—that reflect creative tensions of mind and heart.

Cognitive Dissonance

In brief, the term "cognitive dissonance" describes a disturbed state of mind in the face of unexpected tension between core convictions (beliefs, ideas, values), on the one hand, and contradictory experiences or events, on the other hand. In formulaic terms: cognitive dissonance = core convictions + contrary situations that *do not add up* ($\neq$).

Social psychologist Leon Festinger pioneered the concept of cognitive dissonance, citing the example of "a cigarette smoker who believes that smoking is bad for his health . . . an opinion that is dissonant with the knowledge that he is continuing to smoke."[9] The pleasure of sucking vaporized nicotine into his lungs clashes with acknowledging (cognizing) the potential pain of cancer metastasizing from the lungs. Before symptoms develop, knowing the risks and pushing the

9. Festinger, Reicken, and Schachter, *When Prophecy Fails*, 25–26.

odds spark their own discomfort, begging for relief. Festinger posits three common ways people try to ease the dissonance of challenged cherish beliefs or practices: (1) change their convictions and actions, opinions and habits; (2) gather new data bolstering their original position and debunking counterinformation; (3) push the problem out of mind through denial, delay, diversion, or delusion—whatever it takes to restore equilibrium.[10] We do not like dissonance![11]

"Facts are stubborn things," as prosecutor (and later president) John Adams argued,[12] as are events and situations that do not care how we feel about them. They are what they are, and eventually they press long and hard enough against our contrary viewpoints to create crises of confidence. In turn, however, convictions can also be plenty stubborn and die hard.

The main research project of Festinger's team had nothing to do with tobacco but focused instead on a small apocalyptic sect based in Oak Park, Illinois, led by a woman named Dorothy Martin and a medical doctor named Charles Laughead.[13] Martin claimed to have received an extraterrestrial (ET) communiqué that the world would be hit with a cataclysmic tsunami on December 21, 1954, just before Christmas. But true believers need not fear because they would be rescued at Martin's house on December 17 by special celestial "Guardians" piloting flying saucers. When the "rapture" and "flood" dates came and went without incident, a remnant of the group—deep in the throes of cognitive dissonance—clung to their hopes and beliefs with various tweaks and provisos, including the theory that their alien pilots had in fact made test runs but were not quite ready to complete the rescue mission (safety first!). Persisting to Christmas Eve, a faithful few sang carols in Martin's backyard to herald the coming of their skycap saviors.[14] That's one way to mitigate dissonance—the delusional way.

What does this extreme example have to do with the formation of the New Testament? Let me be clear: I do not believe that Jesus or the New Testament writers were delusional. But the New Testament bears repeated witness to a core belief that Jesus would return to earth on a cloud one day to complete the restoration of God's kingdom (see Mark 13:24–27; Acts 1:9–11; 1 Thess. 4:16–17;

10. Festinger, Reicken, and Schachter, *When Prophecy Fails*, 26; cf. Aronson and Tavris, "Role of Cognitive Dissonance"; Berger and Zijderveld, *In Praise of Doubt*, 32–36; Tavris and Aronson, *Mistakes Were Made*, 15–54.

11. Especially dissonance that challenges "strong deeply held religious or political positions, or convictions that relate directly to their way of life." Berger and Zijderveld, *In Praise of Doubt*, 32.

12. McCullough, *John Adams*, 68.

13. Referred to by the pseudonyms Marian Keech and Dr. Timothy Armstrong in Festinger, Reicken, and Schachter, *When Prophecy Fails*. Festinger's team embedded in the sect for firsthand research.

14. See Beck, "Christmas."

Rev. 1:7; 14:14–16). Naturally, expectations of Jesus's "second coming" gave rise to questions of timing: "When will this be?" (Mark 13:4; cf. Luke 17:20). "Lord, is this the time when you will restore the kingdom?" (Acts 1:6).

Notably, the New Testament sets no specific dates for Jesus's return. God alone knows the schedule, and he's keeping it to himself (Acts 1:7). Not even Jesus or the angels know "about that day or hour" (Mark 13:32 NIV), a fact that self-appointed, pinpointing prognosticators of Jesus's reappearing blatantly ignore. Still, though advancing no fixed timetable, Jesus and his early followers seemed to anticipate his earthly return soon, preferably before too many believers died. "'The time promised by God has come at last!' [Jesus] announced. 'The Kingdom of God is near!'" (1:15 NLT). "The appointed time has grown short" (1 Cor. 7:29). "Surely I am coming soon" (Rev. 22:20; see also 1:3). The watchword is "Watch!" "Be ready!" (Matt. 24:36–44; Mark 13:32–37; 1 Thess. 5:1–7).

But time marches on. Troubles, including poverty, continue and compound. More and more believers in Christ die, and *still* Jesus has not returned to save his people. Hope delayed and deferred—a situation ripe for cognitive dissonance, which the New Testament acknowledges and negotiates in various ways. I will explore this issue in challenge 7. For now, I simply stress that the delay of the *parousia* (appearing/coming) was another key factor in shaping New Testament worldviews.

Significantly, anxious dissonance over issues such as persisting poverty and postponed *parousia* served as *productive challenges*, as *creative tensions*[15] for the New Testament writers, spurring them to refine, reformulate, stretch, and strengthen the fabric of faith in Christ and faithfulness to Christ. Luke Timothy Johnson confirms the formative role of cognitive dissonance: "These [New Testament] compositions emerge from a tension-filled process of human self-interpretation. . . . Believers found themselves in a state of cognitive dissonance that required resolution. . . . For the first believers there was an immediate and obvious dissonance concerning themselves—between their experience of divine power and their actual condition in the world."[16]

Johnson also pinpoints as a cause of "extreme" cognitive dissonance "the way Jesus died" on the cross as an apparently failed Lord and Messiah.[17] Further, the apostle Paul, the principal New Testament letter-writer, wrote out of a profound sense of dissonance over his traumatic transformation to a passionate devotee

15. A major theme in Palmer, *Healing*; see, e.g., 43–45, 71–80, 191–93.
16. L. Johnson, *New Testament*, 3, 21.
17. L. Johnson, *New Testament*, 22–23; cf. L. Johnson, *Writings of the New Testament*, 235.

of Christ after having been a zealous antagonist of Christ believers (Gal. 1:13). By Paul's own admission, his former virulent opposition to Christ made him "the least of the apostles, unfit to be called an apostle" (1 Cor. 15:9). His painful personal history marked him out "alone among the first Christians" as one who most "sharply experienced the cognitive dissonance between religious experience and symbolic world."[18] He wrote his way through this dissonance toward resolution.

In the "challenge" chapters to follow, I adduce in more detail the impact these and other cognitively dissonant issues had on the New Testament writings. I also explore emotional elements of this creative grappling with dissonance.

Emotional Upheaval

The full statement of John Adams's view of "facts" reads, "Facts are stubborn things, and whatever may be our wishes, our inclinations, or the dictums of our passions, they cannot alter the state of facts and evidence."[19] True, how we feel about facts does not change the facts; but it does affect what facts we pay attention to and how we perceive and process them. A tidal wave of recent emotion research has swept away the long-standing divide between reason and passion, cognition and emotion, thoughts and feelings.[20] Advanced studies in social psychology and neuropsychology have refined Aristotle's ancient insight: "The emotions are those things through which, by undergoing change, people come to differ in their [critical] judgments and which are accompanied by pain and pleasure." Understanding experiences of anger, for example, entails determining "what is their *state of mind* when people are angry and against *whom* are they angry and for what sorts of *reasons.*"[21]

While it may appear that vehement outbursts erupt with little forethought, the more accurate picture is that we act—and react—in fits and starts out of an otherwise steady whir of mostly unconscious thoughts and feelings. And naturally, we think, feel, and act with our *bodies*, our interconnected, holistic bodies—not simply with our intel-processing brains or intuitive "guts." Our heart rates may spike in concert with intense anger or fear (Aristotle thought the chest cavity

18. L. Johnson, *New Testament*, 65.
19. McCullough, *John Adams*, 68.
20. See Barrett, Lewis, and Haviland-Jones, *Handbook of Emotions*; Goldie, *Oxford Handbook of Philosophy of Emotion*; Plamper, *History of Emotions*.
21. Aristotle, *On Rhetoric* 2.1.8–9 (1378a) (emphasis original).

literally heated up[22]) and may even stop if the overloaded body-system crashes. But the upshoot in blood pressure and emotive sensation generates from a constantly running embodied network.

For purposes of analysis, we speak of physical, mental, emotional, and behavioral operations, but these are artificial divisions. Descartes's famous dictum, *Cogito ergo sum* ("I think, therefore I am"), is too reductive. Better, "I am who I am because I think and feel and act in my body."[23] The critically acclaimed writer Louise Erdrich elegantly captures the thought-feeling nexus. In one novel, the narrator reports about a character, "A thought, in the form of a feeling, came creeping toward him."[24] In another, a distressed character says, "I now thought, and tears started in my eyes. I let them flood down my cheeks. . . . I stood there in the shadowed doorway thinking with my tears. Yes, tears can be thoughts, why not?"[25]

But no one is an isolated "I" or an "island entire of itself."[26] Looking at our individual selves in the "I" necessarily involves considering "you"[27] and "her, him, they" in some configuration of "us." I am who I am as a thinking-feeling-acting being *in relations* (contexts, events, situations, environments) with other thinking-feeling-acting subjects. And those relations inevitably affect us, not least on an emotional level. Brain scientists speak of "neuroplasticity," the remarkable phenomenon of lifelong neural evolution shaped by interactive experiences.[28] Our hardwired frameworks are constantly rewiring, "softening," shapeshifting in the face of new challenges.

One science writer stresses that we always feel "in situ"—in dynamic situations—that affect not simply what we feel but who we are. Emotions function as "complex acts of meaning-making that show us who we are—tangled and sophisticated, even inscrutable to ourselves."[29] When we encounter extraordinary situations and events, good and bad, our baseline "core affect" becomes "energized or enervated"[30]—that is, boosts or bottoms out with a flood of attendant thoughts and feelings. Cognitive dissonance thus mixes with affective

22. Aristotle, *De Anima* 1.1 (403a.28–31).

23. Descartes himself had a wider assessment of human experience; see his "thoughtful" work, *Passions of the Soul*.

24. Erdrich, *Night Watchman*, 349 (winner of the 2021 Pulitzer Prize).

25. Erdrich, *Round House*, 60 (winner of the 2012 National Book Award).

26. Donne, *Selections*, 272.

27. See the classic work by the Jewish philosopher Martin Buber, *I and Thou*.

28. See Costandi, *Neuroplasticity*; Zerilli, *Adaptable Mind*. To see this principle applied to biblical-theological study, see J. Green, *Body, Soul, and Human Life*, 115–22; J. Green, *Conversion in Luke-Acts*, 40–43.

29. Dermendzhiyskais, "Feeling, In Situ."

30. Russell, "Core Affect," 145.

disturbance—upsetting thoughts with upheaving emotions[31]—to *make meaning* out of our complicated lives.

The unsettling, dissonant situations, such as Jesus's death and delayed return, that engulfed early Christ followers naturally had emotive as well as cognitive repercussions. Jesus's crucifixion naturally evoked feelings of sadness and hopelessness (Luke 24:20–21).[32] Even news of Jesus's resurrection did not eliminate negative emotions. Mark's Gospel ends on the dissonant note of fear that overwhelmed a group of women fleeing from Jesus's empty tomb (Mark 16:8). Likewise, Jesus's dilatory return prompted grief and despair over loved ones who died in the interim (1 Thess. 4:13–18). And remaining on high alert for Jesus's imminent return, despite the delay, carries its own emotional strain. The research psychologist Robert Plutchik includes vigilance—keenly feeling attuned to some prospective event—as one of eight emotions at the hub of his "Emotion Wheel."[33]

Although the New Testament writings do not gush with emotional language, they are scarcely dispassionate and certainly aim to *move* readers to active responses: changing hearts and minds (repentance), strengthening beliefs and practices (faithfulness).[34] To move readers effectively, the writers themselves must be moved with passionate conviction about their subject matter, as the New Testament authors were about the crucified, risen, and returning Christ.

Emotion scientists have confirmed that the link between "emotion" and "motion/motivation" is no linguistic accident. Emotions play a lead role in motivating "action readiness," prompting and guiding movement through a precarious world.[35] Once again, emotions move in the same stream as thoughts, not in some offshoot tributary or crashing counterwave—though emotions can stir up a stormy stream of thought! Emotions involve *evaluations* or *appraisals* of situations: a jolt of fear triggers our thinking and feeling that the thin, curvy object in the grass might pose a threat, thus motivating a quick jump away before finally determining whether we're dealing with a snake or a stick.[36]

Given more time and space, you might even think and feel through the experience more fully in writing. This might be especially helpful if you've determined

---

31. Nussbaum, *Upheavals of Thought*.

32. See Spencer, *Luke*, 616–28.

33. Plutchik, "Nature of Emotions," 349–50.

34. See Hockey, *Role of Emotion*, 253: "By highlighting ... certain emotions," the writer of 1 Peter "is attempting to shape the believers' value system and affect their goals, which should then influence their behavior."

35. Frijda and Mesquita, "Analysis of Emotions," 283–84; Lowe and Ziemke, "Feeling of Action Tendencies"; Fontaine and Scherer, "Emotion Is for Doing."

36. Moors et al., "Appraisal Theories"; Moors, "Flavors of Appraisal Theories."

that it was a poisonous snake, and you're never walking a nature trail again! The therapeutic value of "expressive writing" about traumatic experiences and events is well established.[37] "Putting stress into words"[38] on a page can be a powerful means of "coping with emotional upheavals"[39] and making sense of the mess.[40]

My premise in the present volume is that the Gospel-storytelling evangelists, letter-corresponding apostles, and apocalypse-sketching seers of the New Testament work out cognitive dissonances and emotional upheavals in a tension-filled world through their literary works. They *write to the challenges* of living out Christ-centered faith in a fractured, perplexing environment.

But unlike the writing produced by modern writing-therapy, which encourages trauma sufferers to write freely and privately for themselves without worrying about others' receptions, the New Testament documents were expressly written for fellow travelers on life's hard road, for fellow bearers of Christ's cross (Matt. 7:13–14; Mark 8:34–35). With remarkable humility, honesty, courage, and creativity, the New Testament writers seek to make meaning of the real, rough-and-tumble world in which they and their readers live and move. We are privileged to join this journey but with fair warning: PREPARE TO BE SHAPED BY THE NEW TESTAMENT WRITINGS AND THE LIVING CHRIST THEY PROCLAIM, as they reflect an intelligent, impassioned process of being shaped by challenging experiences and events.

37. Pennebaker and Smyth, *Opening Up*.
38. Pennebaker, "Putting Stress into Words."
39. Pennebaker and Smyth, *Opening Up*, 121, 162.
40. See Goldie, *Mess Inside*.

1

Old and New

The Historical Challenge of Innovation and Evolution

	If anyone is in Christ, there is a new creation: everything old has passed away; see, everything has become new! (2 Cor. 5:17)
Tenet	Jesus Christ is the one in whom "everything has become new," having inaugurated a new era in religious thought and experience.
Tension	How does this new Christ-centered perspective relate to older religious perspectives, especially Jesus's Jewish worldview, which is rooted in the "Old" Testament? And how does Christ's new revelation continue to innovate and evolve?

Although the glory days of classical Greek philosophy had passed, thinkers in first-century Athens still fancied themselves sages. But Athens had dropped from the top ranks of academia and politics and become known, as we might say, for being "flaky" or "new age-y." Or as one New Testament writer comments, "Now all the Athenians and the foreigners living there would spend their time in nothing but telling or hearing something new" (Acts 17:21). On religious matters, Athenians dedicated shrines to every possible deity, even "To an unknown god" for safe measure (17:23). The geographer Pausanias observed their "conspicuous . . . devotion to religion," including erecting "an altar to Shamefastness [Shyness], one to Rumor, and one to Effort."[1] They weren't "shy" about flaunting their religious curiosity.

1. Pausanias, *Description of Greece* 1.17.1.

G. Mochetti, after Raphael, 1794 / Public Domain / wellcomecollection.org

The School of Athens

Paul's preaching in Athens about a strange, resurrected god-figure named Jesus evokes a mixed response. While some philosophers mock Paul as a "babbler" and peddler of "scraps of information,"[2] others want to know more about his "new teaching" (Acts 17:18–19). After acknowledging "how extremely religious [they] are in every way" (17:22), Paul addresses the Athenians' surprising ignorance about the one true "God who made the world and everything in it" (17:24). Obviously, nothing is *older* than this Creator God, this venerable "Ancient One" (Dan. 7:9, 13, 22). Yet given his audience, Paul cites not the Jewish scriptures but rather Greek poetic traditions that "in [God] we live and move and have our being. . . . For we too are [God's] offspring" (Acts 17:28; cf. Aratus, *Phaenomena* 5). In their penchant for newfangled notions, the Athenians have lost sight of the world's foundational existence and sustenance "in God."

Chalk one up for Paul the traditionalist. But Paul is also an innovator. He does advance a "new teaching," even a new god, it might seem—the risen Jesus. Or maybe two new deities: Jesus and Anastasia/Resurrection (Acts 17:18)! Curiously, however, at Ares's Hill in Athens, Paul proclaims Jesus only indirectly as "a man

2. BDAG, s.v. "σπερμολόγος," 937; lit. "seed-picker" (*spermologos*).

whom [God] has appointed" and certified "by raising him from the dead" to be the world's final Judge (17:31). Despite the mixed Athenian responses (17:32–33), readers of Acts and Paul's letters have no doubt that this God-appointed "man" is the Jewish Messiah Jesus, who reveals God in a dramatically *new* fashion. "In Christ, there is a new creation: everything old has passed away; see, everything has become new!" (2 Cor. 5:17).

Such news has a nice ring to modern ears, obsessed as we are with new and shiny objects, constantly updating and rebooting. Old is out. Obsolete is measured in seconds and minutes, not centuries and millennia. While the Jesus movement is now ancient news, yet still attractive to millions, in its formative stages, it was new and fascinating, yet *not* widely welcomed.

The dominant ancient worldview valued old over new, antiquity over novelty, tradition over innovation, as if "nothing can be both new and true."[3] History undergirded faith; chronology vindicated theology. In this respect, Judaism had a lot going for it. The first-century historian Flavius Josephus defends his Jewish religion to his Roman patrons in a twenty-volume encyclopedia titled *Jewish Antiquities*. In another work, he reaffirms the "very great antiquity" of the "Jewish nation," which existed well before Greek ascendancy.[4] For all of Aristotle's intellectual advances and his student Alexander's great achievements, they were comparatively new kids on the block: "Almost all which concerns the Greeks happened not long ago; in fact, one may say, is of yesterday only."[5] The great Jewish prophet-leader Moses predates Aristotle and Alexander by a thousand years.[6]

Although many Gentiles in the New Testament era mocked Judaism's practices as peculiar and outmoded, a substantial number of Greeks, Romans, and other groups were intrigued by this "old-time religion." Many Gentiles attended local synagogues, and some became converts. What to do, however, with this new Jewish offshoot, this "sect of the Nazarenes" (Acts 24:5) that embraced the crucified and resurrected Jesus of Nazareth as God's Messiah?

This strange new movement seemed difficult to reconcile with older traditions. Reforming an established religion to conform with ancient ideals was one thing; refitting it for a new era was another. Exactly how "new" was this new Jesus stuff? Did it have legitimate claims to antiquity and continuity with the Jewish scriptures? Such a challenging issue would have sparked not only disbelief

---

3. Feldman, *Jew & Gentile*, 198.
4. Josephus, *Against Apion* 1.1 (cf. 1.2–4).
5. Josephus, *Against Apion* 1.7.
6. Josephus, *Against Apion* 2.154–56. Moses also predates Homer (eighth century BCE) by centuries.

among outsiders but also dissonance among believers as they thought through and lived out their Christ-centered faith. Did their historical roots sink deep enough to sustain this faith?

The New Testament writings were composed mostly, if not exclusively, by Jewish believers in Jesus. Whatever is "new" in Christ is inherently embedded in its Jewish soil. It's a family affair in two ways. Judaism is both mother and sibling to Christ-centered New Testament faith: *mother* from the formative stream of the Hebrew Bible/Old Testament and *sibling* with adaptive tributaries of early Judaism in the "intertestamental" period.[7] Of course, as both testaments attest, sibling rivalries can be fierce (e.g., Gen. 25–50; Luke 12:13–15; 15:11–32).

The New Testament writings variously negotiate tensions between "old" and "new" Jewish teachings and practices in view of Christ's "new creation." They do not iron out all tensions into a seamless, starched product. They bear the stretch marks of historical challenges of innovation and evolution, even as they strive to keep the "old" and "new" stitched together. Jack Levison states, "In our age, which values novelty and invention, in which the breakneck pace of life continues to accelerate, it may not be possible to grasp how intently the followers of Jesus pored over the *past* to ground their journey into the *future*."[8] We now track this journey via three signposts: word, worship, and world.

New Word

Words matter in religion, especially those codified in sacred canons. Adherents of Judaism, Christianity, and Islam represent People of the Book. But not the same Book, despite shared traditions of the founding father Abraham. The Hebrew Bible featured the Torah (including Abraham stories) and various other historical and poetical writings. The Greek Christian Bible added the New Testament.[9] The Arabic Muslim scriptures incorporated Abraham, Jesus, and many other materials into the Quran.

In these traditions prophets play a major role as inspired mediators of God's word. While Abraham is called a prophet in Genesis 20:7, the prototypical Hebrew prophet is Moses, God's mouthpiece (Exod. 3:10–16; 33:11). Having received the tablets of the law, etched by God's "finger" (Exod. 31:18; Deut.

---

7. See Segal, *Rebecca's Children*.

8. Levison, *Unconventional God*, 194 (emphasis original).

9. Alongside a Greek version of the Hebrew Bible, known as the Septuagint (LXX), which included several additional books. See Carter, *Seven Events*, 21–42.

9:10–11), Moses came to be credited with authoring the five Torah books (i.e., the Pentateuch, Genesis–Deuteronomy). Thereafter God raised up succeeding "prophets like Moses," from Joshua to Jesus (Deut. 18:15, 18; Josh. 1:1–9; Acts 3:17–26; 7:37). The New Testament views Jesus as God's consummate prophet, a prophet greater than Moses—*like* Moses but greater (Heb. 1:1–4; 3:1–6). But how so, and to what degree? The more one stresses Christ's surpassing eminence, the *less* like predecessors he appears. Hence the conundrum of continuity between "old" and "new."

While Jesus Christ is the main subject of the New Testament, he wrote none of it. He was an itinerant storytelling prophet, not a scribe. He was not a Moses, a David, or a Solomon, the traditional authors of the Torah, Psalms, and Proverbs, respectively. He inspired others to interpret his words and deeds for future generations. Put another way, Jesus and the Spirit inspired prophets to speak and write about his God-appointed mission, just as prophets of old spoke and wrote about God's word and work (2 Pet. 1:19–21).

How, then, do the New Testament writings about Jesus's followers square with the message of ancient Hebrew prophets and Jesus's new embodiment of God's word? How faithfully do they interpret Moses and Jesus? The threat of false prophecy (misinformation) persists. Anyone can claim to be a prophet. If they dare, anyone can amplify God's word and amend the canon. The writer of the last New Testament book concludes with a bold curse: "I warn everyone who hears the words of the prophecy of this book: if anyone adds to them, God will add to that person the plagues described in this book" (Rev. 22:18). From a canonical perspective, does this writer perhaps protest too much? Now that we've added twenty-seven books to the Old Testament, that's it! No more! Hmm. Weren't the "old" Jewish scriptures sufficient for Jesus and Paul? Yes and no. As evidenced in various ways, the New Testament grapples with dissonances between "old" and "new" insight.

"But I Say unto You": The Prophet Jesus

On a Galilean mountaintop, Matthew's Jesus delivers his most famous "sermon" in the mode of Moses, who received the Torah atop Mount Sinai. Although he never names Moses, Jesus plays the "new Moses" part by charting God's "blessed" way and commenting on God's revealed law reinforced by prophets (Matt. 5:1–48; 7:12).[10]

---

10. See Allison, *New Moses.*

Jesus offers authoritative commentary on several commandments. With slight variations, he repeats the basic formula, "You have heard it said to those of ancient times . . . but I say unto you" (Matt. 5:21, 27, 31, 33, 38, 43). This old-new distinction has often been interpreted as a clash of "antitheses," making Jesus into someone who is both anti-Moses and anti-law. But far from representing "antitheses" to Torah, Jesus's legal opinions constitute "extensions" or updates to old precedents, fleshing out fuller implications of various mandates.[11] More specifically, his commentary reflects internalizations and intensifications of Mosaic laws.[12] For example, Jesus extends the law "You shall not murder" to a prohibition of anger in the heart (an internalization), which motivates murder (5:21–22), and he excludes all certified grounds for divorce, except sexual infidelity (an intensification) (5:31–32).

Issue	Moses's Mandates	Jesus's Updates
Murder	Murder prohibited, "liable to judgment"	Law extends to angry thoughts and feelings
Adultery	Adultery prohibited	Law extends to lustful thoughts and feelings
Divorce	Required certified due process	Prohibited, "except on the ground of unchastity"
False Witness + Vow-Breaking	Lying under oath prohibited, especially in vows made to God	Lying prohibited under oath or not; always speak the plain truth
Revenge	Proportional, no more/less: "eye for eye/tooth for tooth"	Concessional, no punitive revenge: "Turn the other cheek"
Neighbor Love + Enemy Hatred	Dual track: "Love neighbor"/hate enemy (implied)	One way: "Love enemy/pray for those who persecute you"

In all cases, Jesus both reaffirms and reconfigures Torah traditions along stricter, more "conservative" lines. He aims to out-Torah the best Torah teachers: "For I tell you, unless your righteousness *exceeds* that of the scribes and Pharisees, you will never enter the kingdom of heaven" (Matt. 5:20). According to Matthew's Jesus, the top religious and legal scholars are not so much wrongheaded as weak-minded: they don't go *far enough* in their Torah-keeping! True and faithful scribes in Jesus's book are those who mine the rich treasure of "what is new *and* what is old" (13:52). Jesus supplements rather than supplants Torah; indeed, he

11. Levine, *Sermon on the Mount*, xx, 23–43.
12. Gale, "Gospel according to Matthew," 20.

super-reinforces the "old" word, sinking its roots deeper in the heart and spreading its fruits wider in the world (13:1–43).

That's one way of dealing with dissonance: double down on being the true preservers and practitioners of the "old" ways. Yet this strategy risks overpressing the point. Jesus's Torah extensions are not exactly "new." The Tenth Commandment, "You shall not covet" (Exod. 20:17; Deut. 5:21), already internalized interdictions against murder and adultery, and Moses and other prophets urged holding God's commandments in one's heart (Deut. 6:4–6; Jer. 31:33). Though containing no mandate to love their enemies, the Old Testament commissions Israel to be a "blessing" and "light" to all peoples (Gen. 12:1–3; 22:17–18; Isa. 42:6; 49:6).

But there's more. Consider three factors complicating tensions between "old" scriptural editions and Jesus's "new" revised version. First, the Old Testament itself contains dissonant strains. Take divorce, for example. Moses allowed a man to serve his wife divorce papers on the thin grounds that he "finds something objectionable about her" (Deut. 24:1), thus modifying the creation principle that God instituted marriage as an indissoluble "one flesh" union—as Matthew's Jesus argues (Gen. 1:27; 2:22–24; Matt. 19:3–6). Still, Matthew's Jesus, grants an exception for sexual infidelity (Matt. 5:32; 19:9), even as Mark's Jesus stipulates no such loophole (Mark 10:2–9).

Second, consider another core commandment: "Remember the sabbath day, and keep it holy. . . . You shall not do any work" (Exod. 20:8–10). Although Jesus regularly observes this sacred day (Matt. 4:23; 9:35; 12:9; 13:54), on one sabbath he allows his disciples to "harvest" grain while he engages in healing activity—both "work" violations according to some Pharisees (12:1–2, 10). Here Jesus appears somewhat more "liberal" in his Torah practice. Yet he by no means repudiates sabbath law. He defends sabbath feeding and healing work by citing legal (Num. 28:9–10 // Matt. 12:5; Exod. 23:5 // Matt. 12:11), historical (1 Sam. 21:1–6 // Matt. 12:3–4), and prophetic (Hos. 6:6 // Matt. 12:7) precedents, all aligned with the creational principle underlying sabbath rest. If God "rested" on the seventh day after making a "very good" world (Gen. 1:31–2:4), what better day to make one of God's ailing creatures whole again? So, was Jesus a "liberal" or "conservative" Jew, a "judicial activist" or "strict constructionist" interpreter of scriptural law? Good luck answering that one.[13]

Likewise, to raise our third caution flag, Pharisees ill fit the straitjackets that Christian preachers and teachers—starting with Matthew and other New

---

13. See Spencer, "Scripture, Hermeneutics, and Matthew's Jesus."

Testament writers—assign them. Labeling a whole group as deviant or dangerous is the stuff of polemics, not demographics. The truth is, not all Pharisees agreed among themselves. Distinct rabbinic "schools" or "houses" advanced different interpretations of Torah and routinely cited multiple opinions in their written commentaries, known as the Mishnah and Talmud.[14] Overall, compared with other Jewish factions like the priestly Dead Sea sect, the Pharisees stand out as more *progressive innovators and reformers*[15]—both like and not like Jesus. Sometimes the hottest debates erupt between religious siblings with opposing opinions concerning how best to practice the common faith. What should we "bind" and "loose" (Matt. 18:18), embrace and exclude?[16]

Although we don't know the full state of play between Matthew's community and the Pharisees, an influx of Gentile Christ followers in Matthew's "church," likely in Antioch of Syria,[17] heightened tensions. In the Sermon on the Mount, Jesus bars the Pharisees from the "kingdom of heaven" if they don't up their Torah-keeping game (Matt. 5:20). Later he denounces the Pharisees as "hypocrites . . . blind guides . . . whitewashed tombs . . . snakes . . . vipers" (23:13–36). Did the Pharisees fire back in kind? Probably, but we have no *Against Matthew* volume to prove it. Was Matthew fair to the Pharisees? Of course not, at least not entirely. In impassioned debate you aim to win the rhetorical battle; you paint with bold strokes, highlighting your viewpoints and redlining opponents' positions. You seek to move your audience emotionally as much as logically.

"I Think That I Too Have the Spirit of God": Prophets in Jesus's Name

Although Paul never calls himself a "prophet," he believes God called him to be an inspired preacher. Like Jeremiah, Paul senses that God "set [him] apart before [he] was born" (Gal. 1:15; Jer. 1:5; cf. Isa. 49:5) and tested his mettle in the crucible of suffering and opposition (1 Thess. 2:2–4; Jer. 11:19–20).[18] Paul also identifies himself as a Pharisee who came to believe in and serve Christ (Phil. 3:5; cf. Acts 23:6; 26:6).

God's testing of prophets like Jeremiah and Paul implies the ever-pressing threat of false prophets who claim divine inspiration for prestige and profit. For Paul, the threat extends to those who *pretend* to speak "in Jesus's name." At the

14. Levine, *Sermon on the Mount*, xx.
15. Noam, "Pharisaic Halakah."
16. Volf, *Exclusion and Embrace*.
17. See Meier, "Antioch," 45–72. On the tension *within* Matthew concerning the Gentile mission, compare 2:1–12; 10:5–6; 15:21–28; and 28:16–20.
18. Evans, "Prophet, Paul as," 763.

end of 1 Thessalonians Paul exhorts, "Do not quench the Spirit. Do not despise the words of prophets, but *test everything*; hold fast to what is good" (5:19–20). Prophecy examined, not eliminated.

Similarly, in the Sermon on the Mount, Jesus warns, "Not everyone who says to me, 'Lord, Lord,' will enter the kingdom of heaven, but only the one who does the will of my Father in heaven. On that day many will say to me, 'Lord, Lord, did we not prophesy in your name . . . ?' Then I will declare to them, 'I never knew you; go away from me, you evildoers'" (Matt. 7:21–23). Jesus cites a key criterion for authentic prophecy: doing God's will. Prophetic authority aligns with ethical integrity.

The first Johannine letter advances a doctrinal test—namely, belief that Jesus Christ was a real flesh-and-blood human being: "Test the spirits to see whether they are from God; for many false prophets have gone out into the world. By this you know the Spirit of God: every spirit that confesses that Jesus Christ has come in the flesh is from God, and every spirit that does not confess Jesus is not from God" (1 John 4:1–3). This belief also has ethical implications. True believers love as Jesus loved, walk as Jesus walked, obey Jesus's words, and confess their sins to receive Jesus's forgiveness (1:5–2:6; 3:4–22; 4:7–5:3). Humility is the prophet's anchor, arrogance his Achilles' heel.

Paul knew this from experience. While modern readers often bristle at Paul's strong assertions of authority, they miss his honest expressions of weakness and humility. He writes 1 Corinthians to a vibrant congregation riddled with rivalry about who is the wisest and ablest among them. Though Paul seeks to unify the congregation as its founding apostle (9:1–2) and "master builder" (3:10), he does not lord his position over them or flash his charisma before them. Instead, he appeals to his humble service of the *crucified Christ*—the church's one true foundation (3:11)—who embodied God's wisdom and power *in his suffering* (1:17–30): "I did not come proclaiming the mystery of God to you in lofty words or wisdom. For I decided to know nothing among you except Jesus Christ, and him crucified. And I came to you in weakness and in fear and in much trembling" (2:1–3). Paul is absorbed by God's *grace*, God's *gift*, in Christ (15:10; 2 Cor. 12:9).[19] Grace (*charis*) sources his and others' gifts (*charismata*), leaving no room for boasting or boosterism (1 Cor. 1:28–31; 3:21–4:13).

In Paul's extended teaching on family matters in 1 Corinthians 7, he affords us a rare glimpse into how he applies Jesus's words.[20] Concerning divorce, though Paul

---

19. Barclay, *Paul*.

20. Paul seldom references Jesus's words. That does not preclude, however, a broad coherence with Jesus's teachings. See Evans and White, *Who Created Christianity?*; and Wenham, *Paul*.

affirms Jesus's "command" to maintain the marital bond (7:10–11), he transparently supplements Jesus's teaching: here's what "I say—I and not the Lord" (7:12). Regarding mixed marriages between believers and unbelievers, Paul opines that the believing spouse should not initiate divorce; "but if the unbelieving partner separates, let it be so; in such a case the [believing] brother or sister is not bound" to preserve the marriage (7:15). It's possible Paul again speaks from experience: it would not be surprising if his wife left him after his sudden conversion to Christ. No doubt in Corinth's bustling commercial center, with its multifarious viewpoints and lifestyles, marital tensions intensified when one spouse independently professed, "Jesus is Lord" (12:3).

Paul addresses a new situation in the Greco-Roman world not confronted by Jesus. Although Jesus prohibits divorce (except in infidelity cases, according to Matt. 5:32; 19:9), this does not stop him from challenging disciples to leave everything behind—including spouses—to follow him (Mark 1:16–20; 10:28–31; Luke 14:25–33). Paul modifies Jesus's position both by urging believers to stay married to unbelievers in hopes of saving them (1 Cor. 7:16) and by permitting divorce if unbelievers so choose.

No less than in churches today, matters concerning marriage and divorce created tension in New Testament communities. And things only get hotter when sex comes into play. Paul thought that all things considered—particularly the "present crisis" before Christ's imminent return (1 Cor. 7:26, 29)—it was better to remain celibate and unmarried, like Paul (presently) and Jesus. But Paul does not command others to comply, since "each has a particular gift from God" (7:7): some have the God-given capacity to stay single and celibate, while others are not so "blessed." Again, he freely admits, "I have no command of the Lord," while hastening to add, "but I give my opinion as one who by the Lord's mercy is trustworthy" (7:25). Considered opinion, not absolute law.

Moreover, concerning widows, Paul allows them to marry whomever they wish but "only in the Lord." Still, he hedges a bit: "In my opinion she is more blessed if she remains as she is. And I think that I, too, have the Spirit of God" (1 Cor. 7:39–40 NRSVue). Paul thinks he's right; he hopes he's led by God's Spirit, but he might be wrong. He remains open to further insight.

Paul treats himself as he treats prophetic enthusiasts who claim to speak with Spirit-authority. Worship services included many speakers popping up with "a hymn, a lesson, a revelation, a tongue, or an interpretation" (1 Cor. 14:26). Paul is all for Spirit-inspired speech, but he worries about disorder and dissonance—including literal dissonance. Sometimes too much sound signifies nothing; big noise, little knowledge. He counsels speaking "in turn . . . one by one," not all over each other; only "two or three prophets" should hold the floor in a service, while "others weigh what is said" with both sympathetic consideration and critical assessment "so that all may learn and all be encouraged" (14:27–31).

New Worship

There was no First Church on the corner of Main and Broad in downtown Corinth or in any other first-century city. In fact, there were no purpose-built "church" buildings at all. Christ's earliest followers typically gathered for worship, fellowship, and instruction in believers' residences, though they might also rent a lecture hall (*scholē*) for larger assemblies (Acts 19:8–10).

Otherwise, they continued attending established worship centers—temples, synagogues, or shrines—some recast in new forms. Greek Corinth, for example, was reconstructed on the Roman model by Julius Caesar in 44 BCE. This "new" Corinth became dotted with sanctuaries and statues dedicated to Greco-Roman deities like Aphrodite-Venus, Athena-Minerva, Artemis-Diana, and Apollo, as well as to deified emperors and their families.[21] Christ believers continued to visit these sites, creating dissonances that Paul addresses (1 Cor. 8:1–13; 10:14–33).

Jesus worshiped, taught, and valued prayer in the Jerusalem temple, God's "holy place" (Mark 11:15–12:44; Luke 2:46–47; 18:9–14; John 2:13–25; 5:14; 7:14–31; 8:1–11). After his departure, his followers continued to frequent the temple as well as meet in homes: "Day by day, as they spent much time together in the temple, they broke bread at home" (Acts 2:46). "And every day in the temple and at home they did not cease to teach and proclaim Jesus as the Messiah" (5:42).

Historically, this was the *second* temple, originally constructed in 520–515 BCE when Judahite exiles began returning home years after Babylon destroyed Solomon's original temple in 587 BCE. This second sanctuary, however, didn't match the grandeur of Solomon's (Hag. 2:3) until Herod the Great renovated it as a world-class temple, beginning in 19 BCE. By Jesus's era, the temple had a long, fraught history of old and new iterations. In 70 CE, Rome would raze the second temple to the ground.

How and where should Christ followers worship God in this new Roman imperial environment? Do they keep dreaming of another new Jerusalem temple?

---

21. Cf. Pausanias, *Description of Greece* 2.2.6–2.3.1. See Spaeth, "Imperial Cult."

Or do they reenvision sacred space? In any case, in the New Testament's Jewish worldview, Rome's demolition of God's sacred city and sanctuary stoked cognitive dissonance and emotional upheaval. How does faith in Christ's "new" work help manage this devastating loss?

Your Place or Mine?

Another wrench is thrown into sacred-space claims by another sect, known as the Samaritans, "a third offshoot of ancient biblical religion,"[22] though only a few hundred Samaritans exist today.[23] Rabbinic Jews and Christ followers represented the two other religious branches. Scholars continue to debate fine points about the Samaritans' origins, but they now widely agree that casting the Samaritans as "half-breed" descendants of northern Israelites who intermarried with Assyrian conquerors was a prejudicial tactic by Southern Judahite purists to slur the Samaritans' ethnic heritage. Based near the cities of Samaria and Shechem (Sychar) and Mount Gerizim, the Samaritans regarded themselves as faithful, "pure" worshipers of Israel's God and keepers of Torah.[24]

Around the time Judahite returnees built the second Jerusalem temple, some northern Israelites built an altar on Mount Gerizim,[25] and by the second century BCE, a Samaritan temple was erected there as a rival to Jerusalem's temple. The tyrannical Syrian-Greek ruler Antiochus IV (175–164 BCE) targeted both places for a total Greek makeover, designating the Gerizim sanctuary "the temple of Zeus-the-Friend-of-Strangers" and dedicating the Jerusalem temple to "Olympian Zeus" (2 Macc. 6:1–2; cf. 5:21–23).[26] After the Maccabean reclamation of Jerusalem's temple (167–164 BCE), the priest-king John Hyrcanus launched a military campaign in Samaria, destroying Shechem and the Gerizim sanctuary (110 BCE). From that point on, hostilities spiked between Samaritans based in Samaria/Gerizim and Jews based in Judea/Jerusalem.

Scriptural tensions also mounted as the Samaritans began to produce revisions of Genesis–Deuteronomy. This revised document was known as the Samaritan Pentateuch. This "New Revised Torah Version" accentuated Gerizim as the "blessed mount" (Deut. 27:11–12; 28:1–14; cf. Josh. 8:30–35).[27] Then, as

22. Zangenberg, review of *The Keepers*, 357.
23. Pummer, *Samaritans*, 289–301; UNESCO, "Mount Gerizim."
24. Anderson and Giles, *Keepers*.
25. Pummer, "Was There an Altar?"
26. Novakovic, "Jews and Samaritans," 208–9.
27. R. Anderson, *Samaritan Pentateuch*; Kartveit, *Origin of the Samaritans*, 259–312; Pummer, *Samaritans*, 195–218.

Mount Gerizim and Mount Shechem

now, battles over boundaries and Bibles, sanctuaries and scriptures fueled intense religious strife.

The New Testament Gospels reflect these Samaritan-Jewish frictions. For example, though Luke's Jesus brands a Samaritan as a "foreigner" (*allogenēs*, "another race," Luke 17:18), he uses individual Samaritans as critical foils to unmerciful and ungrateful Jews (10:25–37; 17:11–19). But Luke also acknowledges that some Samaritans had no great love for Jerusalem-bound Jews, including Jesus (9:51–53). Still, this does not warrant violent backlash against Samaritans. Jesus talks down two disciples, James and John, when they want to go all Elijah on an inhospitable Samaritan village and torch the place with a divine thunderbolt (9:54–55; cf. 1 Kings 18:36–40; 2 Kings 1:9–14). The Jesus movement struggled with its own strains of ill-will toward "foreign" Samaritans.

The Fourth Gospel portrays a group of antagonistic Jews—sweepingly labeled "the Jews"—slandering Jesus by calling him a demon-possessed Samaritan (John 8:48); so the evangelist is slamming both (unbelieving) Jews and Samaritans. An extended story in John 4, however, reflects more congenial Jewish-Samaritan relations brokered by Jesus Messiah.

Among various matters Jesus discusses with a Samaritan woman at a well near Sychar, the issue of sacred space is central.[28] This is not just any watering hole: it is the old well of "our ancestor Jacob" (John 4:12), a founding father claimed by Jews and Samaritans. Intrigued by Jesus's prophetic insight (4:10–19), the

---

28. John 4:7–26 represents the longest discussion between Jesus and an individual in Gospel literature. Although the Samaritan woman proves to be a worthy conversant, she has been much maligned in Christian interpretation. See Reeder, *Samaritan Woman's Story*; Spencer, "Feminist Criticism," 307–23.

woman presses him on a critical dividing point: "Our ancestors worshiped on this mountain, but you say that the place where people must worship is in Jerusalem" (4:20). We imagine her gesturing toward "this mountain," Mount Gerizim, which remained focal for Samaritan worship even with its temple in ruins. In effect, she asks, "Where does God meet God's people? Your place or mine? This place (which, by the way, your people demolished) or yours in Jerusalem?"

Jesus takes up her challenge, holding in tension his people's priority over and solidarity with her people in God's family. On the one hand, Jesus affirms that "salvation is from the Jews," who "know" Israel's saving God in a way the Samaritans "do not know" (John 4:22). But on the other hand, he embeds this exclusive argument in an inclusive framework of the approaching "hour" when worshiping the one Father-God "in spirit and truth" will transcend geopolitical and topographical boundaries (4:21, 23–24). The Spirit-filled human heart, individually and communally, is the optimal house of worship (cf. 1 Cor. 3:16; 6:19; cf. Eph. 2:21–22).

Temple, Temple, Temple

Spiritualizing and universalizing tenets of faith whose foundations have been shaken are common ways of soothing qualms. Among those today who are disaffected by anemic and toxic Christian responses to surging social, technological, and environmental changes, many claim to be "spiritual" but not "religious," to prefer interfaith discussion groups in home and community centers rather than institutional services in old church auditoria. Jesus may be "just alright with me,"[29] but I'd just as soon do without crusty churchy business and bureaucracy.

This modern analogy, however, does not quite fit the foundational Old or New Testament. Prophets from Amos and Isaiah to Jesus and Paul valued sincere, heartfelt worship and worried that prayers, sacrifices, and other rituals could become fusty, perfunctory exercises at best or covers for unjust, exploitative actions at worst (Amos 5:21–24; Isa. 1:11–17; Mark 11:15–17; Col. 2:16–23). *But they were not anti-temple.*

- *Reform* the temple system when it fossilizes or fails, yes.
- *Reconfigure* worship practices after the temple's destruction, yes.
- *Rebuild* the fallen temple, even if God uses an alien power as an agent of judgment—yes, that too.

29. As the Doobie brothers sang in their 1972 song "Jesus Is Just Alright with Me," during another antiestablishment era.

But utterly *reject* God's holy house? Perish the thought! What would it say about Israel's God if he forever abandoned his own house, household, and homeland?

JEREMIAH AND EZEKIEL

Jeremiah and Ezekiel, two prophet-priests, operated in the precarious period surrounding Babylon's conquest of Jerusalem. While the temple still stood, Jeremiah challenged the popular presumption that God would never let this sanctuary be dismantled, as if it were a magically invincible refuge for God's people. The people of Judah thought that if they kept up the mantra, "This is the temple of the LORD, the temple of the LORD, the temple of the LORD" (Jer. 7:4), all would be well.[30] But Jeremiah thought that the way some were using the temple as a safe house perverted its charter values of love, mercy, and justice. Violently oppressing immigrants, orphans, widows, and other vulnerable persons, then taking cover in the temple "den of robbers" (7:11)—this is something God cannot tolerate (nor could Jesus, as he quotes this Jeremiah text during his table-toppling demonstration in the temple, Mark 11:17). Unless "you truly amend your ways and your doings" (Jer. 7:5), Jeremiah thunders, you can be sure God will bring this house down on your heads (7:1–15)!

But during the final siege of Jerusalem, while Jeremiah was locked up in the palace prison, he dared to purchase his cousin's field as a sign that even with the coming devastation and displacement, "houses and fields and vineyards shall again be bought in this land" (Jer. 32:15; cf. 31:1–14). Although nothing is said about rebuilding the temple, perhaps it's implied. In any event, Jeremiah's "story of redemption . . . gives the future a *topos*, a location,"[31] a sacred realm to restore God's people.

From his exile post in Babylon, Ezekiel is under no illusions about the "abominable" state of the current temple establishment, which effectively expelled God from God's house and ensured its demise (Ezek. 8:1–11:12). But when Ezekiel anxiously asks if this is the "end" of Israel, God promises to reunite the people with "one heart" and a "new spirit" of faithfulness (8:13–20; cf. 36:26–32) and restore the temple forever: "[I] will set my sanctuary among them forevermore.

---

30. For a modern analogy, see Palmer, *Healing*, 180: "All we Americans need to do is chant 'one nation under God, indivisible, with liberty and justice for all,' and we get a booster shot of national and delusional self-righteousness." Palmer says this as a strong advocate of democracy, urging Americans to live up to the country's ideals.

31. Davis, *Biblical Prophecy*, 164.

My dwelling place shall be with them; and I will be their God, and they shall be my people" (37:26–27).[32] Ezekiel is granted a spectacular "vision of transformation" with detailed blueprints for a new holy city and temple (chaps. 40–48).[33] Neither the original second temple, however, nor Herod's renovated structure follows Ezekiel's complicated plan, suggesting that it represents an ideal, end-time vision.

HEBREWS AND REVELATION

Hebrews situates God's ideal dwelling place (1) *back* before Solomon's fixed city temple to Moses's mobile desert "tent/tabernacle" during the Israelites' trek to the promised land (Heb. 9:2, 6) and (2) *up* to the "greater and [more] perfect tent (not made with hands, that is, not of this creation)" in heaven, where Christ "entered once for all into the Holy Place" to secure "eternal redemption" (9:11–12).[34] Hebrews thus advances the most extreme New Testament position toward the Jerusalem temple by virtually erasing it from the record.

The tabernacle also has a limited shelf life. Its earthly purpose, connected with the "old" covenant between God and Israel, has become "obsolete" (Heb. 8:13) with Christ's once-for-all redemptive act and ongoing high-priestly intercession (7:23–28) in the heavenly sanctuary. The "new covenant" in Christ effectively supplants the "old covenant" (8:1–13; 9:23–28).[35]

But that's not the whole story of Hebrews. Outmoded or obsolescent does not mean useless or worthless. The tabernacle was the vital center of God's relationship with the ancient Israelites through the difficult forty-year wilderness trek from Egypt to the promised land. Now—in the new era inaugurated with Christ's death, resurrection, and heavenly intercession—the "old" wilderness experience continues to shape the identity of God's people on earth as they await Christ's return and to serve as a key analogical aid to understanding Christ's work.[36]

Hebrews extends the analogy to sacrificial offerings. Christ followers must continue to present a "*sacrifice* of praise to God, that is, the fruit of lips that confess his name," and they must "not neglect to do good and to share what

32. Greenberg, "Design and Themes," 216.

33. Darr, "Book of Ezekiel," 1532–36; Stevenson, *Vision of Transformation*.

34. The dualism between perfect mental ideas and imperfect material copies echoes Plato's worldview; see L. Johnson, *Hebrews*, 17–21.

35. John's Gospel also uses tabernacle imagery to illuminate Christ's saving work, but it grounds this work in the *earthly/incarnate* Jesus, who "became flesh and lived [tented/tabernacled, *skēnoō*] among us" (John 1:14).

36. See Moffitt, *Rethinking the Atonement*, 29–45, 117–34.

[they] have, for such *sacrifices* are pleasing to God" (Heb. 13:15–16). These are doxological and ethical sacrifices offered as easily in the world as in the sanctuary, unlike animal blood offerings, which were restricted to sacred altars. Even so, psalms and alms constitute continuing acceptable sacrifices from the "old covenant." As the psalmist intones, "Offer praise as your sacrifice to God. . . . Those who offer praise as a sacrifice honor me" (Ps. 50:14, 23 NAB; cf. 51:15–19).[37]

The book of Revelation offers a new twist on temple figuration by envisioning a new Jerusalem *without* a structural temple, "for its temple is the Lord God the Almighty and the Lamb" (Rev. 21:22). The Lamb represents the slain and raised Jesus Christ (5:6–13; 7:9–17; 14:1–5; 17:14; 19:6–9). The "Lord God" thus bodily personifies the temple meeting "place." Such ultimate re-placement of the earthly temple does not, however, downgrade the sacred function it performed while it lasted, as Hebrews seems to do.

New World

The spoken (word) and spatial (worship) issues considered thus far coalesce in expansive visions of creation: "In the beginning when God created the heavens and the earth, . . . God said, 'Let there be . . .'" (Gen. 1:1, 3). God "sustains all things by his powerful word" (Heb. 1:3), which New Testament writers believe is expressed most powerfully in Jesus Christ, the creational and incarnational Word (John 1:1–5, 14; Col. 1:15–20; Heb. 1:1–3; Rev. 19:13). God's perfect world has been tarnished, however, by human negligence and avarice. The "old" world has been poorly maintained by its God-appointed caretakers (Gen. 1:26–31; 2:15). Hence, God longs for a "new creation," which Paul believes is fulfilled "in Christ," through whom "everything has become new" (2 Cor. 5:17). So that's a wrap—*if* you ignore all the persisting evil and suffering in the world *after* Christ, which Paul certainly does not.

How do believers deal with this dissonance between the present world and both the good "old" creation and the "new" not-yet order? What exactly would this "new world" involve? Repairing and retooling the "old" into Creation 2.0? Re-creating and reconstructing the "old" into a "new" brand? No idea is bigger— this is as big as all creation!

---

37. On almsgiving as sacrificial service to God, see G. Anderson, *Charity*, 150–52; cf. Sir. 35:4 CEB; Rom. 12:1; 1 Pet. 2:5.

"New Things I Now Declare": Isaiah and Creation

No book influenced New Testament writers more than Isaiah, and among Isaiah's ideas and images, none are more formative than those related to God as Creator and Redeemer. Although Isaiah's creation theology is concentrated in chapters 40–55 (Second Isaiah), which are set during the Babylonian exile, the book has a cosmic outlook from beginning to end.[38]

> Hear, O heavens, and listen, O earth;
>   for the LORD has spoken. (Isa. 1:2)

> The new heavens and the new earth,
>   which I will make,
> shall remain before me, says the LORD. (66:22)

Second Isaiah particularly reflects old/new and past/present/future tensions. Things have been rough for God's people in the wake of Babylon's destruction of Jerusalem and deportation of Judah's leading citizens. Desolation and despair dampen survivors' spirits, which the prophet aims to reinvigorate with a panoramic view of history and therapeutic message of renewal.

Isaiah doesn't sugarcoat the past: "[Jerusalem] has received from the LORD's hand double for all her sins" (Isa. 40:2). But she has now "served her term. . . . her penalty is paid," and God's condemnation and sternness give way to comfort and tenderness (40:2). The "originating" and "continuing" Creator God partners with creation in the perpetual process of re-formation and revitalization.[39] Jerusalem stands on the threshold of creation renewal, if she remembers "the LORD, [her] Maker," whom she's tragically "forgotten" (51:13), if she embraces the creative tensions and evolutions of old/new, former/latter experiences.

> Remember this and consider,
>   recall it to mind, you transgressors,
>   remember the former things of old;
> for I am God, and there is no other;
>   I am God, and there is no one like me,
> declaring the end from the beginning
>   and from ancient time things not yet done. (46:8–10)

---

38. Fretheim, *God and World*, 181.
39. Fretheim, *God and World*, 180–90.

> For I am about to create new heavens
>   and a new earth;
> the former things shall not be remembered
>   or come to mind.
> But be glad and rejoice forever
>   in what I am creating. (65:17–18)

Isaiah paradoxically challenges the people both to remember and to forget the old/former things God has made. But above all, they must delight in what God is still "creating" (Isa. 65:18) anew, according to God's good "purpose," which "shall stand" (46:10). Isaiah's joyous prospect of new creation counterpoints Ecclesiastes' cynical ennui that "all things are wearisome; . . . there is nothing new under the sun" (Eccles. 1:8–9).[40]

"Everything Has Become New": Christ and Creation

The Gospels of Mark and Luke open against the backdrop of Isaiah's vision of exiled Israel traveling toward home through a transformed wilderness. The heading of Mark ("The beginning of the good news about Jesus the Messiah, the Son of God, as it is written in Isaiah the prophet," 1:1–2 NIV) echoes and extends the creation story ("In the beginning," Gen. 1:1). Christ's story begins in medias res, within the ongoing cosmic saga, with particular attention to Israel:

> See, I am sending my messenger ahead of you,
>   who will prepare your way;
> the voice of one crying out in the wilderness:
>   "Prepare the way of the Lord, make his paths straight." (Mark 1:2–3,
>   quoting Isa. 40:3)[41]

Luke extends the Isaiah quotation to expand the scope of God's remaking work:

> Every valley shall be filled,
>   and every mountain and hill shall be made low,
> and the crooked shall be made straight;
>   and the rough ways made smooth;
> and all flesh shall see the salvation of God. (Luke 3:5–6 // Isa. 40:4–5)

40. W. Brown, *Seven Pillars*, 197, 210.
41. Mixed with allusions to Exod. 23:20 and Mal. 3:1; see Spencer, *Reading Mark*, 11–14.

In their own struggles under an imperial regime—Rome now, instead of Babylon[42]—these Gospel writers seek "emotional refuge"[43] in Isaiah's comforting message of re-creation. Such refuge, however, remains more aspirational than actual, as Rome retains its repressive power throughout the New Testament period. By any measure, the path of "new creation" is not all that straight and smooth. But it never has been—not for refugees and returnees in Isaiah's time, and not for Jesus and his followers.

So how do New Testament writers respond constructively to the tension created by persisting evidence of a crooked, not-so-new creation? In some way, this question affects all seven challenges explored in this study. But we now consider two approaches, one focused on *growing*, the other on *groaning*.

Jesus: Birthing and Growing

As the creative Word made flesh, bone, and blood (Luke 24:39–40; John 1:14), "Jesus emerged by way of evolution, just as you and I did."[44] The biblical-theological worldview celebrates an evolving creative process through the ages, generated by the divine Spirit or "wind" power (Gen. 1:2) rather than (merely) raw electric energy and random adaptive forces.[45] In Jesus's case, while Matthew and Luke report his conception by the Holy Spirit, apart from male human seed (Matt. 1:20; Luke 1:31–35), it still took place in the womb of a young woman who carried Jesus to full term and delivered him through natural processes. No full-formed mythic figure magically sprouted from Mary's body.

Thereafter "the child grew and became strong" and "increased in wisdom and in years," not beginning his messianic work until he "was about thirty years old" (Luke 2:40, 52; 3:23). Although a precocious adolescent with emerging consciousness of God as his Father (2:46–49), Jesus still has to grow into his vocation as a human being. Moreover, Jesus's developing view of God's realm is saturated with creative agricultural images, reminiscent of Isaiah (Isa. 5:1–7; 35:1–2; 42:9; 43:19; 51:3). Jesus conceives of God's proclaimed word as seed sown into hearts and minds, sprouting, growing, and bearing fruit to different degrees in different environments (Matt. 13:1–23; Mark 4:1–20; Luke 8:4–15). He likens the

42. "Babylon" is used as a cipher for Rome in 1 Pet. 5:13; Rev. 17:5; 18:2.
43. Historian William Reddy defines "emotional refuge" as "a relationship, ritual, or organization . . . that provides safe release from prevailing emotional norms and allows relaxation of emotional effort, with or without an ideological justification, which may shore up or threaten the existing emotional regime" (*Navigation*, 129); cf. Spencer, "Song of Songs."
44. Delio, *Making All Things New*, 71 (cf. 72–89).
45. Delio, *Christ*, 4; cf. Haught, *Making Sense of Evolution*.

progress of God's domain to the inexorable growth cycle of scattered seed from stalk to head to full grain to harvest (Mark 4:26–29), the gritty persistence of "good seed" to bear fruit among "enemy"-sown "weeds" (Matt. 13:24–30, 36–43), and the amazing potential of a tiny mustard seed to become a substantial shrub that accommodates bird nests (Matt. 13:31–32; Mark 4:30–32; Luke 13:18–19).

These images characterize Jesus's life-giving word in creational terms, re-forming the world in multiple shapes and sizes amid variable conditions. Ap-pearances of dormant, limited, obstructed growth give way to assurances of God's persisting regenerative purpose in Christ.

In the Fourth Gospel, Jesus not only speaks in creational language; he veri-tably personifies creation. "In the beginning," Jesus the creative divine Word brought everything "into being" (John 1:1–5), priming the flow of ever-renewing life. Eventually, Jesus entered earthly experience more personally as a full-fledged human being in life—*and death*—but death as reproductive and transformative, not terminal: "Very truly, I tell you, unless a grain of wheat falls into the earth and dies, it remains just a single grain; but if it dies, it bears much fruit" (12:24). Just so, Jesus's death leads to his fruitful resurrection and first reappearance in a *garden* (20:11–16; cf. 19:40–42). Hope springs eternal for new creation *out of* death.

But what about other people? The Old Testament offers select glimpses of afterlife: direct ascensions to heaven of two figures, Enoch (Gen. 5:24; Sir. 44:16; cf. Heb. 11:5) and Elijah (2 Kings 2:11–12; Sir. 48:9); resuscitation of two deceased sons (1 Kings 17:17–24; 2 Kings 4:32–37; Sir. 48:4–5); restoration of Israel, pic-tured as reassembling and reviving bones from a mass graveyard (Ezek. 37:1–14); and a general end-time resurrection (Dan. 12:1–4).[46] John's Gospel affirms Jesus's role as Son of God and Son of Humankind, who rebirths and renews God's children through the Spirit (John 1:12–13; 3:3, 5) in advance of a final resurrec-tion and reckoning (5:25–29; cf. 11:24), prefigured "now" (5:25) in revivifying Lazarus after four days of entombment (11:23–27, 38–44). The Johannine Jesus also features birthing women as models of creative "labor," assuring his followers that the pain and suffering they will endure in his absence "will turn into joy . . . [when] I will see you again," just as a mother's "anguish" soon dissipates "because of the joy of having brought a human being into the world" (16:20–21).

In the Synoptic Gospels, Jesus also reflects on another kind of natural growth pattern, this time from the material-textile world, aligned with Isaiah's imagery of

---

46. See Levenson, *Resurrection.*

God's stitching and stretching the *fabric* of creation.[47] Jesus spins
two short parables illustrating tensions between "new" and "old"
materials: one involves sewing a new patch on an old coat; the
other involves storing new wine in an old wineskin, which was typically made from a goat hide (Matt. 9:16–17; Mark 2:21–22; Luke
5:36–39). Mixing new and old materials doesn't always work well:
when a new patch shrinks after washing, it "pulls away" from old
cloth, "and a worse tear is made" (Matt. 9:16); as new wine
ferments, it emits expanding carbon dioxide gas
that bursts old, brittle containers. In both cases, a
thoughtless blend of old and new damages *both*.[48]

Jesus speaks these parables in a debate over "old"
spiritual practices of fasting, which he suspends
temporarily for his followers: no fasting during his
brief, urgent earthly mission, though it will be resumed
after his death (Matt. 9:15; Mark 2:20; Luke 5:35; cf.
Acts 13:2). In short, Jesus does not create his gospel
out of whole cloth but aims to hold older and newer
elements together in creative tension, striking a balance between shrinking and bursting, contracting and expanding.

Ancient Middle Eastern
wineskin
Borya Galperin / Shutterstock

Paul: Suffering and Groaning

Alongside Paul's sweeping statement about the "cosmic 'new creation'" of
"everything" in Christ,[49] he makes no bones about continued suffering in the
world. What gives? If this "new creation" comes with the same old pain and
suffering, who needs it? Better the devil you know than a new set of troubles.

But Paul doesn't see it that way. While following Christ's way brings *more
difficulties* for Paul in a harsh world often hostile to the gospel, he maintains
remarkable resilience. Notice two assessments flanking the "new creation" text
in 2 Corinthians 5:17:

> We are afflicted in every way, but not crushed; perplexed, but not driven to despair;
> persecuted, but not forsaken; struck down, but not destroyed. (4:8)

47. See Isa. 40:22; 42:5; 44:24; 45:12; 48:13; 50:9; 51:6, 8, 13, 16; W. Brown, *Seven Pillars*, 197–220.
48. Spencer, *Reading Mark*, 45–46.
49. Horrell, Hunt, and Southgate, *Greening Paul*, 169; they also discuss whether Paul views the "new
creation" in 2 Cor. 5:17 in individual or corporate terms (167–69). While both readings are possible,
the collective, "cosmic" perspective appears primary.

As servants of God we have commended ourselves in every way: through great endurance, in afflictions, hardships, calamities, beatings, imprisonments, riots, labors, sleep-
less nights, hunger. . . . We are treated . . . as dying, and see—we are alive; as punished,
and yet not killed; as sorrowful, yet always rejoicing; as poor, yet making many rich;
as having nothing, and yet possessing everything. (6:4, 8–10)

In sum, "We have spoken frankly to you Corinthians; our heart is wide open"
(6:11). Frankly, yes, but maybe foolishly too! While wearing his heart on his
sleeves, has Paul lost his mind? Is he dealing with dissonance through sheer
delusion?

To use one of Paul's favorite rejoinders: By no means! He knows exactly what
he's thinking and feeling within a complex paradoxical and panoramic worldview.
The *paradoxical* angle focuses on life-generating elements of death. Like John,
Paul uses agricultural images of buried-and-dying seeds sprouting life (1 Cor.
15:20–23, 36–45) and maternal language of labor pains producing birth (Rom.
8:22; Gal. 4:19; 1 Thess. 5:1–4).[50] But he also asserts that he is "always carrying
in the body the death of Jesus, so that the life of Jesus may also be made visible
in our bodies" (2 Cor. 4:10; cf. Gal. 2:19–20) and that Christ's "power is made
perfect in weakness" (2 Cor. 12:9–10). Straightforward statements, yes; simple to
understand, not so much. We will return to this weak/strong, death/life paradox
in challenge 3.

Paul's *panoramic* perspective pushes beyond stifling strictures of suffering.
The terms rendered "crushed" (2 Cor. 4:8) and "calamities" (6:4) come from
stenos, meaning "narrow, constricted."[51] Envisioning suffering as narrowing leads
to metaphors like being "crushed," "hard pressed," or "in a bind." Paul releases this
pressure by ex-pressing an expansive view of the Creator God.

In Romans 8:18–39, Paul sets "the sufferings of this present time" (8:18) in the
broad horizon of past and future creation, with accompanying blues soundtrack.
The epic music of the spheres features three groups in a mournful, soulful—yet
hopeful—chorus of *sighing/groaning*. Creation itself appears as active subject,
along with humankind and the Creator God in concert with the Spirit. All voice
their anguish over a suffering world:

All Creation: "We know that the whole creation has been *groaning* [*systenazei*]
    in labor pains until now." (8:22)

50. See Gaventa, *Our Mother Saint Paul*, 3–75.
51. Cf. the English "stenography," a short form of writing, and "stenosis," as in spinal stenosis, com-
pacted vertebrae.

Humankind: "And not only the creation but we ourselves, who have the *first fruits* of the Spirit, *groan* [*stenazomen*] inwardly while we wait for adoption, the redemption of our bodies." (8:23)

Creator God/Spirit: "Likewise the Spirit helps us in our weakness. That very Spirit intercedes with *sighs/groans* [*stenagmois*] too deep for words. And God, who searches the heart, knows what is the mind of the Spirit." (8:26–27)

Notice that these terms for groaning/sighing also derive from *stenos*, reflecting inner pressure erupting outwardly in vocal moans that are "too deep for words." Notice, too, the commingling of cries, which evince shared, sympathetic suffering among Creator and the "whole creation."

However, such cosmic groaning, while honest and realistic, is not defeatist or nihilistic. It releases pressure, presses through the ordeal to hope of "redemption." It reprises evolutionary processes of painful childbearing and cyclical fruit-bearing (Rom. 8:22–23) evoked by Jesus. This is no naive, pie-in-the-sky hope but rather a gritty, down-to-earth "hoping against hope," as Paul characterizes Abraham's hope that he and Sarah would produce many descendants, despite having aged bodies "already as good as dead" (4:18–19). The Creator God never stops "giv[ing] life to the dead and call[ing] into existence the things that do not exist" (4:17).[52]

As Isaac became the firstborn person among the new people of Israel, collectively imaged as God's firstborn (Exod. 4:22),[53] so God's Son Jesus became "the firstborn within a large family" (Rom. 8:29; cf. Col. 1:15, 18), born and reborn out of deadly pain and suffering: "It is Christ Jesus, who died, yes, who was raised, who is at the right hand of God, who indeed intercedes for us" (Rom. 8:34). Jesus thus teams with the Holy Spirit (8:26–27) in interceding to God on behalf of suffering humanity, in invoking God's compassionate, restorative action. "If God is for us, who can be against us?" (8:31 NIV). God is not just rooting for us and encouraging us to endure but is perpetually *working* for, in, and with us in a dynamic, cosmic forcefield of love (8:28, 37–39).

Critics might still charge Paul with special pleading in facing the dissonant challenges to Christ's "new creation" posed by persisting suffering in the world, not least his own considerable afflictions *for* Christ. But Paul cannot be charged with superficial pleading. He confronts reality head-on, without cheap revisionism or hopeless resignation. Paul's persevering faith flows from firm conviction and deep experience of God's intimate involvement in creational life through Christ and the Spirit.

52. See Caputo, *Hoping against Hope*.
53. See Isa. 41:8–10; 43:1–7; 44:21–24; 45:10–11; 46:3; 49:1–5; 51:2; 54:1.

2

Right and Wrong

The Moral Challenge of Hypocrisy and Apostasy

Clothe yourselves with the new self, created according to the likeness of God in true righteousness and holiness. (Eph. 4:24)	
Tenet	Jesus Christ is the "Righteous One" who came to reveal God's righteous way and bring sinful people into "right" relationship with God, leading to "right," Christlike behavior.
Tension	If Jesus Christ has transformed repentant sinners into righteous followers of God's way, why do they still stumble into sin, cause each other to stumble, cover up missteps, and sometimes fall away entirely from the "right" path?

Today "righteous" and "righteousness" are rarely used in everyday conversation. They are mostly limited to religious speech, and not always in a positive way. The biblical scholar Marcus Borg reports, "When I have asked Christian audiences about their associations when they heard the word *righteous*, some terms they used were *holier-than-thou, judgmental, condemnatory, hypocritical, priggish, legalistic, moralistic, full of themselves, pompous,* and *arrogant*."[1] That's quite an ugly, "unrighteous" list!

Righteousness is a major biblical theme, one rooted in the character of God. Simply put, "The LORD is righteous; he loves righteous deeds" (Ps. 11:7). Being righteous basically means doing what is right, acting according to God's nature.

1. Borg, *Speaking Christian*, 133 (emphasis original).

Legal dimensions also come into play: God makes righteous judgments, both punishing and pardoning wrongdoers but always with the goal of promoting good, virtuous lives. As Psalm 23 states, "The LORD . . . leadeth me in the paths of righteousness for his name's sake" (23:1, 3 KJV).

The New Testament regards Jesus as the consummate "Righteous One" (Acts 3:14; 7:52; 22:14), who came to earth to "fulfill all righteousness" (Matt. 3:15) and to enable his followers to "become the righteousness of God" (2 Cor. 5:21), clothed "with the new self, created according to the likeness of God in true righteousness and holiness" (Eph. 4:24). Jesus realized his right-making vocation by (1) teaching and demonstrating the right way, (2) forgiving unrighteous sinners, and (3) gifting the Holy (Righteous) Spirit to his spiritual children (John 16:7–11; Rom. 8:4–17).[2]

With all this biblical touting of righteousness, how has it gotten such a bad rap today? Although some preachers rail against modern society's pervasive wickedness, most people still care about right and wrong. They especially don't like being lied to or deceived; they don't like fakes and frauds. Truth and transparency matter. And here's the rub: for all our embracing Jesus as "the way, the truth, and the life" (John 14:6), we Christians can fall woefully short of Jesus's way of "true righteousness and holiness" (Eph. 4:24). Although complaints about church hypocrites can be overblown, there's often evidence to convict us.

Thus we fuel not only external ridicule and resistance but also internal cognitive dissonance and emotional tension. Not living up to one's own truth is disorienting, so much so that we deny it, excuse it, spin it, or do anything to sidestep it. We pile dissonance on top of dissonance, trying to bury the hard truth in a whitewashed tomb or unmarked grave, as Jesus metaphorically blasts some religious teachers for doing (Matt. 23:27–28; Luke 11:44).

But Jesus not only exposes opponents' hypocrisy. He also warns his disciples to beware of arrogant, self-righteous hypocrisy (Matt. 6:1–18). The New Testament writers are not shy about calling out lapses in integrity and even confronting betrayal and denial among Jesus's followers.

On the flip side, the New Testament also examines gray areas between right and wrong, including cases where those who first appear to be wrong wind up being right. This business of righteousness is not easy to get right! But it's too important not to try. Overall, the New Testament strives to be moral without being moralistic. It wrestles with "situational ethics"—not in the free-wheeling

2. In his in-depth study of Rom. 8, Wright unpacks Christ's "putting-right project for the world" (*Into the Heart of Romans*, 19, 23).

sense that "anything goes" but in the commonsense approach that real-life situations inevitably shape people's assessments of right and wrong.

More Right Than Wrong: The Prospect of Higher Righteousness

We noted in challenge 1 how Matthew's Jesus internalizes and intensifies various Torah standards of righteousness. He offers Torah "extensions," not detours or detractions. But aspects of Jesus's career—including some practices adapted by his followers—raise ethical questions and open possible side roads to the straight paths of righteousness. Put another way, sometimes wrong seems right, or at least not *so* wrong, as with ethically dicey traditions about Jesus's (1) *birth* to an unwed young woman engaged to a man who was not Jesus's father, (2) *ministry* of fellowship with known sinners, especially eating with them, and (3) *death* by crucifixion alongside two criminals and insistence that his disciples take up their crosses with him.

The third issue poses the biggest challenge to New Testament writers. What can possibly be *right* about Jesus's horrible, unjust death? How does this death not run crosswise to all standards of decency and morality? We will consider this thorny problem in challenge 3.

We now take up the first two issues, related to Jesus's birth and table fellowship, which skate the right/wrong edge.

What's a Righteous Man to Do with a Pregnant Fiancée in Nazareth?

Ancient biographies of great figures often started with their noble, extraordinary births. Bastards and commonfolk need not apply. Stories of nobodies' hardscrabble rise to prominence did not appeal to the ancients as much as they do to Americans. Better to be wellborn with special touches of divine intervention in their nativities.

So where does that leave Jesus, born of an ordinary young woman in backwater Nazareth of Galilee? Paul all but ignores Jesus's birth, only commenting in passing that "when the fullness of time had come, God sent his Son, born of a woman" (Gal. 4:4). No mention of Mary, Bethlehem, or other details. But "the fullness of time" opens a cosmic view of Jesus's origins—his *originality*—as God's "pre-existent" Son. No earthly emperors, even ones claiming divine adoption, can compete with Jesus's priority over all creation (Phil. 2:6–11) as the world's divine Cocreator (Col. 1:15–20). The poetic prologues in Hebrews 1:1–4 and John 1:1–18 also extol Jesus as Creator. More than enough said—without a birth narrative. In fact, these lyrics about Jesus were not simply said but sung as early hymns, the first noels.

As mentioned in challenge 1, while Mark may hint that Jesus's story traces back to the "beginning" of the world, it officially opens with Isaiah's expectation of a wilderness prophet who will "prepare the way of the Lord" (Mark 1:2–3; Isa. 40:3–5). We promptly learn that this prophet is John the Baptizer, and the Lord is Jesus of Nazareth (1:4–9). While receiving John's baptism, the adult Jesus is affirmed by his divine Father and God's Spirit (1:9–11). Nothing is said about Jesus's birth or childhood.

That would not do, however, for Matthew and Luke: Jesus's great calling demanded a great nativity. Enter the tradition of Jesus's virgin birth or, rather, his conception by the Holy Spirit in the virgin Mary's womb (Matt. 1:18–25; Luke 1:26–38). His birth followed natural processes after the normal period of pregnancy. But Jesus's formation as a divine-human being within the ordinary body of an ordinary village girl—apart from human male seed—is big news! And this news was ripe for gossip, because Mary became pregnant with Jesus *while* she was engaged to Joseph *before* they had consummated the marriage. As Mary began to show, tongues began to wag, even if the Nazarenes assumed that fiancé Joseph was the father. But what if he weren't? Joseph was known as a decent and honorable man. What happened to Mary then? Was she unfaithful? Was she raped?[3] In any event, no one's first thought—least of all Joseph's—would have been, "Praise the Lord! The virgin Mary has conceived the Messiah!" No, something's not right here.

Matthew's first direct reference to righteousness applies to Joseph, Mary's betrothed husband: "Joseph, being a *righteous man*" (1:19). What's a righteous man to do when he discovers that his bride-to-be is pregnant—and not by him? He finds himself in the throes of a cognitive and emotional crisis. Religious law seemed to require breaking off the engagement and besmirching Mary's reputation. But Joseph can't easily disavow his commitment to Mary, regardless of what she has done or what has happened to her. He decides to compromise, to "dismiss" Mary "quietly," privately, without exposing her to public humiliation (1:19–20). Doing the right thing, sort of. Doing the least damaging thing to Mary and struggling to uphold a moral foundation of care versus harm.[4]

3. According to the church father Origen (ca. 185–ca. 254), Celsus, a second-century Greek critic of Christianity, floated the unsubstantiated rumor that the Roman soldier Panthera impregnated Mary (Origen, *Contra Celsum* 1.32, 69). See also later Jewish references in b. Sanhedrin 67a; b. Shabbat 104b.
4. In his major work, *The Righteous Mind: Why Good People Are Divided by Politics and Religion*, social psychologist and ethicist Jonathan Haidt develops a comprehensive "Moral Foundations Theory" (MFT) around five core areas of tension: (1) Care/Harm, (2) Fairness/Cheating, (3) Loyalty/Betrayal,

We might view Joseph's decision as taking the path of "lower" righteousness, doing the least he can do to keep the law under difficult circumstances. But that low bar does not suit Jesus's pattern of "fulfil[ling] all righteousness" (Matt. 3:15), fulfilling the law of Moses to a tee (5:17–18) and then filling it out further (5:20–48). Nor does it suit Jesus's ancestry, his "genealogy" (*geneseōs*), which Matthew traces from Abraham and David (1:1). Jesus's Spirit-conception in Mary's womb does not so much "begin" Jesus's earthly life as extend it via his ancestors.

Much could be said about Abraham and David as righteous—yet far from perfect—forefathers. But more remarkably, this genealogy includes four fascinating *foremothers*—Tamar, Rahab, Ruth, and the wife of Uriah (Bathsheba)—who all appear to have some "foreign" connection (Matt. 1:3–6). Tamar and Rahab were associated with the Canaanites, Ruth was a Moabite, and Bathsheba was first married to the Hittite Uriah. But more notably, three of these women—Tamar, Ruth, and Bathsheba—became pregnant by a Jewish man in an irregular situation of questionable righteousness, and Rahab was a prostitute in Jericho (though the Bible cares less about her profession than her protection of Israelite spies).[5]

The first case may be the wildest (Gen. 38). The patriarch Judah arranges his son Er's marriage to Tamar. But God strikes the wicked Er dead before Tamar bears him any children. Following custom, Judah then gives Tamar to his second son, Onan. But Onan refuses to perform his marital duty and is also killed. Judah then hesitates to give a third son to Tamar, leaving her a vulnerable childless widow. Tamar has little choice but to take matters into her own hands, which she does with cleverness and courage. She positions herself in veiled disguise along the road where Judah is traveling. Taking her to be a prostitute, Judah pays for her sexual services with his signet ring and other forms of ID (think license and credit card). What he does not count on, however, is that she becomes pregnant and keeps his IDs as proof of paternity.

Although Judah is incensed when he learns Tamar has "played the whore" and become pregnant—"Bring her out, and let her be burned" (Gen. 38:24)—he changes his tune when she shows him the goods—*his* goods! He owns up to his misdeed and says, "She is *more in the right* than I, since I did not give her to my [other] son" (38:26). She isn't perfectly righteous, as there's nothing ideal about this mess on the Fairness/Cheating spectrum.[6] But she makes the best of a bad

(4) Authority/Subversion, and (5) Sanctity/Degradation. These binary categories reflect a spectrum of attitudes and actions, not absolute polarities; cf. Graham et al., "Moral Foundations Theory."

5. For these women's fascinating stories, see Gen. 38 (Tamar); Josh. 2:1–21; 6:22–25 (Rahab); the book of Ruth; 2 Sam. 11 and 1 Kings 1:11–31 (Bathsheba).

6. The second category of Moral Foundations Theory (see note 4).

situation, even rising above it to *higher righteousness* that promotes life out of death, hope out of despair, and honor out of shame.[7]

But what do Tamar and the other intrepid foremothers have to do with *Jesus's* identity, other than spicing the family tree? Matthew positions these women at the top of the tree, celebrating their high standard of doing the *more-right* thing in a stressful world, as Joseph must do. These women in the Abraham-Judah-David line are Joseph's foremothers. In contrast to Luke's emphasis on Mary's critical role in Jesus's nativity, Matthew stresses Joseph's response to his fiancée's "irregular" pregnancy.

But doesn't "righteous" Joseph act more like Judah than Tamar in deciding to dismiss Mary, even if discreetly? What is poor Mary to do? What would Tamar and company have done to compel Joseph to do the right thing? Enter the Lord's angel, commanding Joseph to buck up (fear not), do right by Mary, and embrace her "as your wife." The angel assures Joseph that God's Spirit has generated in Mary's womb one who embodies God's saving presence "with us," as Isaiah prophesied (Matt. 2:20–23; Isa. 7:14).

In truth, an angelic dream message with scriptural prooftext is not a lot to go on, though it's more than Tamar and Judah got. Skeptics would require more evidence. Again, no one was expecting a virgin-conceived Messiah in Nazareth, and Isaiah 7:14 hardly clinched the deal.[8] Even with the dream, Joseph must choose to act with courage and confidence that God is genuinely with them in their strange situation, as God was with Joseph's foremothers. And act Joseph does, taking Mary as his wife and taking care of her and her son, whom Herod aimed to kill (Matt. 1:24–25; 2:13–15, 19–23)! Tamar would have been proud.

A strange way to fulfill all righteousness. But normal ways don't always work, especially in times of dissonance and upheaval, when wrong seems to prevail at every turn. Yet through and above the morass, God uses bold, even bizarre, human actions to realize God's righteous aims.

What's a Righteous Meat-Lover to Eat in Corinth and Rome?

We're used to hearing parents and doctors tell us, "Eat right! You are what you eat." Seems like good advice, but it doesn't typically rise to the level of a moral imperative or religious duty. We know about kosher and halal dietary rules, like abstaining from pork, and about religious practices of fasting or eating certain foods

---

7. See Levine, "Gospel of Matthew," 467–68; Spencer, *Dancing Girls*, 24–46.
8. The Hebrew text features a child-conceiving/-bearing "young *woman*." The "virgin" (*parthenos*) comes from the later, Greek version. Neither says anything about a divine Spirit-conception.

on special occasions. But many Westerners view these dining habits as quaint and outmoded, not recipes for righteous conduct. We're more likely to take cholesterol-lowering drugs than to give up bacon or, alternatively, to follow the latest fad diet guaranteed to produce the fittest bodies. Morality, perhaps juiced with righteous indignation, might fuel some vegetarians, though not necessarily due to religious conviction.

But the Bible was shaped in the milieu of ancient Israel where food laws composed part of the "Holiness Code" (Lev. 17–26) for good reasons, however arcane they might seem to us. Right eating was righteous and ritualized in traditions that marked out God's people. Violating kosher norms was not so much morally wrong as it was spiritually lax and socially shameful. Outside the community, however, Jews were ridiculed for their strange diets and other odd practices, such as circumcision and sabbath observance.[9] Tyrannical rulers like Antiochus IV were not beyond killing Jews who refused to defile themselves with nonkosher meat, even on pain of death (1 Macc. 1:41–64; 4 Macc. 4–8).[10]

Kosher meat seal
North Lincolnshire Museum / CC BY 2.0 / Wikimedia Commons

When early congregations of Christ followers began to mix Jewish and Gentile members, tensions inevitably affected table fellowship, a central component of community. What do we serve at church suppers? Do we have separate kosher and nonkosher tables, or do we serve "family style"? Do we ever get any succulent meat, pork or otherwise? Meat was less available in the ancient world than it is in modern supermarkets, and it usually required state-religious certification. That is, prime meat portions were sacrificed to deities and rulers in pagan temples before the less-choice cuts were offered to the public. As believers in one God and the Lord Jesus Christ, can we, Jew or Gentile, eat this "idolatrous" meat in good conscience? A situation ripe for cognitive, emotional, and social dissonance.

The book of Acts reports a major conference in Jerusalem where attendees debated Gentile believers' obligations to keep Jewish laws (Acts 15:1–35). While Gentiles were welcomed as full members of Christ's community on the basis of their faith in Christ, not their compliance with Jewish law, they were nonetheless

9. See Feldman, *Jew & Gentile*, 153–70; Feldman and Reinhold, *Jewish Life*, 366–80.
10. See Gupta, "1 Maccabees."

urged to be considerate of their Jewish sibling-believers by abstaining from immoral and idolatrous practices, such as swearing off eating meat that had been improperly slaughtered and impiously dedicated to other gods (15:19–20). According to Acts, this policy was "unanimously" confirmed and codified in a memorandum sent to all Christ congregations (15:22–30).

So that was that—or not. No church conference goes that smoothly! Paul continues to deal with dietary issues, as his letters to Corinth and Rome demonstrate, negotiating persisting tensions between so-called weak and strong members. It's not clear whether Paul coins or appropriates these labels. In any case, in 1 Corinthians 8–10 and Romans 14–15, these categories do not relate so much to political power (see challenge 3) as to ethical conscience.

Those dubbed "weak" have more sensitive consciences, while the "strong" are more open-minded—specifically about eating meat processed and consumed in pagan temples, which flourished in Corinth and Rome. The "weak" comprise Jewish and Gentile believers who want nothing to do with food that has any whiff of idolatry about it.[11] By contrast, the "strong" see nothing wrong with consuming locally produced meat. Which group is right? To eat meat or not to eat meat? Which diet marks the path of righteousness?

Enter Paul the arbitrator, who's no nutritionist or meat inspector but rather a servant of Christ. Theologically, Paul takes the "strong" side. The many "so-called gods" are all empty suits, figments of superstitious imaginations, and the idols representing them nothing but wood and stone sculptures with no capacity to smell or eat animal sacrifices or bless those who offer them (1 Cor. 8:5). "Yet for us," Paul asserts, "there is one God, the Father, from whom are all things and for whom we exist, and one lord, Jesus Christ, through whom are all things and through whom we exist" (8:6). Since all flesh, human and nonhuman, derives from this divine God-Christ union, the will of this Creator is all that counts in "meaty" matters. God's gracious provisions cannot be tainted by nonexistent gods and impotent idols. Thus, all Paul requires is, "Whether you eat or drink, or whatever you do, do everything for the glory of God" (10:31).

Except that's not quite all. Paul continues, "Give no offense to Jews or to Greeks or to the church of God, just as I try to please everyone in everything I do, not seeking my own advantage, but that of many, so that they may be saved"

---

11. Paula Fredriksen argues that Paul writes "to gentile Christ-followers about sacrifices to idols"— i.e., "former idol-worshippers [who] might still feel anxious around such sanctified foodstuffs." This is an issue that Diaspora Jews had long wrestled with and accommodated in various ways. Fredriksen, *Paul*, 69; cf. 211n17.

(1 Cor. 10:32–33). "Weak" Pastor Paul moderates Professor Paul, the "strong" theologian, with keen "discernment as a situated participant, in the context of human relationships."[12] He considers two situations: one involves in-house temple dining, and the other involves "take-out" meat-market options consumed in people's homes.

First, although pagan gods, idols, and temples amount to nothing, the cosmic evil forces behind these entities are another story. In Paul's mind, eating meat at social functions and worship services within Greco-Roman temples is getting too close for comfort to demonic environments and making a mockery of the Lord's Supper, which was meant to honor Jesus's crucified-risen body. "You cannot partake of the table of the Lord and the table of demons" (1 Cor. 10:21). You can't be that "strong" (10:14–22).

Second, while it's acceptable to shop at the general market and eat meat purchased there at home (1 Cor. 10:25–27), Paul prioritizes "giving no offense" to anyone in the process. No believer should do anything, even what may be technically right, that might prompt "weak"-minded believers to "stumble" or "fall" (8:7–13). Paul is not worried that "weak" members will feel bad but rather that they will *act* bad by going against their consciences and doing what's wrong *for them* before they're ready to take a "stronger" step. Right knowledge is good, but considerate love is better—*more right* (8:1; 12:31–13:13). Accordingly, if "weak" congregants believe that eating meat sacrificed to idols is wrong, then it *is* wrong for them; they "sin against Christ" (8:12). Until persuaded otherwise, they should not be browbeaten with "strong" theology or tempted by other believers' dietary freedom. The "strong" must make concessions to the "weak," not the other way around: "Therefore, if food is a cause of their falling, I will never eat meat, so that I may not cause one of them to fall" (8:13).

Put another way in Romans, "We who are strong ought to put up with the failings of the weak [un-strong, *adynaton*], and not to please ourselves. Each of us must please our neighbor for the good purpose of building up the neighbor" in the spirit of Christ, who served weak humanity and "did not please himself" (Rom. 15:1–3). Thus, Paul further develops his Christ-shaped "relational, other-regarding ethic."[13] Again Paul deals with "weak" and "strong" opinions about food but with menu changes, now focused on vegetarian-omnivore and abstinence-gluttony polarities. He seems to do so tongue-in-cheek, lightly mocking fanatics on both ends: the "weak" veggie-munchers and the "strong" all-you-can-eaters

12. Horrell, *Solidarity and Difference*, 207.
13. Horrell, *Solidarity and Difference*, 190.

(14:2). The "vegetables" term (*lachana*) strictly refers to leafy greens and herbs, and "eating anything" suggests scarfing down everything in sight.[14] Hence, Paul sets up a snarky contrast between "lettuce-eaters" and "garbage-bellies," as one commentator quips.[15] We might substitute kale for lettuce or go even snarkier with "Prigs versus Pigs."

Again, Paul is no dietitian or health consultant. His aim is not to manage food groups but to moderate tensions between people groups with different eating habits, giving special consideration to those with "weaker" sensibilities. The point is "never to put a stumbling block or hindrance in the way of another" (Rom. 14:13), never to coax others to break their stricter "right" diets because they seem "wrong" to you. What truly "*is wrong* [is] for you to make others fall by what you eat" (14:20). Bottom line: "The kingdom of God is not food and drink but righteousness and peace and joy in the Holy Spirit"—righteousness that "makes for peace and mutual upbuilding" in the Christ community (14:17, 19).

All Right, No Wrong: The Problem of Self-Righteousness

One strain of biblical teaching denies human self-capacity for righteousness. The postexilic prophet confesses, "All our righteous deeds are like a filthy cloth" (Isa. 64:6). Paul flatly admits that, despite his strict religious upbringing, he does "not hav[e] a righteousness of [his] own" but only "the righteousness from God based on faith" (Phil. 3:9). In sum, "There is no one who is righteous, not even one" (Rom. 3:10).

Religious people, however, tend to find this "no righteous" diagnosis a hard pill to swallow. Even if they concede a sinful past before being "saved," that's behind them now; henceforth, they stride in paths of righteousness, with God's help, of course, but also with a little too much strut in their new (self-)righteous step. To be sure, "walk[ing] in newness of life" is a worthy goal for baptized believers in Christ (Rom. 6:4). But in reality no one follows Christ perfectly, and whatever righteousness emerges owes to continuing immersion in divine grace, love, and power. No room for self-glorification: "Let the one who boasts, boast in the Lord" (1 Cor. 1:31; cf. Jer. 9:24).

As discussed in challenge 1, Christians have commonly equated Pharisaism with self-righteousness, hypocrisy, and hyper-legalism. Apart from distorting the

---

14. Jewett, *Romans*, 837–38; BDAG, s.v. "λάχανον," 587.
15. Gaventa, *When in Romans*, 108, 109–10.

Pharisees' piety, this stereotype distracts from noticing serious moral lapses within the Jesus movement, exposed by various New Testament writers. Easier to brand other groups than to blame one's own.

Peter and Fellow Disciples Who Think They're Loyal

In one of the most infamous Gospel episodes, while Jesus undergoes a late-night trial before the high priest, the apostle Peter vehemently denies three times that he's ever met Jesus. This profile in cowardice follows only a few hours after Peter's bodacious protest to Jesus: "Even though I must die with you, I will [absolutely] not [*ou mē*] deny you" (Mark 14:31). Likewise, the other disciples chime in, rebuking Jesus for suggesting they would "all become deserters" (14:27). But desert him they do after Jesus's arrest (14:50). Some women follow Jesus to the cross, albeit only "from a distance" (15:40), but they hadn't made a point of touting their devotion to Jesus.

Deserters, deniers, and distancers are scarcely ideal disciples. Credit the Gospel writers' honesty about Jesus's first followers and the dissonance their failings create for future ones. Gospel readers can't help but notice a critical crack in the Loyalty/Betrayal moral foundation.[16] If Peter the "Rock," to whom Matthew's Jesus entrusted the foundation of "my church" (Matt. 16:18), couldn't stand up under fire, what hope do average believers have? Consider some ways the New Testament negotiates this tension.

- *Endless love.* The Gospels indicate that Jesus senses beforehand that Peter will deny him, a premonition he communicates to Peter, prompting vociferous objection.[17] Jesus knows that Peter and company aren't strong enough yet to take up their crosses with him. But he simply discloses this fact without berating their weakness. As the Johannine narrator describes Jesus's disposition toward his fickle disciples, "Having loved his own who were in the world, he loved them to the end" (John 13:1). They might fail him, but his love for them will never fail.

- *Renewed faith.* Luke adds some memorable touches. Accompanying Jesus's prediction of Peter's denials is his prayer for Peter: "I have prayed for you that your own faith may not fail; and you, when once you have turned back, strengthen your brothers" (Luke 22:32). Acts shows that Jesus's prayer was

16. The third plank of Moral Foundations Theory (see note 4).
17. Matt. 26:31–35; Mark 14:27–31; Luke 22:31–34; John 13:36–38.

answered, as Peter demonstrates bold faith in the risen Christ amid continuing opposition, including imprisonment, by the Jerusalem authorities
(Acts 3–5).

- *Spirit power.* Acts makes clear that Peter's resurgence has nothing to do
  with his own resilience, repentance (he never says "sorry"), or his "own
  power or piety" (3:12). The power generating Peter's renewal comes from
  the Holy Spirit, poured out by Jesus upon "all flesh" (2:17–18, 32–33). This
  Spirit does not create righteous robots but provides guidance and strength
  for following the challenging path of the "Righteous One" (3:14; 7:52).

- *Pastoral care.* Denier and deserter disciples would seem to be the last people
  "Good Shepherd" Jesus would entrust with his vulnerable "flock" (John
  10:1–18). But that's precisely what happens when the risen Jesus commissions Peter to tend and feed the "lambs/sheep" in loving fellowship
  with Jesus. Peter "felt hurt" that Jesus asked him three times, "Do you love
  me?"—one time for each of Peter's previous denials (21:15–19)! Jesus thus
  drives home the dissonance and distress of Peter's past in order to reorient
  him toward sympathetic pastoral ministry. The letter of 1 Peter portrays
  the elder-apostle as a faithful senior shepherd, acquainted with both "the
  sufferings of Christ" and "the glory to be revealed"; he exhorts fellow shepherds, subject to "anxiety" in their demanding work, to "tend the flock of
  God" with humility and trust in the "chief shepherd" Jesus (1 Pet. 5:1–7).

Paul's Competitors Who Think They're More Qualified

While Christians have long touted Paul as the epitome of the gospel's transformative, right-making power, he was not so esteemed in his own time. Paul was
a disruptive, dissonant figure whom various ministers of Christ distrusted and
tried to diminish. Their suspicions were not unreasonable. The path from arch-
persecutor of the "church of God" (Gal. 1:13) to apostolic missionary is hard to
believe. Paul wasn't one of Jesus's original twelve apostles, and reports of private
visionary encounters with Christ (Gal. 1:12, 15–16) are hard to verify.

As Acts tells the story, when Paul first presented himself to the Jerusalem congregation as a dedicated Christ believer and proclaimer, almost everyone doubted
his sincerity and remained afraid of him. Only when a respected member named
Barnabas "took [Paul], brought him to the apostles, and described for them how
on the road he had seen the Lord, who had spoken to him," did the community
begin to accept him (Acts 9:26–27). But tensions persisted.

Paul and Barnabas eventually teamed up as a dynamic ministerial and missionary duo, based in the growing Jewish-Gentile congregation in Antioch of Syria (Acts 11:19–30; 13:1–3; 15:12). Their partnership did not last forever, though, as they came to fall out over adding a third member (John Mark) to their team (15:36–42). Or so Acts reports. Paul's own version of the conflict targets Barnabas—and Peter—as hypocrites for their table conduct in Antioch.

One time, according to Paul, when Peter visited the Antioch assembly, he declined to dine with Gentile believers, opting to segregate with stricter Jewish members, presumably at a kosher table. On this occasion, Paul did not encourage Gentile accommodation to Jewish sensibilities. To the contrary, he publicly "opposed [Cephas/Peter][18] to his face" for "not acting consistently with the truth of the gospel" or with his table fellowship with Gentiles in other settings. Paul was further appalled that "even Barnabas was led astray by their hypocrisy" (Gal. 2:11–14). As Margaret Mitchell has noted, "This text was a thorn in the side for Christian exegetes, from very early on, a problem that could not be avoided . . . because the charge at issue . . . in this passage—hypocrisy—could undermine the whole religious movement with which they were associated."[19]

Paul found himself isolated in this situation, which contributed to his frustration in the original moment and in his current dealings with dissonant Jewish-Gentile relations in Galatia, which focused more on certain leaders' pressure to circumcise Gentile believers than on changing their eating habits. Paul becomes so beside himself toward the end of Galatians that he blurts out a vicious wish that those promoting circumcision "would castrate themselves!" (5:12). So much for the sensitive, conciliatory writer of 1 Corinthians and Romans. Who exactly is the hypocrite here?[20]

By time he wrote 2 Corinthians 10–13, Paul's relationship with this congregation had become more precarious, as a group of rival leaders emerged, claiming to be superior to Paul. He derisively dubs these competitors "super-apostles," using a compound superlative adjective, "hyper-super/super-duper" (*hyperlian*, 2 Cor. 11:5; 12:11). These rivals did not press pet doctrinal or ritual issues so much as their personal charisma and authority,[21] evidenced in eloquent speech, brilliant wisdom, spectacular miracles, dramatic visions, and forceful leadership. In turn,

18. "Cephas" is the Aramaic version of Peter's Greek nickname, meaning "Rock."
19. Mitchell, "Peter's 'Hypocrisy,'" 214.
20. Mitchell ("Peter's 'Hypocrisy'") discusses how the fourth-century church father John Chrysostom recognized and negotiated the potential problem of *both apostles' hypocrisy* in the Antioch incident.
21. The fourth component of Moral Foundations Theory is Authority/Subversion (see note 4).

they demeaned Paul as a dull speaker, weak leader, and altogether pathetic figure who hides behind a domineering avatar in his letters (10:1–2, 10; 11:5–6, 20–29; 12:1–13).

For his part, Paul blasts these bombastic boasters as "false apostles, deceitful workers, disguising themselves as apostles of Christ. And no wonder! Even Satan disguises himself as an angel of light. So it is not strange if his ministers also disguise themselves as *ministers of righteousness*" (2 Cor. 11:13–15). In a rhetorical tour de force, Paul occasionally counters with his own achievements—for example, as a special seer into the mysteries of paradise (12:1–5) and a "true" worker of apostolic "signs and wonders" (12:12). But he only plays his opponents' chest-thumping game as a "fool"—on their level! His main claim to authority rests in his weaknesses, his myriad sufferings as minister of the crucified Christ (12:9–10; see challenge 3).

Does Paul have a chip on his shoulder? Does his clever rhetoric betray an underlying current of jealousy and resentment? Perhaps. But at the core of his being beats the passionate heart of a reconciling servant of the crucified Christ, who gave himself "so that in him we might become the righteousness of God" (2 Cor. 5:21; cf. 5:11–20).

Johannine "Children" Who Think They're Perfect

The Fourth Gospel identifies its primary witness as the "disciple whom Jesus loved" (John 21:20, 24–25). He is the only disciple who follows Jesus to the foot of the cross (19:26–27). No denying or deserting Jesus. He typically outshines Peter, including outrunning him to Jesus's empty tomb (20:1–8). Though this special disciple is never named in the Fourth Gospel, perhaps signifying his ideal status, early tradition associated him with the apostle John. The three letters known as 1–3 John, attributed to "the elder/presbyter" (*presbyteros*, 2 John 1; 3 John 1), circulated in the Johannine "community of the beloved disciple," which is committed to the foundational teaching of John's Gospel.[22]

Love marks a leading theme across the Johannine Gospel and letters. Since God "*is* love" (1 John 4:8), the righteous ways of God reflect multifaceted love: perfect love exists between God and Jesus, between Father and Son (John 17:23–26; 1 John 1:3); God's gracious love for the world invites our grateful love for God in return (John 3:16; 1 John 4:7–9); and Christlike love for one another abounds within the beloved community (John 13:34–35; 1 John 3:16;

---

22. R. Brown, *Community*.

4:7–12). But Jesus's "sermonic" call to love one's enemies (Matt. 5:43–48; Luke 6:27–36) is conspicuously absent in the Johannine writings, where charity starts—and stays—at home, with us and with others like us. Such an insular perspective may reflect a tight-knit community that feels threatened by the wider society.

Unfortunately, however, this fear of outsiders can spill into the community and be directed toward insiders who break from family values. Such internal conflict split the "loving" Johannine fellowship. Dissonance festered into division. "We" fragmented into a smaller circle of "us" divorced from "them." Lovers became "exes," who were *ex*communicated: "They went out [*exēlthan*] from us [*ex hēmōn*], but they did not belong to us [*ex hēmōn*]; for if they had belonged to us [*ex hēmōn*], they would have remained with us. But by going out they make it plain that none of them belongs to us [*ex hēmōn*]" (1 John 2:19).

The Johannine elder writes from the "we" side as a concerned father to his "little children" (1 John 2:1, 12–14, 28; 3:18; 4:4; 5:21). But this beloved father figure has precious little love for defectors, called "antichrists" (2:18) and "deceivers" (2 John 7) in the letters and "secessionists" and "schismatics" by scholars.[23] Of course, secession is in the eye of the beholder. Who left whom? Who expelled whom? Who stands as the faithful tradition-bearer? A letter from Diotrophes, a ringleader of "them" (3 John 9–10), would doubtless tell a different story from the elder/father, who simply dismisses dissenters: since "they" were never really with us in the first place, good riddance!

Does this distinctly unloving attitude toward defectors not betray the elder's hypocritical blind spot, similar to what beset Peter and Paul according to Galatians? Might we rightly charge the elder with violating Jesus's core love commandment and blowing his own self-righteous horn?[24] Perhaps he puts on an overconfident face for "the children" to ease the cognitive dissonance and emotional upheaval of his fractured community. Or perhaps love has limits; perhaps "they" can drift too far from "us"?

This raises the key question, What is so wrong with "them"? The elder pinpoints his opponents' main problem as their arrogant belief that they are so right! Of course, both sides claim to be right. But the elder denounces his rivals' extremist views concerning their—and Jesus's—righteousness. Though rightly affirming Jesus's sinlessness, they wrongly imply that he could not have sinned

23. Painter, *1, 2, and 3 John*, 5 (he prefers the more generic label "opponents").
24. Notice the self-assured drumbeat of "we know/we may be sure" in 1 John 2:3–5, 18; 3:2, 14, 19; 4:13; 5:2, 15, 18–20.

because he never truly assumed human nature ("became flesh," John 1:14) but only appeared to have a human body. This denial of Jesus's humanity marks antichrist ideology (1 John 2:18, 22; 4:1–3; 2 John 7).

Closely tied to this hyper-spiritualized view of Christ is the secessionists' presumption of their own idealized perfection in Christ. Here and now, in this world, they claim to have already attained complete righteousness: no more sin, striving, or struggling; no need for forgiveness or spiritual growth. To which the elder retorts, "If we say that we have no sin, we deceive ourselves, and the truth is not in us. If we confess our sins, he who is faithful and just [or righteous] will forgive us our sins and cleanse us from all unrighteousness" (1 John 1:8–9). We can continue to be forgiven because "we have an advocate with the Father, Jesus Christ the righteous," who pleads our case *as one of us,* who gave his flesh and blood "for our sins" (2:1–2). By no means, however, does the elder excuse believers' sinful behavior. Because Christ "is righteous," his children should "walk just as he walked" and "do what is right" (2:6; 3:7); and when they don't, they confess their failures, receive forgiveness, and keep moving forward in the way of love.

From Right to Wrong: The Peril of Renouncing the Righteous Way

Temporary deviations from the righteous path are one thing; total renunciations are another. Whereas hope of restoration remains alive for occasional deniers, deserters, and dissenters, it seems forever lost for adamant repudiators. Defectors (apostates) create a defensive (apologetic) crisis. It's hard enough to hold together as a minority, countercultural community, like the early Christ followers, without having to deal with outright traitors to the faith and wholesale assimilators to the dominant culture. As encouraging as it was to have a hardened Christ-resister like Saul/Paul experience a dramatic turnaround and a craven Christ-denier like Simon Peter rebound with robust commitment, it was devastating to have former believers utterly turn against Christ and his community, whether out of antipathy or apathy.

The Benedict Arnold of the nascent Jesus movement was Judas Iscariot, one of Jesus's twelve apostles. Judas betrayed Jesus to authorities who orchestrated his crucifixion. But others "shrink back and so are lost" in other ways (Heb. 10:39). How do the New Testament writings deal with these crises of defection that potentially expose defective elements in the Jesus movement? This poses no small challenge for the fledgling community.

Falling Headlong: The Judas Factor

In listing Jesus's chosen apostles, the Synoptic Gospels start with Simon Peter and end with Judas Iscariot (Matt. 10:1–4; Mark 3:13–19; Luke 6:12–16). In Simon's case, they note the nickname "Peter" (Petros/Rock), which Jesus gave him, and they label Judas "the one who betrayed him" (cf. John 6:71). The traitor tradition was too well known to gloss over. Best admit it early in Gospel accounts, although Judas receives no further mention until he hatches the plot for Jesus's arrest. Except for the Fourth Gospel's parenthetical comment that Judas "was a thief; he kept the common purse and used to steal what was put into it" (John 12:6), no evidence emerges of sinister character before he betrays Jesus. He just seemed to snap.

By contrast, although Peter's denial of Jesus was also well known, he did not bear the "denier" label for life. He remained Petros/Rock, despite his petrification with fear at Jesus's trial. Although Peter has his ups and downs, he stands out in the Gospels as the apostles' leading spokesperson. As we've seen, Peter's denials create considerable tension for New Testament writers, but not as much as Judas's betrayal does. Fairly or unfairly, Peter gets a second chance, resumes his leadership among Jesus's followers, and even superintends the business of filling Judas's vacated apostolic position (Acts 1:15–26)!

Replacing Judas was necessary not only because of his nefarious betrayal but also because of his horrendous death: "Falling headlong, he burst open in the middle and all his bowels gushed out" (Acts 1:18). Matthew tells a different tale than Acts, less gory but just as horrible: "Throwing down the pieces of silver in the temple, he departed; and he went and hanged himself" (Matt. 27:5). Both versions make the same point: Judas got what he deserved.

Archibald Tuttle / CC BY-SA 4.0 / Wikimedia Commons

Depiction of the death of Judas (on the left) on a column at the basilica in Vézelay, France

But did he really? Is the matter as simple as that? Any movement can have one bad apple. Solution: pluck it off the tree, drop it, and move on. But the Gospels and Acts don't leave it there. The Judas problem is too serious to bury. Though the don't elaborate at length, the narratives drop various hints of causes and motives driving Judas's betrayal and add details about his character and actions.

	Driving Factors: Causes and Motives	Added Details: Character and Actions
Matthew	• Judas seeks and receives money from chief priests (26:14–16) • Scripture fulfilled: "as it is written" (26:24)	• Payment amount: thirty pieces of silver (26:15) • Judas "dipped his hand into the bowl" with Jesus at the Last Supper (26:23) • Upon learning that Jesus was condemned to death, Judas "repented" of "betraying innocent blood" and returned the silver coins to the priests, who rebuffed him (27:3–4) • Judas threw down the coins, left, "and hanged himself" (27:5) • The chief priests used the coins to buy a field "as a place to bury foreigners" (27:7)
Mark	• Judas receives money from chief priests (14:10–11) • Scripture fulfilled: "as it is written" (14:21)	• Jesus and Judas "dip bread into the bowl" at the Last Supper (14:20)
Luke	• Satan enters Judas (22:3) • Judas receives money from chief priests (22:4–6) • Divine purpose: "as it has been determined" (22:22)	• Judas's "hand is on the table" with Jesus's at the Last Supper (22:21)
John	• Jesus announces, "Did I not choose you, the twelve? Yet one of you is a devil" (6:70) • The devil "had already put it into the heart of Judas" to betray Jesus (13:2) • Scripture fulfilled: "The one who ate my bread has lifted his heel against me" (13:18; Ps. 41:9) • Satan enters Judas (13:27) • Jesus prays, "I guarded them, and not one of them was lost except the one destined to be lost, so that the scripture might be fulfilled" (17:12; cf. 6:39; 18:9)	• Judas "was a thief; he kept the common purse and used to steal what was put into it" (12:6; cf. 13:29) • Jesus signals his knowledge of Judas's imminent betrayal by giving him a piece of bread dipped in a common dish (sauce) (13:26–27, 30)
Acts	• Judas is rewarded for his "wickedness" (1:18) • Scripture fulfilled: "'Let his homestead become desolate, and let there be no one to live in it'; and 'Let another take his position'" (1:20; cf. v. 16; Pss. 69:25; 109:8)	• With his reward money, Judas buys a field, which comes to be known as "Field of Blood" (1:19)

We may well imagine that Judas suffered cognitive dissonance and emotional upheaval. He did not sign on for a defeatist Messiah who was heading toward execution and calling followers to bear their crosses with him. Although Jesus proved to be a powerful teacher and healer, he mobilized no armed revolution, no forceful overthrow of the empire—as Judas may have hoped. Therefore, Judas may have become disillusioned with Jesus's pacific mission and decided to cut his losses. A plausible theory but not what the Gospels and Acts present.

Instead, they variously attribute Judas's betrayal to three causes or motives: money, Satan, and Scripture; or financial greed (follow the money), diabolical control (the devil made him do it), and biblical prophecy (it was predestined). Matthew adds a more sympathetic picture of Judas but at the steep price of smearing Jewish priestly leaders. Matthew's Judas has a sudden change of heart about "betraying innocent blood" (Matt. 27:4). He confesses his sin to the chief priests and returns the thirty pieces of silver, hoping to receive forgiveness and perhaps forestall Jesus's execution. But to no avail, as the priests couldn't care less about Judas's conscience, and Judas couldn't carry the burden of his guilt and resorted to suicide (27:5). In an ironic and anti-Judaic move in Matthew's literary plot, Judas—whose name means "Jew/Judean"—becomes a tragic casualty of Jewish bloodlust.

John's Gospel takes another tack, focused not on eliciting pity for Judas but on exonerating Jesus of responsibility for Judas's defection. In this case, multiple dissonant problems arise. If Jesus was so prescient about human nature (John 2:24–25), why choose Judas as an apostle? Or, if he knew Judas's vulnerability, why didn't Jesus train him better, steer him down the right path? Maybe most disturbingly, how could Jesus lose one of his chosen emissaries? What does that say about believers' security? Jesus acknowledges that his difficult teachings may cause "many of his disciples" to drop out (6:60). He even wonders about the twelve disciples: "Do you also wish to go away?" Right after Peter reaffirms their commitment, Jesus adds, "Did I not choose you, the twelve? Yet one of you is a devil" (6:67, 70). Jesus acknowledges Judas as the devil's agent from the start (cf. 13:2, 27). This assessment fits the Johannine letter's demarcation of secessionists as never really belonging to us (1 John 2:18). Still, the question nags concerning why Jesus selected Judas in the first place.

Jesus affirms that he has faithfully "guarded" his followers and made sure "not one of them was lost"—"*except* the one destined to be lost, so that the scripture might be fulfilled" (John 17:12; cf. 18:9). Destined to be lost? Why? Beyond echoing Scripture (13:18; Ps. 41:9), perhaps Judas's "lost" destiny meshes with

Jesus's destiny to lay down his life for his "sheep" (John 10:11–18, 27–28). Someone must catalyze the events leading to Jesus's saving death. Judas just happens to fulfill that tragic role—for the greater good, we could say.[25]

The Gospels and Acts offer no wholly satisfying answers to the Judas problem. At times, they skate close to the edge of special pleading. Only Matthew gives Judas any benefit of the doubt, and then only to the detriment of Jewish authorities. But again, we should give the New Testament narratives credit for showing their messy work in a difficult moral case rather than sweeping it under the rug. Judas's shocking betrayal of the righteous Jesus's "innocent blood" affected the writers deeply—and dissonantly.

Falling Away: The Hebrews Crisis

From the singular problem of Judas, we turn to a congregational crisis addressed in Hebrews concerning those who have already abandoned the faith or are strongly considering it. Unlike in the Johannine letters, the issue here is not secession provoked by doctrinal disputes and personality conflicts but rather total defection and disaffection, apostasy and apathy.

For the Hebrews community, probably based in Rome (Heb. 13:24), the moral foundation of Loyalty/Betrayal intertwined with Care/Harm as the suffering that believers experienced for their faith raised doubts about its saving benefits. Was it worth staying with a religion that cost so much? Hebrews acknowledges the hardships while attempting to mitigate their dire effects: "After you had been enlightened, you endured a hard struggle [*athlēsin*] with sufferings, sometimes being publicly exposed [*theatrizomenoi*] to abuse and persecution, and sometimes being partners with those so treated. For you had compassion for those who were in prison, and you cheerfully accepted the plundering of your possessions, knowing that you yourselves possessed something better and more lasting" (10:32–34).

Because believers have been "enlightened" about Jesus's true nature (he is no criminal meriting execution) and have come to trust him as Lord and Christ, they suffer societal attacks in three arenas: (1) "athletic" defeat and injury, (2) "theatric" humiliation and shame, (3) economic deprivation and confiscation of property. Hebrews tries to buoy the flagging spirits of depleted, disaffected congregants by reminding them of their past emotional resilience and maturity, which are

---

25. The later, apocryphal Gospel of Judas, written from a Gnostic perspective, completely whitewashes Judas, portraying him as Jesus's closest confidant. At the end, Jesus commends Judas, "But you will exceed all of them. For you will sacrifice the [fleshly] man that clothes me" (Gospel of Judas 56); see Kasser et al., *Gospel of Judas*.

manifest in their "compassion" toward imprisoned fellow believers and "cheerful" acceptance of confiscated possessions.

Although the addressees no doubt remained concerned about those jailed for Christ's sake, they might well scoff at blithe assumptions about how "cheerfully" they lost their livelihoods. In any event, they have now ceased putting on a happy face. The price is too steep. Better to cut their losses and ties with the Jesus movement. Or in the more pejorative terms Hebrews uses, they've begun to "drift away" (2:1), "go astray in their hearts" (3:9), "turn away from the living God" (3:12), "fail to enter [God's rest] because of disobedience" (4:5–6), "harden [their] hearts" (3:8; 4:7), "fall away" (6:6), "willfully persist in sin" (10:26), "shrink back" (10:39), "grow weary or lose heart" (12:3), and "fail to obtain the grace of God" (12:15).

Most seriously, if they break with Christ—after having "been enlightened" (Heb. 6:4; 10:32) and "formerly received the good news" (4:6) and "knowledge of the truth" (10:26)—"it is impossible to restore [them] again to repentance" (6:4). There's no turning back after turning away—not without making a mockery of Jesus's redemptive death, without virtually "crucifying again the Son of God" (6:6). Their fates will be sealed. They will forfeit security as surely as Israel's rebellious exodus generation failed to enter the promised land (3:7–4:11) and the "immoral and godless" Esau failed to reclaim the birthright he sold, "even though he sought the blessing with tears" (12:16–17).

Yet all hope is not lost. It's not too late for fence-sitters to come down on the right side, bear "the peaceful fruit of righteousness" (Heb. 12:11), and "make straight paths for your feet" (12:13) in the Jesus-led "race that is set before us" (12:1). Despite dire warnings about defectors, Hebrews remains optimistic that strugglers in the faith will persevere: "Beloved, we are confident of better things in your case, things that belong to salvation. . . . We want each of you to show the same diligence so as to realize the full assurance of hope to the very end, so that you may not become sluggish, but imitators of those who through faith and patience inherit the promises" (6:9–12).[26]

So the author gives his flagging audience a pep talk: "Hang in there. I believe in you!" But he also undergirds his motivational speech with affective and cognitive counsel. The emotional turmoil embroiling the Hebrews congregation because of societal sanctions imposed for their commitment to Christ centered on fear and shame: fear of severe loss of livelihood and shame of public ridicule

26. For a helpful discussion of tension between hope and judgment in Hebrews' warning passages, see Bateman, *Four Views*.

and ostracism (Heb. 10:33).[27] Hebrews aims to treat these emotional symptoms with a heavy dose of Jesus's powerful experience and a kind of reverse psychology.

Jesus the Son has been anointed and vindicated by God as the "righteous scepter" of God's realm who "loved righteousness and hated wickedness" (Heb. 1:8–9; cf. Ps. 45:6–7). But the righteous way blazed by Jesus on earth before his heavenly exaltation is a way of human suffering "in every respect . . . yet without sin" (4:15; cf. 2:17), to the point of humiliating crucifixion. And he does not simply plod through this suffering to the bitter end; he enters it, engages it, learns from it (5:8), and presses through it. Jesus pioneers and perfects the way of faithful righteousness and salvation (2:10; cf. 12:2), transforming "fear of death" into hope of redeemed life (2:14–15; cf. 13:12) and "disregarding [the cross's] shame" in hope of "the joy that was set before him" (12:2) and the glory/honor of God, whose image he bears (1:3).[28] Since "Jesus is not ashamed to call them brothers and sisters" (2:11; cf. 11:16)—not ashamed to share fully their suffering and humiliation—they should not be ashamed of him; they should not recoil from following and fellowshipping with him en route to a joyous, glorious rest. Put another way: if ashamed of anything, they should have proper shame about abandoning Jesus, who gave everything for their salvation.[29]

Similarly, the shaky believers' fear of persecution and dispossession should be countered by a proper fear, a "godly fear" (*eulabeias*, Heb. 5:7 RSV) demonstrated by the suffering Jesus, a grateful attitude of "reverence [*eulabeias*] and awe" toward God, who welcomes Jesus's spiritual siblings into an unshakable kingdom (12:28).[30] Such God-fearing should not be trivialized, however; it carries an element of dread as well as awe, of potential destruction as well as salvation. "Those who have spurned the Son of God . . . and outraged the Spirit of grace" merit "worse punishment" than those who never followed Jesus in the first place; Hebrews offers no cheap comfort for defectors: "It is a fearful thing to fall into the hands of the living God" (10:29–31; cf. 12:25–29).

Since emotions motivate cognitive deliberation and purposeful action, the writer of Hebrews aptly uses emotive rhetoric to persuade readers to keep the faith and "hold firm/fast" (Heb. 3:6; 10:23). But the author doesn't simply try to scare or shame them into remaining loyal. Negative emotional manipulation is insufficient to sustain group commitment and cohesion. For those already

---

27. On fear in Hebrews, see Gray, *Godly Fear*; on shame, see deSilva, *Despising Shame*.
28. See deSilva, *Hope of Glory*, 144–77; L. Johnson, *Hebrews*, 33–38.
29. Cf. Hockey, *Role of Emotion*, 226–50.
30. See Gray, *Godly Fear*, 187–214.

terrorized and stigmatized by outsiders, a strategy of stoking fear and shame within the community can easily backfire if not supplemented by positive emotional and practical support. Fortunately, Hebrews offers such support, cultivating vital emotions of hope and love via central practices of prayer and fellowship (see 4:14–5:9; 6:10–20; 10:23–39; 13:1–3).

3

Weak and Strong

The Political Challenge of Authority and Tyranny

We proclaim Christ crucified, a stumbling block to Jews and foolishness to Gentiles, but to those who are the called, both Jews and Greeks, Christ [is] the power of God and the wisdom of God. (1 Cor. 1:23–24)	
Tenet	Jesus Christ is God's anointed "strongman" who proclaimed and embodied God's supreme rule over all worldly kingdoms and ultimately conquered humanity's most powerful enemy: death.
Tension	How can belief in Jesus's august power and authority be reconciled with his humiliating death on a Roman cross and the empire's persisting oppression?

Around 30 CE a fiery preacher named John stations himself at the Jordan River in the Judean wilderness, calling people to repent and be baptized so they might receive forgiveness of sins and escape the coming judgment of God (Matt. 3:1–12; Mark 1:4–8; Luke 3:1–20). From Jerusalem and the surrounding countryside, many throng to John, hoping he is the prophet Elijah (John dresses and speaks like him) returned to earth to signal the restoration of God's kingdom.

Could he even be the Messiah (Luke 3:15)? John emphatically answers, No! His Elijah-style mission is preparing the way for God's anointed agent, Jesus. John first describes Jesus in functional terms: "I baptize you with water; but one who is more powerful than I is coming; I am not worthy to untie the thong of his sandals" (3:16). More simply, "one who is more powerful" designates the "stronger man" (*ischyroteros*). The Gospels portray Jesus as a "stronger" prophet and proclaimer of God's rule who performs life-restoring miracles and embodies God's life on earth. Yet as surely as John the Baptizer was beheaded by the Galilean tetrarch Herod Antipas (Matt. 14:1–11; Mark 6:17–29; Luke 9:7–9), Jesus the Messiah was crucified by the Roman Judean governor Pontius Pilate.[1] Obviously, stringing up a putative strongman on a cross would strip him of any legitimate claim to power. A crucified emperor has no clothes.

By all normal measures, Jesus seems to be a defeated strongman, a failed Messiah. Yet his New Testament story does not end with crucifixion. He is resurrected on the third day after death. Although no one sees Jesus's release from tomb and graveclothes, numerous witnesses claim to see him alive and well, to eat with him, and to hear him teach until he ascends into heaven (Luke 24:13–53; Acts 1:1–11; 1 Cor. 15:3–7). Undoubtedly, this testimony about the risen-exalted Jesus Messiah, confirmed by believers' experience of Christ's Spirit among them, goes a long way toward managing the cognitive dissonance and emotional upheaval of his excruciating death. As Paul says, "If Christ has not been raised, your faith is futile" (1 Cor. 15:17). But glory be, he has been raised, as "we proclaim and so you have come to believe" (15:11). "Thanks be to God, who gives us the victory through our Lord Jesus Christ" (15:57). The Strong One lives!

Yet, as reassuring as Christ's resurrection is, it doesn't overcome all doubts, fears, and tensions. Consider three nagging matters.

First, Christ's followers do not immediately believe in his resurrection. According to the Gospels, Mary Magdalene and other women are the first to see Jesus's empty tomb and later meet him in his risen body (Matt. 28:1–10; Mark 16:1–8; Luke 24:1–11, 22–23; John 20:1–2, 11–18). But they are expecting neither of these experiences, and no one else, least of all the male disciples, is inclined to believe a wild "idle tale" from grief-stricken women (Luke 24:11). Paul doesn't bother to include the women in his list of witnesses to the risen Christ (1 Cor. 15:5–8). The eleven apostles (the twelve minus Judas) eventually believe when they see the living Jesus for themselves, though Thomas needs an extra nudge toward faith (John 20:24–29). And Paul needs a gobsmacking encounter with Christ to get him on the right course (1 Cor. 15:8–10). Yet after his ascension, Christ did not normally make personal appearances on earth. People came to faith by hearing about Christ, not seeing him in the flesh. "Blessed are those who have not seen and yet have come to believe" (John 20:29). Blessed, yes, but not immune to pangs of doubt.

---

1. With Herod's assistance in Luke 23:6–25; Acts 4:27.

Second, even staunch believers in Jesus's resurrection might wonder why he would leave them before returning some indefinite time later to finalize God's righteous realm. Since Jesus has conquered death, why not consummate victory *now* over all pain, suffering, and death-dealing forces? What better time than "this time" to "restore the kingdom" (Acts 1:6)? Why let evil strong men continue to weaken, oppress, and attack God's people? We will focus on this problem of Jesus's delayed return in challenge 7. Here I simply acknowledge the tension of continuing to live in a troubled world while Jesus sits securely at God's right hand. His sympathetic intercession for his earthly suffering siblings (Heb. 2:14–18; 4:14–15; 7:25) is most welcome. But why not cut straight to the heart of the problem and solve it, once for all?

Third, the empty tomb does not erase the bloody cross; the resurrection does not eradicate the crucifixion. Though having a restored and glorified body, Jesus still bears the marks of crucifixion in his nail-printed hands and sword-pierced side (John 20:25, 27; cf. Gal. 6:14, 17). Far from repressed as a traumatic memory overshadowed by resurrection, Jesus's crucifixion is memorialized in a sacred meal-ritual signifying believers' communion with the broken and bleeding body of Christ (Matt. 26:26–29; Mark 14:22–25; Luke 22:14–23; 1 Cor. 11:23–26). The cross of Christ becomes the core symbol—the *crux*—of Christian identity. We do not string little rocks around our necks or put boulders atop our churches to symbolize an open rock-hewn tomb. We wear and display *crosses*. We follow Jesus's example and exhortation to "take up [our] cross daily and follow [him]" (Luke 9:24), though most American Christians, accustomed to religious freedom and a dominant Christian heritage, have no real connection to the cross as a sign of physical debilitation, social oppression, and political execution—except for African Americans scarred by the horrific history of lynchings.[2]

There was only one reason to carry a cross in the Roman Empire: to certify Rome's absolute power and any resister's abject weakness. The New Testament writers know and feel this in their bones. They couldn't miss it, as Rome flooded its social media with bloodstained crosses along roadways and hillsides.[3] Those who shaped the New Testament had to come to grips with the crucified Jesus's persisting weakling image, complicated by the poor, weak status of most of his followers (1 Cor. 1:26–28). The cross of Christ could not be buried and forgotten; it must be borne and remembered "as often as you eat this bread and drink the cup" (11:26).

2. See the trenchant work of the theologian James Cone, *Cross and the Lynching Tree*.
3. See Carter, *Seven Events*, 87–106.

A weak Messiah for a weak people. What was God thinking? What kind of political strategy is that, except for continued depredation under the iron thumb of Strongman Caesar and his powerful deputies? The New Testament writers aren't the first or last of God's people to wrestle with this perplexing "power paradox."[4] The Old Testament has a markedly mixed view of political rulers *within* Israel. While historians, prophets, and poets in the Bible come to view David as God's anointed king and adopted son (2 Sam. 7:12–16; Ps. 2:6–7), the establishment of monarchic rule in Israel is not viewed so favorably, to say nothing of the fact that David and his descendants prove far from perfect. When the people clamor for "a king to govern [them], like other nations" (1 Sam. 8:5), the prophet-priest Samuel conveys God's displeasure over this request. As Israel's true king who has rescued them from enslavement, God feels "rejected" (8:7). Plus, God knows exactly how earthly kings operate, using their power to extract money, resources, labor, and soldiers from the people for royal gain and glory (8:4–18). In other words, kings typically become tyrannical strongmen who exploit the weak and vulnerable.

When the people keep insisting on having their own king, God gives in, and they mostly get exactly what God said they would: a line of rapacious, self-serving strongmen. Even David has his abusive, acquisitive moments (2 Sam. 12, 24) and only functions as "a man after [God's] own heart" (1 Sam. 13:14) when he serves and shepherds God's people. David's son Solomon ramps up the super-strongman routine to extreme levels of self-aggrandizement, sparking a labor revolt that splits the kingdom (1 Kings 11–12).

The twentieth and twenty-first centuries have witnessed a resurgence of autocratic strongmen. The names are all too (in)famous: Mussolini, Franco, Hitler, Pinochet, Amin, Hussein, Gaddafi. Though these are all dead now, a harrowing cadre of others remain, intermittently in and out of power, but always lusting for more. Historian Ruth Ben-Ghiat tells these strongmen's terrible stories, showing how they were motivated by their "common drive to exercise as much personal power as their political systems allowed and to appear to the world—and each other—as virile."[5] They also trade on building up false hopes of betterment, which they have no interest in realizing: "These rulers promise a bright national future, but the emotions they elicit are bleak. The line between everyday life and horror in their states can be razor-thin."[6]

---

4. Cf. Keltner, *Power Paradox*.
5. Ben-Ghiat, *Strongmen*, 1.
6. Ben-Ghiat, *Strongmen*, 14.

So it was with Roman and Herodian rulers in Jesus's day. But what difference did Jesus make in this political system that remained intact after his death and resurrection? Again, did Jesus's crucifixion not trigger more cognitive dissonance and emotional upheaval than it eased? What do you do with a seemingly weak(ling) king stigmatized by scars of crucifixion? How can he save us from the dreadful onslaughts of vicious strongmen?

Rule as a Weak King

As Jesus enters Jerusalem at Passover season in the last week of his life, a crowd hails him as "King of Israel" (John 12:13; cf. Luke 19:38), the blessed heir to the "coming kingdom of our ancestor David" (Mark 11:10; cf. Matt. 21:9). At his trial before the Jewish high council, Jesus answers the loaded question "Are you the Messiah?" with a straightforward "I am," then announces his future coming from the "right hand of the Power [God]" (Mark 14:61–62; cf. Matt. 26:63–64; Luke 22:67–68). Before the Roman tribunal, Jesus answers Governor Pilate's question "Are you the King of the Jews?" more obliquely but without denial: "You say so" (Matt. 27:11; Mark 15:2; Luke 23:3). Soldiers tack a mocking placard to his cross: "This is Jesus, the King of the Jews" (Matt. 27:37). This is what happens to would-be kings in Caesar's realm.

Yet for all this final hullabaloo about Jesus's kingship, he does not go around promoting himself as Messiah or King. Even the Johannine Jesus, known for making bold "I am" claims supported by miraculous signs, promptly escapes to a nearby mountain when a multitude he has bountifully fed aims to "take him by force and make him their king" (John 6:15). He wants no part of their royal scheme. According to the Synoptic Gospels, Jesus proclaims the gospel and kingdom *of God*, not himself. Israel already has a king—the Lord God, who has redeemed and covenanted with them since the days of Abraham and Moses.

To be sure, Jesus performs mighty acts signaling that God's realm has been restored from the clutches of inimical forces. A battle is at hand in which Jesus leads the charge against nefarious cosmic powers commanded by Satan and his demonic agents, who, in turn, control earthly tyrants. The Gospels consistently portray Jesus as stronger than any demonic spirit or despotic strongman. But it's not simply a question of Jesus's superior firepower, of might makes right, but rather a question of how Jesus *uses his power* as God's viceroy.

Binding the Devil

Jesus's public service begins at his baptism, where he receives his heavenly Father's approval and the divine Spirit's anointing (Matt. 3:16–17; Mark 1:9–11; Luke 3:21–22). Without allowing Jesus a moment, however, to bask in this glorious initiation, the Spirit propels him into the wilderness for an intense forty-day clash with Satan/the devil (Mark 1:12–13). The battle is on!

Matthew and Luke report three tests Satan poses to Jesus, each designed to get him to use his divine power for selfish gain and satanic aims (Matt. 4:1–11; Luke 4:1–13). Two of the tests—zapping stones into bread and flying off the temple's pinnacle—combine popularity and power. Imagine the crowd appeal of these demonstrations. "Bread and circuses" for all! Stop fasting and satisfy your hunger, Jesus, by turning a few desert rocks into delicious buns. Then do a freestyle dive off the temple top before the angels catch you and land you safely. The people will go wild! You'll be a sensation!

These proposed culinary and acrobatic moves are just warm-up acts, however, for Satan's coup de grâce, offering Jesus all the world's kingdoms "if [he] will fall down and worship [Satan]" (Matt. 4:9; cf. Luke 4:6–7). Whatever Satan's actual capacity to enthrone Jesus over all earthly realms, his main scheme is to get Jesus to renounce allegiance to God, derail God's plan for the world, and submit himself to Satan's authority—with a colossal benefit package!

But no amount of earthly popularity, possessions, or power can divert Jesus from his devotion to God's word, realm, and service: "Away with you, Satan! For it is written, 'Worship the Lord your God, and serve only him'" (Matt. 4:10, quoting Deut. 6:13). Jesus resolutely commits himself to never use his power to serve himself. He will provide abundant bread for others who are hungry but not for his own private consumption (Matt. 14:13–21; 15:32–39; Luke 9:10–17). His ultimate "big top" public spectacle will be on Skull Hill (Golgotha), where he will be lifted on a cross to

The Third Temptation

die, not atop the temple mount to stage an aeronautic feat. Jesus will promote God's kingdom by "soft power"[7] that graciously gives and nudges, not by strong power that rapaciously grasps and steamrolls.

Yet it remains hard to understand why Jesus's nonviolent resistance of evil and advancement of good lands him on a cross and leaves an evil empire and its satanic patron intact. More immediately, why does Jesus let Satan set the agenda, whisking him from wilderness to temple to mountain? Why not just destroy Satan from the start? Why does Satan deserve "soft" treatment, especially since he will not cease to undermine Jesus at every turn and continue to harass vulnerable people?

As it happens, though Jesus does not shield himself from Satan's assault, he does strongly intervene to deliver people weakened and damaged by demonic possession, not least stricken children (Mark 7:24–30; 9:14–29). There's nothing soft about Jesus's exorcistic ministry. One time he dispatches a "legion" horde of demons from a man they'd tortured into a herd of pigs, which hurtle to their deaths in the sea (Mark 5:1–20).

But some malign Jesus for his liberative use of power. Not surprisingly, the swineherds who lost their livestock urge Jesus to leave their region. But also, closer to home, some scribes charge him with abetting "the ruler of the demons" (Mark 3:22). In their twisted logic, they think Jesus has struck some deal with Satan to gain control over demons. But Jesus's only aim with demons is to evict them from their "host" victims and restore health and freedom. To this end, he minces no words in exposing his accusers' muddled thinking: "How can Satan cast out Satan? If a kingdom is divided against itself, that kingdom cannot stand" (3:23–24). In Matthew and Luke, Jesus adds a statement directly linking his exorcising work with the dynamics of God's compassionate commonwealth: "If it is by the Spirit/finger of God that I cast out demons, then the kingdom of God has come to you" (Matt. 12:28 // Luke 11:20).

Jesus punctuates his defense with a parable featuring a strongman (*ischyros*) representing Satan. In the worldview of Jesus and the Gospels, Satan, the evil one, is a formidable but by no means invincible foe. Though he and his demons may overtake a human body, they in turn may be overcome by a stronger one who binds the diabolical invaders, strips them of ill-gotten gains, and kicks them out of the "house" (Mark 3:27)! Recall that Jesus is the quintessential Stronger One (*ischyroteros*, 1:8).

7. Nye, *Soft Power*.

Luke sets this vignette in a royal military context where an armed "strongman" guards his fortified "castle/palace" (*aulē*) and conquered possessions until "one stronger [*ischyroteros*] . . . overpowers [or conquers] him" and divests him of his illicit holdings (Luke 11:21–22).[8] Satan usurps power for nefarious ends. He has no legitimate right to rule and no beneficent gifts to offer. He and his evil allies flaunt their powers and claim their turfs. But they will ultimately be displaced by the relentless righteous realm of God, coextensive with all heaven and earth (cf. 10:21). Jesus Messiah acts as the vanguard of God's strong power to save the world.

But why, again, does the liberative Jesus not finish off oppressive enemies—even, as we've seen, going so far as to advocate loving them (Matt. 5:43–44; Luke 6:27–28)? This does not preclude strong intervention on behalf of those who suffer enemy attacks. But it does signal a "soft," bleeding-heart side to Jesus, which he takes to the cross as he literally gives his lifeblood for others and prays that his executioners' would be forgiven (Luke 23:34). Why go down this self-defeating road? Why not fight with all God's might to eradicate evil forces and usher in a peaceful paradise? Why not ride the wave of royal acclamation Jesus receives at Passover all the way to the throne of Israel, Rome, and the world?

Riding the Donkey

The annual Passover festival commemorates God's deliverance of ancient Israelites from Egyptian enslavement, culminating in drowning Pharaoh's cavalry in the Red Sea (Exod. 14:26–15:21). At his final Passover, Jesus enters Jerusalem riding a borrowed donkey. Along the way a crowd spontaneously assembles, lays down their coats and "leafy branches" before Jesus as a kind of red carpet, and hails him as the saving "Son of David" (Matt. 21:7–9; Mark 11:7–10) and "blessed . . . king who comes in the name of the Lord!" (Luke 19:38; cf. John 12:13). The stage is set for a triumphal coronation of King Jesus and new emancipation of Israel.

Initially Jesus seems poised to seize the moment. He does not rebuke the people for their outburst. In Luke's account, when some Pharisees urge him to stop this commotion, probably to avoid Roman reprisals for disturbing the peace, Jesus affirms the crowd's enthusiasm and even gets the rocks into the act: "I tell you, if these [people] were silent, the stones would shout out" (Luke 19:40). The next day he enters the temple, where he enacts a housecleaning demonstration, toppling tables, disrupting business, and echoing prophetic words demanding a spiritual overhaul of God's house (Mark 11:15–17). Over the next few days, he returns to

---

8. Spencer, *Luke*, 307.

the temple, where he teaches the people, debates with officials and scholars, and acts very much like he owns the place as God's Son and David's heir (11:27–12:37).

But these authoritative displays do not reveal the whole picture. Jesus's overturning the money changers' and merchants' tables makes a strong symbolic point but is a comparatively minor incident. Normal temple business quickly resumes. For all his temple pontificating on critical issues, Jesus never claims to be high priest or king. Although riding a donkey recalls Solomon's royal procession into Jerusalem on his father David's mule (1 Kings 1:33, 38) and realizes the prophet Zechariah's vision of how Jerusalem's "triumphant and victorious" king will arrive to destroy Israel's enemies (Zech. 9:9–10; Matt. 21:4–5; John 12:14–15), Jesus does not follow Solomon's enacted or Zechariah's envisioned monarchic, militant rule. Jesus assumes the "humble" role associated with the donkey (Zech. 9:9; Matt. 21:5), without the heroic overlays. He amasses no stockpile of battle steeds and chariots (like Solomon, 1 Kings 10:26–29), drives no enemy horses and chariots into the sea (like Moses, Exod. 14:26–15:10), brandishes no conquering sword, and orchestrates no preplanned imperial parade with armed soldiers at hand and chained captives in tow.

In Luke's account, Jesus weeps over the city's imminent demise because he knows that, despite the crowd's present show of hospitality, they do "not recognize the time of [their] visitation from God" (Luke 19:44). Before week's end, he will sweat in profound agony over his impending arrest and death (22:44).[9] Though knowing that he is destined for betrayal and execution (9:22, 43–44; 18:31–33), Jesus still pleads with his Father at the eleventh hour to alter this fate (22:39–46; cf. Mark 14:32–42). He does not want to lose his life; he does not seek the glory of martyrdom. Yet he ultimately accepts the way of the cross.

Palm Sunday does not depict a Triumphal Entry, as it's commonly called, and Good Friday, the day of Jesus's death, is not all good, even from the retrospective of Jesus's resurrection and ascension. Jesus enters Jerusalem as a humble servant-ruler who soon dies a humiliating, excruciating, unjust death. From a chorus of "Hail to the King" on the road to the placard of "King of the Jews" on the cross, Jesus's final way is marked by jolting irony and mockery. He is the anti-king, the weak king, the antithesis of worldly strongmen.[10]

The Gospel narratives do not mount a systematic theological or philosophical defense of Jesus's kingship. They tell the story of Jesus's character and actions in contrast to the character and actions of Satan, Caesar, Herod, and other evil

9. On the authenticity and interpretation of this text, see Spencer, *Luke*, 561–66.
10. See Wilson, *Unmanly Men*, 190–242.

powers. The Gospels are not ashamed to show Jesus's "weak" side; they do not mythologize him into some airbrushed superhero or fantasize a utopian version of his kingdom. The Gospels render the highest, most honest honor to God and Jesus, merited by their solidarity with a struggling people, not a perfunctory or begrudging honor like that coerced by narcissistic Caesars and other strongmen.

The Power of the Cross

In straightforward declarative form, Paul dares to claim, against common sense and strict logic, the power of the cross: "The message about the cross . . . is the power of God" (1 Cor. 1:18). He does not make this bold assertion naively, however. Paul knows that the formula "Cross = Power" normally counts the cross as an instrument of Roman power against enemies. On its face, claiming the power of a crucifixion victim is absurd, foolish/moronic (*mōron*) and offensive/scandalous (*skandalon*) (1:18–25). But God rules by God's rules, not those of rulers set against God.

Accordingly, "God's foolishness is wiser than [*sophōteron*] human wisdom, and God's weakness is stronger than [*ischyroteron*] human strength" (1 Cor. 1:25). If earthly rulers had a clue, "they would not have crucified the Lord of glory" (2:8); and when they did, they had no idea they were revealing God's greater, gracious power in weakness—God's soft, saving power. Again, Paul grants the difficulty of grasping this concept via human logic. It must be revealed by God's Spirit, who "comprehends what is truly God's" modus operandi (2:11).

Though Paul mounts a rhetorical tour de force touting the power of the cross, the twin problems of cognitive dissonance and emotional upheaval persist. At its root, cognitive dissonance is a *logos*-problem, and by any reckoning, viewing a crucifixion victim as strong and mighty stretches logic. And nothing is more *pathos*-laden, more wrenching to the human spirit, than the violent public execution of an innocent person. Enduring commitment to the mystery of the crucified Christ's saving power demands a full-orbed faith, one that is intellectually probed (belief), emotionally connected (trust), actively lived (faithfulness), and rooted in a conceptual framework of paradox.

The Power of Paradox

Paradox may be defined as "an apparently unacceptable conclusion derived by apparently acceptable reasoning from apparently acceptable premises." Everything hinges on negotiating "apparent" elements. Some "appearances have to deceive" to some degree for the paradox to work.[11] From a New Testament perspective, Christ's cross cannot be what it appears to be or, more precisely, not *only* what it appears to be. It *is* a brutal means of death that Jesus palpably suffered. But it is also *something more* than what is apparent at first sight and thought—something strong, powerful, saving, and liberative , something of God's greater purpose that "no eye has seen nor ear heard, nor . . . heart conceived" (1 Cor. 2:9).

Very well, *if* you buy into the paradox, *if* you accept the unseen, unheard, unapparent conclusion; of course, a skeptic may add, *if* you're gullible enough to swallow the fantasy. Yet, since the complexities of life and death strain the capacity of language and reason, paradox has long served as a serious stimulus to creative insight. The fifth-century BCE Greek philosopher Zeno of Elea posed paradoxes, such as the paradox of Achilles and the tortoise, positing that the swift-running warrior Achilles could never completely catch up to a slow-slogging tortoise that had been given a head start. Why not? Because however quickly Achilles reached the tortoise's starting point, the animal would have moved on some distance from that point. On it would go ad infinitum or until the tortoise stopped (but tortoises live a lot longer than warriors!).[12] Of course, if I were given a fifty-meter head start over Usain Bolt, he would still beat me to the one-hundred-meter finish line! But in the "race of life," a common philosophical metaphor (Phil. 2:16; 3:12–16; Heb. 11:39–12:4), we know well the frustration of striving and never completely arriving due to ever-shifting goalposts.

The Liar Paradox is another logician's favorite. Its simplest form runs like this: "This statement is a lie." Is it true or not? A more contextualized version is "Cretans are always liars," which Paul (or someone writing in his name) mentions in his letter to Titus, who was stationed on the island of Crete (Titus 1:12).[13] Of course, this stereotype exaggerates (are Cretan infants liars?) and becomes more paradoxical if we understand it as derived from the Greek poet Epimenides, who himself came from Crete![14] Was Epimenides lying about all Cretans being liars, or was he just pulling our legs? More germane to our interests, what is Paul

11. Sainsbury, *Paradoxes*, 1.

12. Sainsbury, *Paradoxes*, 4–19; see also an interesting modern use of this paradox in Amor Towles's novel *Lincoln Highway*, 439–40.

13. Scholars continue to debate the authorship and addressees of 1–2 Timothy and Titus, commonly called the Pastoral Letters. Many regard the putative writer "Paul" and recipients, "Timothy" and "Titus," as pseudonyms or literary fictions (see the discussion in Powell, *Introducing the New Testament*, 413–20). In the present section, I leave aside this historical issue, focusing on the content of the canonical Pauline letter to Titus.

14. See Clement of Alexandria, *Stromata* 1.14; Jerome, *Commentary on Titus* (on Titus 1:12–14).

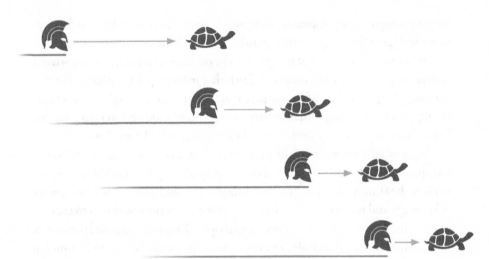

Paradox of Achilles and the tortoise
Baker Publishing Group, based on figure by Martin Grandjean / CC BY-SA 4.0 / Wikimedia Commons

aiming to teach Titus by citing "their very own prophet" (1:12)? As rhetorically deft as Paul is, it's difficult to believe that he simply attacks the Cretan populace as inveterate liars. Both proponents and critics realize the loaded nature of paradoxical statements. On the satirical side, "the works of Plutarch, Lucian, and the comic playwrights . . . provide evidence that, in uttering or alluding to a paradox (including the Liar), writer and speakers could wink at their audiences while simultaneously broaching some weightier subject or concern."[15]

Paul writes to Titus "for the sake of the faith of God's elect and the knowledge of the truth" anchored in "God, who never lies" (Titus 1:1–2). Paul especially worries about certain teachers who have infiltrated the Crete congregations and peddled lies inimical to "sound doctrine." "The testimony" about Cretans' penchant for lying is "true" *enough* (1:13)—without being "always" true (1:12)—to make Paul anxious about community integrity. If Paul winks his eye at labeling Cretans pathological liars, he follows it with a sharp glare of rebuke.[16]

In no way is Christ's crucifixion a winking matter, and no language game or logical trick adequately addresses the inscrutable dissonance of the "crucified God."[17] Yet paradox is one way of opening the flawed, finite human mind to positive potentialities of the cross.

15. Gray, "Liar Paradox," 309.
16. Gray, "Liar Paradox," 307–9.
17. See the monumental work of Jürgen Moltmann in *Crucified God*.

Lose It or Lose It

"Use It or Lose It," as the popular fitness saying goes, makes sense. "Lose It or Lose It" doesn't, and yet that's effectively what Jesus claims about taking up the cross: "If any want to become my followers, let them deny themselves and take up their cross and follow me. For those who want to save their life will lose it, and those who lose their life for my sake, and for the sake of the gospel, will save it" (Mark 8:34–35). This statement comes on the heels of Peter's bold confession to Jesus, "You are the Messiah," which is directly followed by Jesus's first disclosure of his fatal destiny: "The Son of Man[18] must undergo great suffering . . . and be killed, and after three days rise" (8:31).

Peter either doesn't hear or doesn't care about the "rising" after three days; he's appalled that Jesus dares suggest he's on the road to execution. That's not what Peter signed on for. He sharply rebukes Jesus for uttering such defeatist claptrap. In turn, Jesus rounds on Peter, "Get behind me, Satan!" (8:33). At this moment, Peter unwittingly aligns himself with satanic, strongman rule instead of suffering-servant rule. Jesus then punctuates the point by insisting Peter and the disciples *themselves* must follow Jesus's cross-bearing way of *life*.

Come again? A puzzling paradox, to be sure, but one that is borne out in biology every day. As we saw in challenge 1, the Johannine Jesus invokes the life cycle of a "grain of wheat" that falls on the earth, sinks underground, and sprouts to produce "much fruit" (John 12:24–26). The Synoptic Jesus, however, uses an economic image with a psychologic twist: "What will it profit them to gain the whole world and forfeit their life [*psychēn*]? Indeed, what can they give in return [or exchange] for their life [*psychēs*]?" (Mark 8:36–37; see also Matt. 16:26; Luke 9:25). Holistic, healthy "psychic" life—body-soul-spirit, present-life and afterlife—cannot be bought with money or worldly goods. From a cost-benefit analysis, it makes no sense to amass financial wealth at the expense of flourishing life.

But does such a dichotomy always apply? Can you not use wealth wisely to promote a genuinely good life for yourself—and, through charitable giving, for those less fortunate? Why for goodness' sake must a redeeming life end on a cross, unless it stakes all its chips on postmortem paradise? Such questions seem apt for those who profess allegiance to Christ today without fear of persecution and who may even profit from Christian alliances.

---

18. Or "Son of Humankind" (*huios tou anthrōpou*), Jesus's favorite term of self-reference in the Synoptic Gospels; see Spencer, *Luke*, 140–43.

But the New Testament was forged in a less congenial milieu. The Johannine Jesus warns his followers, "If the world hates you, be aware that it hated me before it hated you" (John 15:18). The letter of James flatly states that "friendship with the world is enmity with God" (James 4:4). This ungodly "world" is not the natural world of God's creation but rather the perverted world of God-defying, death-dealing powers. Jesus's uncompromising commitment to God's saving, loving rule for all, not least the least well-off (Matt. 25:40, 46), put him and his followers on a collision course with the corrupt, cross-wielding strongmen of his day. But in God's calculus, this cross was "worth" suffering to redeem the world.

Lifted Up Crosswise

John's Gospel uses a wordplay on "lifting up" and a prooftext to support the paradox of Jesus's cross as a "high"-powered instrument of salvation. All four Gospels feature Jesus's uplifting ministry, raising the lowly (Luke 1:52), especially those confined to a mat (Matt. 9:1–8; Mark 2:1–12; Luke 5:17–26; John 5:1–18), deathbed (Matt. 9:23–26; Mark 5:35–43; Luke 8:49–56), or funeral bier (Luke 7:11–17). Yet "stand up, take your mat and walk" (John 5:8) strikes a dissonant tone from "take up your cross, and die." Or maybe not, as John dares to envision Jesus's "lifting up" on a cross within a complex of *exaltation* events (crucifixion-resurrection-ascension) that are all of a piece in God's plan of salvation: "'And I, when I am *lifted up* from the earth, will draw all people to myself.' He said this to indicate the *kind of death he was to die*" (12:32–33; cf. 8:28).

This brazen vision of the cross as glorious attraction, not gory spectacle, recalls the bronzed serpent-image Moses erected on a pole: "Just as Moses *lifted up* the serpent in the wilderness, so must the Son of Man be *lifted up*, that whoever believes in him may have eternal life" (John 3:14–15). An odd precedent indeed, involving God's strange use of snakes. First, God dispatched "*poisonous serpents* among the people, and they bit the people, so that many Israelites died" (Num. 21:6). These serpents were instruments of God's punishment for the journeying Israelites' incessant complaining about the "miserable food" in the Sinai desert. But then God answered Moses's plea for relief with the bronze serpent totem pole: "Everyone who is bitten shall look at it and live" (21:8).

The parallel with Jesus's crucifixion is strained. A crossbeam is not a pole; Jesus is a flesh-and-blood human being, not a bronze-cast figure; Jesus causes no one's death and suffers death himself; God does not first harm or punish anyone through Jesus before turning around and saving them. And John's Gospel

William Blake, 1800–1803 / Public Domain / Wikimedia Commons

Moses Erecting the Brazen Serpent

does not regard the cross as a site where God vents holy wrath on sinful people. Indeed, the text associating Moses's pole-mounted serpent-image with the crucified Jesus directly leads to the classic statement of *God's saving love* in John 3:16–17.[19]

John's interpretation of Numbers 21 aligns with the Wisdom of Solomon's, presenting the serpent-attack as a temporary "warning" and the pole setup as a God-fashioned "symbol of deliverance" (Wis. 16:6).[20]A serpent coiled around a rod also serves as a healing symbol in the medical profession's caduceus, rooted in the iconography of the Greek gods Asclepius and Hermes. The deadly serpent thus represents a "contradictory symbol" of life, not unlike the cross of Christ.[21]

Although the use of a clever wordplay ("lifted up") and a prooftext (Num. 21) fires the imagination, are these techniques sufficient to explain the paradoxical power of the cross? Not entirely, but they contribute to the rich symbolic universe that shapes the New Testament.

19. Dodd, *Interpretation of the Fourth Gospel*, 307.
20. Dodd, *Interpretation of the Fourth Gospel*, 306; cf. Philo, *Allegorical Interpretation* 2.76–93.
21. Lenchak, "Exaltation of the Cross," 311.

Lifting a Curse

Two New Testament authors draw on another Torah text to make sense of Jesus's crucifixion: "When someone is convicted of a crime punishable by death and is executed, and you hang him on a tree, his corpse must not remain all night upon the tree; you shall bury him that same day, for anyone hung on a tree is under God's curse" (Deut. 21:22–23). Two sermons by Peter image Jesus's death as "hanging . . . on a tree" (Acts 5:30; 10:39), and Paul directly quotes the Deuteronomy text as evidence that "Christ redeemed us from the curse of the law" (Gal. 3:10, 13).

Again, the analogy is not perfect. Deuteronomy implies a sequence of execution, probably by stoning, followed by hanging the corpse from a tree as a public display of shame.[22] But unlike the Romans, who allowed crucified bodies to hang on the cross for extended periods, exposed to predatory animals and inclement weather, the Israelites buried executed criminals the same day, so as not to "defile the land" (Deut. 21:23). The Torah is less concerned with punishing the individual malefactor than with restoring communal and terrestrial wholeness.[23]

Still, hanging on a tree was readily associated with crucifixion in the ancient world. General readers would understand Peter's arboreal allusion to Jesus's death, and Torah-literate readers would pick up Deuteronomic threads.[24] But to what end? Why does Luke's Peter refer to Jesus's crucifixion this way in strategic addresses before the Jewish council in Jerusalem (Acts 5:27–32) and before the Roman officer Cornelius and his household in Caesarea (10:34–43)? Peter makes no Deuteronomic connection between Jesus's tree/cross and "God's curse," as Paul does in Galatians. Peter blames two sets of human authorities—priestly leaders (Acts 5:30) and Roman soldiers (10:39)—while proclaiming *God's vindication* of Jesus by raising him from death and exalting him to God's right hand (5:30–31; 10:39–40).

Although Peter both shames Jesus's enemies who "hanged him on a tree" and honors Jesus as God's "right hand man,"[25] his primary goal is not accusative or vindictive but rather redemptive and restorative. God authorized Jesus as "Lord of all," through his crucifixion-resurrection-exaltation, to "give repentance to Israel and forgiveness of sins" (Acts 5:31) and to provide "peace" and "forgiveness

22. See Josephus, *Antiquities* 3.380.
23. See Reardon, "'Hanging on a Tree.'"
24. Keener, *Acts*, 1805.
25. See Wright's discussion of Daniel's Son of Man and Paul's Jesus (in Rom. 8) as "God's right-hand man." Wright, *In the Heart of Romans*, 192–95.

of sins" to "anyone" from "every nation" (10:34–36, 42–43). Peter tracks the progress of Christ's peacemaking from hanging on a tree to the empty tomb to the heavenly throne without explaining its *process*.

Here Paul adds a key interpretive element: "Christ redeemed us from the curse of the law by becoming a curse for us—for it is written, 'Cursed is everyone who hangs on a tree'" (Gal. 3:13). This comment caps Paul's complex argument involving another Deuteronomy text: "Cursed is everyone who does not observe and obey all the things written in the book of the law" (3:10; see also Deut. 27:26). Despite the "everyone/all" language, the Deuteronomy and Galatians contexts are quite particular. In Deuteronomy 27, "all the things written in the book of the law" meriting God's curse refers to twelve transgressive "things" enumerated in 27:15–25, ranging from secretly crafting an idol to committing murder for hire. None of these applies, however, in Galatians, where the core legal issue is whether Gentile believers in Christ must be circumcised and keep other "works of the law" to be fully incorporated into God's covenant. In other words, do Gentiles remain under the "curse of the law" if they do not submit to circumcision, the original sign of Israel's covenant with God (Gen. 17)?

As Christ's chief apostle to Gentiles (Gal. 1:1, 15), Paul—though himself a devout, circumcised Jew (Phil. 3:4–6)—is adamant that circumcision must not be imposed on Gentiles as a condition of salvation. Faithful commitment to Christ is both necessary and sufficient. Paul argues that Christ's curse-bearing crucifixion served a specific purpose: "in order that in Christ Jesus the blessing of Abraham *might come to the Gentiles*, so that we [Jew and Gentile] might receive the promise of the Spirit through faith" (Gal. 3:14).

Paul's Deuteronomy-based arguments are rather ad hoc, pulling together various strands to score his point.[26] But that's what good rhetoricians do. Moreover, in Galatians Paul is vexed over what he believes is a perverted, "accursed" message, a "different gospel" (1:6–9) peddled by meddlesome "influencers"[27] aiming to coerce Gentile congregants to become Jewish proselytes. Paul's prosecution unfolds hot and fast, niceties and fine points be damned. He believes in his bones that Christ's torturous cross—the locus of violent enmity *against* God's Son—bore the brunt of divisive hostility *among* God's people. The real proof of the cross's reconciling power is less in prooftexts and legal briefs than in Paul's experience of preaching to the Gentiles the gospel of Christ, whom they embrace by faith, apart from "work of the law." The proof is in the people!

26. See Gombis, "Arguing with Scripture"; Gombis, "'Transgressor'"; cf. Willson, "'Cursed.'"
27. Gombis, "Arguing with Scripture," 82, 86, 90.

Lowering the Crossbar

Those empowered by Christ's cross include not only "foreign" Gentiles but also people who are "foolish" and "weak" by normal social standards. Not that God feels saddled by them. These are God's people by God's choice—a "'royalty' of outcasts . . . a kingdom of the low-down and lowborn, the 'excluded,' the very people who are precisely the victims of the world's power."[28] These are most believers in Corinth, who embraced the illogical "message [*logos*] about the cross" (1 Cor. 1:18). As Paul reminds them, "Not many of you were wise by human standards, not many were powerful, not many were of noble birth. But God chose what is foolish in the world to shame the wise; God chose what is weak in the world to shame the strong; God chose what is low and despised in the world, things that are not, to reduce to nothing things that are" (1:26–28).

Via a radical sociology of the cross, Paul envisions a reality antithetical to that presumed in standard wisdom philosophies of power politics.[29] Despite his more privileged background, Paul includes himself in this low company of fools and weaklings, *with the crucified Christ*: "I decided to know nothing among you except Jesus Christ, and him crucified. And I came to you in weakness and in fear and in much trembling" (1 Cor. 2:2–3).[30]

Again, proof of the cross's power and wisdom is not in mathematical proofs but in the experiential lives of those who count for nothing in worldly terms—the X-ed outs, the have-nots, the "scum" of the earth[31]—who have found their true value in Christ's suffering and dying with them. God in Christ has come down to their level in compassion, not condescension.

It may be objected, of course, that this lowly, cruciform mentality keeps deplorables right where the authorities want them: down and out. But by no means does Paul encourage wallowing in self-pity or languishing under the cross-burdens borne for Christ's sake. Call it what you will—paradox, oxymoron, nonsense, scandal—the word (*logos*) of the cross means *life* for, through, and from death. Not bare-bones life but strong life, strengthened life (cf. Phil. 4:13) to resist oppressive powers and reinforce ties of love that bind cross-bearers into one strong body of Christ (cf. Eph. 4:16).

---

28. Caputo, *Weakness of God*, 46.

29. See Barclay, "Crucifixion as Wisdom," 5: "The wisdom of the cross is not just an alternative wisdom but an anti-wisdom, refuting or subverting what would normally be taken for granted."

30. Cf. Welborn, *Paul the Fool*.

31. Barclay, "Crucifixion as Wisdom," 8.

Strong as a Lamb

Though we humans' higher intelligence and cooperative ingenuity have allowed us to survive and tame parts of the wild kingdom, we remain vulnerable creatures—like weak, wandering sheep/lambs. We need the guiding and guarding watch-care of our Divine Shepherd (Ps. 23) and faithful human under-shepherds, like David, who pursued a predatory lion or bear "and struck it down, rescuing the lamb from its mouth," just as he defeated the super-nemesis Goliath (1 Sam. 17:35), and like Jesus, who knows his human flock by name, leading them to nurturing pasture and protecting them from thieves and wolves (John 10:1–18).

Good shepherds like David and Jesus are strong figures but not political strongmen. David's model-shepherd role stems from his youth. He first learns of his kingly destiny after being summoned from his sheep-keeping post by the prophet-priest Samuel (1 Sam. 16:1–13). Yet after David becomes king and amasses the trappings of royal power, he himself falls prey to strongman desires. Case in point: he forces himself on soldier Uriah's wife, Bathsheba; deploys Uriah in the fiercest battlefield sector, where he's killed; and commandeers Uriah's widow for his harem. The prophet Nathan, however, accuses David of acting like a rich man with abundant flocks who callously seizes a poor man's single pet lamb to roast and serve to a guest (2 Sam. 11:1–12:15). The good shepherd boy has become the wicked lion-king.

As the *consistently* Good Shepherd, Jesus Messiah dramatically diverges from his royal ancestor (John 10:11): he is not only moved with compassion to feed his flock (Mark 6:34–44) and to seek and save every lone lost sheep (Matt. 18:10–14; Luke 15:3–7) but also committed to laying down his own life to save his sheep (John 10:11–18; 15:13; 1 John 3:16). Jesus takes up the cross as his shepherd's staff. His solidarity with his flock extends to becoming the weakest among them. John the Baptizer first identifies Jesus in this way: "Look! The *Lamb of God* who takes away the sin of the world!" (John 1:29 CEB). Not the strong Ram of God but the weak Lamb of God.

The book of Revelation develops a complex portrait of Jesus the Lamb/Shepherd (Rev. 7:17) as weak/strong, slain/risen, and combative/conquering (5:6, 12; 12:11; 17:14). But it also identifies Jesus as "the *Lion* of the tribe of Judah" (5:5). The utopian prophetic vision of the lion lying down peacefully with the lamb is fulfilled in Christ, the leonine Lamb and ovine Lion.

Yet this hybrid vehicle does not smoothly hum along Revelation's highway, not least because Jesus the Lion-Lamb still bears the marks of having been slaughtered

The Visit of the Queen of Sheba to King Solomon

on a cross. In the ongoing struggle of world politics, economics, and ecology, lions lie down with lambs only to eat them! This is why self-styled strongmen, like Benito Mussolini, trumpeted the adage "Better to live a day as a lion than a hundred years as a lamb,"[32] even though Mussolini's wife is purported to have said after his death, "My husband appeared to be a lion, but instead he was a rather sad and small man."[33]

The Lion Bleats

The powerful roaring lion-king, "mightiest among wild animals" (Prov. 30:30), is a long-standing image of domination. King Solomon, Israel's quintessential strongman, had a gold-overlaid ivory throne, flanked at each armrest by standing lion statues, sitting atop a platform with six descending steps with more standing lion figures on each side. Reaching Solomon's throne required climbing a gauntlet of fourteen lions! The biblical historian cannot help boasting, "Nothing like it was ever made in any kingdom" (1 Kings 10:20).

For other biblical writers, however, lionizing human rulers was not so noble. Lions symbolized wicked, wrathful, voracious use of power against helpless

32. Keller, *Facing Apocalypse*, 29; cf. Serri, "Dear Trump."
33. Ben-Ghiat, *Strongmen*, 229.

victims: "Like a roaring lion . . . is a wicked ruler over a poor people. A ruler who lacks understanding is a cruel oppressor" (Prov. 28:15–16; cf. 20:2). The true Lord God King is envisioned as the Savior/Rescuer of God's people oppressed by ravenous leonine forces (Pss. 22:21; 35:17), as young David rescued his sheep from lions' mouths and as God rescued Daniel from the lion's den of the Persian king (Dan. 6:10–28).

The prophet Amos, however, stunningly turns this scenario on its head. Because of the people's unfaithfulness to God, the divine oracle is "spoken *against* you, O people of Israel," as the roar of a fearsome lion (Amos 3:1). God exposes the abuse of power by Israel's leaders "who store up violence and robbery in their strongholds" (3:10). Consequently, these strongmen will be stripped of their power, and their "strongholds shall be plundered" by a stronger conqueror (3:11). Eerily flipping the image of God as Israel's saving shepherd, Amos warns, "Thus says the LORD: As the shepherd rescues from the mouth of the lion two legs, or a piece of an ear, so shall the people of Israel . . . be rescued, with the corner of a couch and part of a bed" (3:12). Pieces of Israel—pieces of flesh and furniture—will be "rescued," if one can call it that, from the lion's maw! This is no time to "want the day of the LORD[.] It is darkness, not light; as if someone fled from a lion, and was met by a bear" (5:18–19). The goodly Shepherd has become the deadly Lion.

Shapeshifting and role reversal accompany disruptions in power relations. Vulnerable lambs too often become vengeful lions when they assume authority, and deposed lions whimper for mercy. Lying down together in a peaceable kingdom remains an idyllic vision. In the meantime, identities and potentialities of lambs and lions remain volatile and aversive.

The New Testament compares both the *devil* and *Jesus* to lions, though in distinctive ways. First Peter warns readers to "keep alert" to predations of "your adversary the devil," who "like a roaring lion . . . prowls around, looking for someone to devour" (1 Pet. 5:8). Revelation envisions Jesus in the heavenly throne room as "the Lion of the tribe of Judah, the Root of David," who "has conquered, so that he can open the scroll and its seven seals" (Rev. 5:5). This is a striking image of Jesus's sovereignty that stresses his noble pedigree derived from patriarch Judah and monarch David, his eminent power as "ruler of the kings of the earth" (1:5), and his unique purpose to disclose the scripted ("scroll") drama of world events, culminating in saving God's suffering people.

Jesus's lion-king position is buttressed in Revelation's heavenly portrait by "four living creatures" encompassing God's throne (4:6–11; cf. 5:6–14; 19:4). These beings resemble a lion (naturally mentioned first), followed by an ox, a human face, and a flying eagle—each turbocharged with super-velocity (six wings) and super-vision ("full of eyes all around and inside," 4:6). Each being represents creation in its *strongest* dimensions—a power portrait, if there ever were one, with Lion Jesus reigning supreme at God's right hand.

But no sooner does Revelation identify Jesus as the Judahite Lion than it pivots to the counterimage of Jesus "between the throne and the four living creatures" as "a *Lamb* standing as if it had been *slaughtered*" (5:6)—that is, still standing or standing again despite bearing the stigmata of slaughter and representing the crucified-resurrected Christ. It is this paradoxical standing-slain Lamb image that dominates the rest of Revelation.[34] The Lion never reappears. Jesus is not the strong lion fighting his way to victory. He is the weak lamb who dies, defeated by unjust powers for a time until God raises him to stand up for the least and lowly, even unto death. As "the Lamb," Jesus "will conquer" all beastly powers that are attacking his people, "for he"—as the Lamb—"is Lord of lords and King of kings" (17:14; cf. 19:16).

The Lion's roaring blast has modulated into the Lamb's dying bleat—just as powerful and just as violent but in a different register, if deadly violence has different calibrations and decibel levels. A silencer on a gun makes it no less lethal a weapon. Blood is blood; dead is dead. The slain Lamb is a complicated figure, offering no easy resolution to the dissonance of a crucified Messiah, as we'll see in the next section.

Before further examining the Lamb Jesus, however, it's worth noting early Christian applications of the four living creatures to the four Gospels. Matthew's Jesus became associated with the human-faced figure and Luke's with the ox. The roaring lion and the soaring eagle alternately represented Mark or John, and since Jerome's Latin Vulgate, Mark's lion stamp and John's eagle image have dominated artistic illuminations of the Gospels.[35]

Although Mark contains no lion language, Jesus's featured role as one who speaks and acts with unique authority and power accounts for the lion logo. But in the middle of Mark's story, the lion's destiny takes an ominous turn, as Jesus begins to predict his suffering and killing by human authorities (8:31–32; cf. 9:31; 10:33–34). Richard Burridge captures the shocking irony of this capture-and-kill plot: "A lion's story should always end with a kill, but the narrative has warned us that it is the lion who will die."[36]

---

34. See G. Carey, *Death*, 40–41; Keller, *Facing Apocalypse*, 28–34; Rossing, *Rapture Exposed*, 109–22.
35. See Burridge, *Four Gospels*.
36. Burridge, *Four Gospels*, 58.

The Lion of Venice on Scuola Grande di San Marco's facade, Venice, Italy

Mark leaves us with a fearful image of the fearsome Lion Jesus executed on a cross and buried in a tomb—his final lair, it seems. Yet when some women come on the third day to anoint Jesus's corpse, his body is gone, and a strange "young man" reports that Jesus "has been raised" and will meet them in Galilee (16:1–7). The lion has bounced up to new life and bounded out to his old stomping grounds. At least that's one young man's version of things. The women become hopeful but also fearful. Although Jesus claimed he would rise again, a missing corpse is no proof of a resurrected one. They'll believe it when they see it, when they see him, but Mark's most likely original ending (16:8) leaves that scenario to others' imaginations.

The Lamb Bleeds

The book of Revelation first identifies Jesus Christ as "the firstborn of the dead, and the ruler of the kings of the earth," worthy of worship: "To him be glory and dominion forever and ever. Amen" (Rev. 1:5–6). But again, Jesus's death was no incidental glitch in an otherwise powerful campaign but instead was *instrumental* to his saving work. "*By* his blood" he demonstrated how much he loved us and loosed us "from our sins" (1:5). Such language evokes redemptive sacrifices.

The Fourth Gospel presents the crucified Jesus as the sacrificial "Lamb of God who takes away the sin of the world" (John 1:29; cf. Heb. 9:11–10:18). The exilic prophet Isaiah also imaged the suffering servant figure—whom various New Testament writers associate with Jesus—as "an offering for sin," a slaughtered lamb "wounded for our transgressions, crushed for our iniquities. . . . The righteous one, my servant, shall make many righteous" (Isa. 53:5, 10–11).[37] From a Christian perspective, Jesus became the innocent lamb slain to forgive us, who "like sheep have gone astray" (53:6).

In the only New Testament story, however, that directly applies Isaiah's slaughtered lamb to Jesus, the emphasis falls not on redemption from sin but on redressing the shame or "humiliation" of one to whom "justice was denied" (Acts 8:33, quoting Isa. 53:8). The crucified Jesus veritably embodies the innocent victim of brutal public ignominy, whose shame is "taken away" as God raises him to new life and honor (Acts 8:33, quoting Isa. 53:8). This Isaiah text marks the perfect "starting" Scripture for Philip the evangelist to preach "about Jesus" (Acts 8:35) to an Ethiopian eunuch he encounters on a desert highway, because the image of a shorn, slain lamb resonated with the eunuch's "shorn," shameful physical condition, which "cut" him off from the covenant assembly (Deut. 23:1). Jesus's crucifixion-and-resurrection thus removes obstacles that might "prevent" the eunuch's inclusion into Christ's community (Acts 8:36–38). Further support for welcoming faithful eunuchs and other "outcasts" comes a little later in the Isaiah scroll (56:3–8).[38]

Further evoking the Jewish sacrificial system, Paul proclaims Christ as "our paschal lamb" (1 Cor. 5:7). The sacrifice of the Paschal/Passover lamb signified freedom from slavery rather than forgiveness of sin. On the night God delivered the ancient Israelites from Egyptian enslavement, they marked their homes with blood from a slaughtered "unblemished" lamb, roasted the meat with bitter herbs, and ate it hastily before dashing to freedom (Exod. 12:1–13). This freedom meal became the hallmark of the annual Passover festival.

It was this meal that Jesus celebrated with his disciples at his Last Supper. The main lamb course, however, is conspicuously absent in the Gospel reports. The menu features two items—bread and wine—which Jesus explicitly links with *his* broken body and shed blood about to be offered "for you/many" in an act of covenant renewal (Matt. 26:28; Mark 14:28; Luke 22:20). Only Matthew announces the added benefit of "forgiveness of sins" (Matt. 26:28). It's hard not to see Jesus himself standing in as the Lamb of God. John's Gospel strengthens Jesus's paschal Lamb role by setting his crucifixion at noon on "the

---

37. See Matt. 8:17; Luke 22:37; Acts 8:32–33; 1 Pet. 2:21–25.
38. See Spencer, "Ethiopian Eunuch"; Spencer, *Journeying through Acts*, 101–4.

day of Preparation"—that is, the time Passover lambs were slaughtered in the temple (19:14, 31).[39]

While Revelation affirms the sin-freeing operation that Lamb Jesus performs "by his blood" (Rev. 1:5), it does not unpack his sacrificial atoning work in any detail. Revelation, as *prophecy* in the sense of preaching justice as much as predicting events (1:3; 22:7, 9, 18–19), calls its addressees to *repent* of their sinful ways (2:5, 16, 21; 3:19). The aim is right action more than ritual atonement.[40]

Revelation's slain Lamb Jesus operates more as deliverer from cosmic and political evils than as forgiver of social and personal sins. He battles the beasts of Satanic/Roman oppression—including the mighty-tailed dragon (12:1–18) in league with the colossal tri-beast with a leopard's body, a bear's feet, and a lion's mouth (13:1–4)—*as* a scarred Lamb on behalf of fellow besieged lambs. While the dragon-serpent killed some of Jesus's flock, they nonetheless "have conquered him by the blood of the Lamb and by the word of their testimony [*martyrias*], for they did not cling to life even in the face of death" (12:11). That is, these martyrs remained faithful to Christ unto death, even as the crucified Christ exemplified God's "faithful witness" or "martyr" (1:5; 3:14; cf. 2:13). As they joined Christ in death, they would join him in resurrection, ultimately conquering *by/because of* (*dia*) the blood of the Lamb, not despite it.[41] The paradox lives.

But it is also moderated by the Lamb's powerful features. Revelation's Lamb not only sheds blood but sprouts "seven horns" (horns = power) and "seven eyes" (eyes = perception) (5:6), explodes in "wrath" against God's enemies (6:16), and "will conquer" all beastly forces who "make war on the Lamb" (17:13). This Lamb seems less meek than mighty, less lamb than ram! Strong similarities appear with the Animal Apocalypse (1 En. 83–90), which envisioned Judas Maccabeus, the rebel leader against the tyrant Antiochus IV, as a sheep with a "great horn," defending Jewish lambs against their vicious raptor-attackers as deputies of the wrathful "Lord of the sheep" (90:6–19).[42]

As the thundering "Word of God," Christ smashes the persecutors of God's people as a sword-wielding, white-horse rider commanding the "armies of heaven" (Rev. 19:11–21). Revelation's imagery remains fluid; roaring warrior Rider-Ram and groaning weak Lamb run together.[43] Revelation's Jesus is both victim and

39. See Koester, *Symbolism*, 219–21.
40. See Bowden, "Getting Jesus off the Altar."
41. See G. Carey, *Faithful & True*, 9–31.
42. Nickelsburg and VanderKam, *1 Enoch*, 132–34.
43. Middleton, *Violence of the Lamb*, 65–96.

perpetrator of violence, though from the Seer's perspective, the victim of *unjust* violence and perpetrator of *righteous* violence.

Catherine Keller treads a fine line in interpreting the converged "Lamb and the (endlessly lionized) Judge and Warrior-Word." She opts for no easy resolution but rather the "mindfulness of a dangerous paradox [and] bipolarity . . . a schizopocalyptic tension." Keller candidly acknowledges that Revelation's "bloody Lamb doesn't roll over and play dead or march to inevitable defeat. And it certainly does not sheepishly retreat to safer pastures." Instead, the "metaforce" of Lamb-Ram Jesus dares to advance the "transformative" cause of "just love" governing "a whole social order, a new world, a renewed 'heaven and earth.'"[44]

---

44. Keller, *Facing Apocalypse*, 141.

4

Weal and Woe

The Material Challenge of Infirmity and Poverty

	For you know the generous act of our Lord Jesus Christ, that though he was rich, yet for your sakes he became poor, so that by his poverty you might be become rich. (2 Cor. 8:9)
Tenet	Jesus Christ is the world's whole-making Savior, anointed by God's Spirit to feed the hungry, heal the sick, and free the oppressed—a mission his followers continue in his name.
Tension	If Jesus Christ's saving mission prioritizes holistic well-being, why do many believers (to say nothing of outsiders) continue to fall ill, struggle to make ends meet, and die prematurely?

For many Christians today, the first answer to "What does Jesus mean to you?" would be "He's my Savior." This title has a solid basis in the New Testament, though not as direct as we might assume. "Savior" (*Sōtēr*) appears only three times in the Gospels, and the first reference applies to *God*, as Jesus's mother "rejoices in *God my Savior*" (Luke 1:47).

In the other two texts, Jesus is identified as "Savior": first, by an angel to certain shepherds on the night of Jesus's birth ("To you is born . . . a Savior, who is the Messiah, the Lord," Luke 2:11); second, by a group of Samaritans after hearing a woman's report about Jesus and then meeting him for themselves ("We know that this is truly the Savior of the world," John 4:42). Two cases do not a pattern make, but it's notable that the Gospels highlight Jesus's Savior role on behalf of nomadic shepherds and ethnic Samaritans, two groups on the margins of Jewish life. Jesus is the Savior of all Israel and the whole world.

Among Pauline writings, apart from Philippians 3:20, "Savior" references cluster in the Pastoral Letters; otherwise, the title appears sporadically in 2 Peter, 1 John, and Jude and is applied to both God and Jesus.[1] The letter to Titus stands out for multiple close affiliations of "God our Savior" and "Jesus Christ our Savior" (see Titus 1:3–4; 2:10–13; 3:4–6). Of course, "Savior" should be more than a brand name. Roman Caesars glibly advertised their Savior status on coins, statues, and other public media, all the while securing their imperial positions at their subjects' expense. An authentic Savior must actually do the job of saving (*sōzō*), of providing salvation (*sōtēria*) for those who cannot save themselves. The relatively few New Testament "Savior" references to Jesus are counterweighted by a flood of allusions to his *saving work*.

What precisely does Jesus save people *from*? Modern Christians would likely answer, "He saved me from my sins," with many appending, "and from eternal suffering in hell," presuming hell as God's punishment for unforgiven sins, for *not* being saved. But the New Testament never explicitly applies "salvation" terminology to rescue from "hell" as a place of eternal damnation. It does, however, occasionally associate "salvation" with deliverance from sin and its deadly consequences. Matthew defines Jesus's very name in terms of saving sinners: "[Mary] will bear a son, and you are to name him Jesus, for he will save his people from their sins" (Matt. 1:21). James encourages seeking out and restoring lost persons, in the assurance that "whoever brings back a sinner from wandering will save the sinner's soul from death and will cover a multitude of sins" (James 5:20).

But save/salvation (*sōzō/sōtēria*) language in the Gospels and Acts most often refers to Jesus's many-faceted works of *healing* diseased and disabled people. In two cases, Jesus mediates remarkable life-saving cures—one for a woman with a long-term bleeding disorder (Mark 5:25–34) and the other for a blind beggar (10:46–52). Both times he declares that they have been healed/saved from chronic maladies: "Your faith has made you well [or saved you, *sesōken*]" (5:34; 10:52).

Overall, Jesus's saving mission seeks to realize God's kingdom on earth as a *commonwealth* promoting the common good (weal) of God's creation, especially in therapeutic (wellness) and economic (wealth) dimensions of life.[2] Forgiveness

---

1. 1 Tim. 1:1; 2:3; 4:10; 2 Tim. 1:10; Tit. 1:3, 4; 2:10, 13; 3:4, 6; 2 Pet. 1:1, 11; 2:20; 3:2, 18; 4:4; 1 John 4:14; Jude 25.

2. Cobb, *Salvation*, 1–35; Griffin et al., *American Empire*.

and freedom from sin are integral to this mission. In treating a disabled man, Jesus addresses him and the surrounding audience: "Which is easier, to say to the paralytic, 'Your sins are forgiven,' or to say, 'Stand up and take your mat and walk'?" (Mark 2:9). Neither is "easy" from a human perspective. Forgiving inevitable sins and healing intractable infirmities are tandem works of God channeled through Jesus Christ. *Not* that the man's sins *caused* his paralysis but that sinfulness and sickness mutually reinforce human pain and suffering.

Key summaries in Luke and Acts further illustrate the holistic therapeutic and economic thrust of Jesus's saving ministry:

- In his first adult public appearance, Jesus announces, "The Spirit of the Lord is upon me because he has anointed me to bring good news to the poor. He has sent me to proclaim release to the captives and recovery of sight to the blind, to let the oppressed go free, to proclaim the year of the Lord's favor" (Luke 4:18–19; cf. Isa. 58:6; 61:1–2).

- When messengers from the imprisoned John the Baptizer ask Jesus about his mission, he says, "Go and tell John what you have seen and heard: the blind receive their sight, the lame walk, the lepers are cleansed, the deaf hear, the dead are raised, the poor have good news brought to them" (Luke 7:22).

- In a Roman officer's home, Peter encapsulates the dynamics of Jesus's saving operation: "How God anointed Jesus of Nazareth with the Holy Spirit and with power; how he went about doing good and healing all who were oppressed by the devil, for God was with him" (Acts 10:38).

In short, Jesus proved to be a true Savior, restoring the health and well-being of many sufferers. He even raised a few people back to (finite) life shortly after they died (Mark 5:35–43; Luke 7:11–17; John 11:38–44), and three days after Jesus's own death, God raised him to glorious eternal life. In this powerful position, nothing would seem to limit what Jesus could now do to save the world, ease infirmity, end poverty, and perfect God's peaceable realm.

And yet, in the increasing span between Jesus's resurrection and the consummative "times of refreshing" and "universal restoration" (Acts 3:20–21), the beat goes on with jarring downbeats of pain and suffering clashing with joyous upbeats of miraculous healings performed in Jesus's name. This fibrillating situation is ripe for cognitive dissonance and emotional upheaval among Christ's early followers, not least because of their precarious status as a minority group—devoted to a crucified Messiah!—in a Roman Empire with no health-care system or social safety net.[3] How do New Testament writers cope with this persisting tension between weal and woe?

In Sickness and in Health

Is following Christ good for one's health? Although rigid forms of Christianity can prove traumatic and toxic for nonconformists, modern studies of well-being have confirmed the salutary benefits of religious faith and practice—physically, psychologically, and socially.[4] The New Testament certainly affirms Christ's gospel as good health news for adherents, promising access to critical cures and compassionate care in Christ's name. Any health hazards believers might face in a hostile world, including physical assaults and occasional executions, would be overcome by Christ's restorative love and power.

Except at times when love and hope break down. Although the New Testament touts the saving and health benefits of being "in Christ," it does not squelch counterconcerns about health care. As with other challenges, the New Testament debates out loud, in plain print, various complications in believers' daily experiences.

Before considering three key examples that tackle serious terminal health issues, it is useful to sketch a broad framework for health analysis. The field of medical anthropology identifies three interrelated dimensions of health-related phenomena: physical, social, and environmental. On the pathology side, according to one model, these areas coordinate with disease, illness, and disorder, respectively.[5] Put another way, we become *sick/diseased* with some bodily malady, which *ails/disrupts* relations with family, friends, and others and extends to *alienate/disintegrate* us from the eco-cosmic order of things. In short, health and sickness are multifaceted, multi-affective conditions for good or "ill."

Cross Purposes

We return to the conundrum of the crucified Messiah (challenge 3), now focused on the paradox of Jesus's death as the *means of salvation* from sin. Among various atonement doctrines formulated by Christian scholars through the

3. See Rhee, *Illness*, 193–223.
4. See DeSteno, *How God Works*; Myers, *Pursuit*, 177–204; Myers and Jeeves, *Psychology*, 146–58; Prinzing, "Religion."
5. See J. Green, "Healthcare Systems in Scripture," 358–59; Rhee, *Illness*, 5–9.

centuries, "satisfaction" and "substitutionary" theories have been especially influential. The former claims that Jesus's death satisfied humanity's crushing sin-debt, "paid back what was due God because of the sins of human beings, allowing divine mercy to flow."[6] The latter claims that Jesus's death substituted for the penalty we sinners deserved. Some contemporary theologians have challenged these as inadequately grounded in scriptural thought and modern sensibilities.[7]

Leaving these arguments aside, I take up a more basic issue complicating belief in Jesus the crucified Savior: How can he save others if he cannot save himself? Martyrdom may provide a partial answer: heroic figures who give their lives for a noble cause can shore up followers and shame the enemy. Resurrection provides a better solution. Jesus overcomes death and guarantees the general resurrection. But why would God's Son, who has a record of restoring diseased and even deceased people, accept death in the first place *if* he could avoid it?

The Synoptic Gospels provide poignant accounts of Jesus on the eve of his crucifixion pleading for God to save him from death, to "remove" this poison "cup" (Mark 14:36). Yet this just places the burden more heavily on God, since Jesus takes God's eerie silence as signing his death warrant, which Jesus finally accepts as God's "will" (Matt. 26:37–39; Mark 14:33–36; Luke 22:41–44). We're back to wondering why and how Jesus's death effects salvation, or more fundamentally, why *should* Jesus's death be necessary for salvation when other means already operated in his life? Further, if he wouldn't or couldn't save himself, why should we trust his will and power to save us *through his death*?

Although the Gospels' portraits of Jesus are unabashedly positive, they are by no means naive. Jesus is no superhero; the cross is not kryptonite. He is God's Son, who became human flesh and blood with all its potential for pain and suffering. Jesus's saving power, while formidable, was not unlimited (Mark 6:5). And the problem of a dead Savior, even one raised from the dead, was not lost on the Gospel writers.

Luke especially wrestles with this problem. Two strategic incidents—one, inaugurating Jesus's public mission in the Nazareth synagogue (4:16–30); the other, extinguishing Jesus's life on a Roman cross (23:26–49)—feature various groups who taunt Jesus to heal or save himself. These challengers range from his hometown folk to Jewish leaders, Roman soldiers, and a criminal executed alongside Jesus. Although they are cast as antagonists, their challenge that Jesus

---

6. E. Johnson, *Creation and the Cross*, xiii.
7. E. Johnson's *Creation and the Cross* mounts a compelling challenge to St. Anselm's "satisfaction" theory.

should validate his savior bona fides is not unreasonable. Nor is it unreasonable that those more sympathetic to Jesus might still be bothered by his seeming incapacity for self-help.

Although Luke offers no formal legal defense, the two challenging episodes feature counterexamples of persons who support Jesus's healing/saving power. In the opening incident, Jesus discerns the synagogue audience's fickle "amazement" at his self-identification with Isaiah's portrait of a liberating, Spirit-anointed prophet and exposes their underlying skepticism: "Doubtless you will quote to me this proverb, 'Doctor, cure yourself!' And you will say, 'Do here also in your hometown the things that we have heard you did at Capernaum'" (Luke 4:23; cf. 4:16–22). Eschewing his townspeople's desire for him to perform miraculous feats on demand, Jesus stokes their irritation into rage by referencing select acts of healing administered by Elijah and Elisha to a *non-Israelite* destitute widow in Sidon and a leprous officer from Syria, respectively (4:25–30). Jesus thus seems to care little not only about curing himself but about helping fellow Israelites. He not only transcends personal, familial, and national boundaries; he refuses to favor them.

This incendiary rhetoric overstates the actual ministry Luke's Jesus undertakes. Although he heals a valued servant of a Roman officer (7:1–10), delivers a demon-possessed man "opposite Galilee" (8:26–39), and cures a Samaritan "leper" (17:11–19), he primarily seeks and saves (cf. 19:6) fellow Jews in Galilee and Judea. Just a few miles from Nazareth in Nain of Galilee (not across the border), he raises a widow's only son from his coffin and restores him to his mother (7:11–17). Though envisioning a wider mission "to all nations" (24:47), Jesus personally does little to enact it. Moreover, though he "take[s] up the cross," calls his followers to do likewise (9:23), and even states that his disciples must "hate" their families (14:25–27) if need be, he also loves life, resists the cross until the very end (22:39–44), and affirms the biblical command to love "your neighbor as yourself" (10:17; Lev. 19:17). Jesus is no hater of himself or others, nor is he traitor to his people.

But he's also no proponent of cheap love. Embracive love toward all ethnic groups, even one's enemies (Luke 6:27–36), can create considerable tensions within tight-knit circles who feel, for various reasons, threatened by outsiders. Why is Jesus so concerned about needy widows and other unfortunates elsewhere when we have plenty of strugglers right here in Nazareth? Shouldn't charity begin at home? No doubt, but in Jesus's view it shouldn't end there. God's salvation is not some special blessing for me and mine but a gift of grace offered to all, especially to the last and least, those who rank first and greatest in God's realm (9:46–48; 13:30; 22:24–27).

The triple cluster of "Save yourself!" taunts directed at Jesus on the cross (Luke 23:35, 37, 39) drip with scorn and also poke Jesus to push back with force against the unjust system the scoffers represent. Enough is enough! It's high time to bring down the whole wicked empire and to save himself and God's persecuted people with "a mighty roar—nay better, by a soft word—from his mouth [that would] spring the nails from his hands, thrust away the spears from the hands of the soldiers, heal the wounds of his flesh, and shatter the cross into a million splinters in a dazzling display of sheer might."[8] That would show them real salvation power!

Except, back to challenge 3, that's not what Christ's saving power is about. Jesus's power is shown in weakness on the cross; it's "soft power" that absorbs the hammer blows of imperial violence. Are we back to trying to quell the dissonance of a crucified Messiah through paradox? Not entirely, since Luke also highlights someone from each taunting group who believes in Savior Jesus on some level.

- One criminal advocates Jesus's innocence and pleads to be given a secure place in Jesus's coming kingdom, which Jesus promises to do (23:40–43).
- Just after Jesus expires, the centurion supervising the crucifixion "praise[s] God" and also proclaims Jesus's innocence; something about the way Jesus died deeply affects the Roman officer (23:47).
- One Jewish councilmember, "a good and righteous man named Joseph" from Arimathea who "was waiting expectantly for the kingdom of God," has opposed the ruling against Jesus. Now he requests Jesus's body and provides it a decent burial. Though Joseph does not declare Jesus to be the Messiah, he seems to believe Jesus played a significant role in advancing God's realm (23:50–53).

These three men are scarcely ideal disciples or full converts to Jesus's movement. The criminal makes a "deathbed" confession of faith. The centurion corrects his misjudgment after superintending Jesus's crucifixion, and as far as we know, he never resigned his military commission and joined Jesus's group. Likewise, though Joseph of Arimathea takes a maverick stand for Jesus, we're never told he left his council post to follow Jesus.

Moreover, Luke leaves ambiguous their motivations for sympathizing with the crucified Jesus. We might imagine that Jesus's prayer that his Father would forgive his executioners and enemies (23:34) convinced the criminal and centurion of

8. Caputo, *Weakness of God*, 42–43.

his extraordinary saving purpose. But Luke does not explicitly make that connection. Though affirming it is "necessary that the Messiah should suffer" and die to fulfill his Scripture-rooted, saving-oriented vocation, Luke never details *why* that woeful way is necessary (24:26–27, 44–47). Luke wrestles with the challenge of a crucified Savior without resolving all of its questions and tensions.

Table Trouble

For all its Spirit-inspired giftedness and enthusiasm (1 Cor. 1:4–7), the Corinthian congregation had serious problems of divisiveness, disease, and death—problems largely of its own making, in Paul's view. Obviously, these bad experiences contravene Jesus's saving, healing purpose. Something has gone terribly wrong in this community, threatening both their well-being and their witness to Christ.

Paul diagnoses a complex "body" problem infecting the corporate "body of Christ" composed of individual members nested and networked within Christ's communal body (1 Cor. 6:12–20; 12:12–31). The fellowship table provides a key site for nurturing the body *physically*, through consuming food; *socially*, through conversing; and *spiritually*, through reenacting Jesus's last meal—the Lord's Supper—where he identifies bread and wine with his body and blood given in redemptive death (11:23–26). But in Paul's view, the Corinthians have been effectively toppling this table and making a travesty out of the Supper by celebrating it in an "unworthy manner," "without [properly] discerning the body." Consequently, they "eat and drink judgment against themselves"; "for this reason" many became ill, and some died (11:27, 29–30).

The Corinthians' "unworthy" practice of the Lord's Supper is commonly assessed in moral-spiritual terms: they come to the Lord's table without proper preparation, without confessing their sins and contemplating Christ's death. Yet Paul most directly targets material-nutritional habits that negatively affect their physical bodies. Health care and economics intertwine. When various "house churches" in Corinth gather for their communal "love feasts" (not simply a religious rite with token elements), wealthier members, accustomed to throwing big parties, lay out a spread and load up their plates without leaving enough for poorer members (1 Cor. 11:33–34)!

As a result, David Downs argues, these poor folks, many barely eking out an existence, suffered malnutrition and maltreatment by rich congregants: "The practice of the Lord's Supper" at Corinth "was not merely shaming the poor; it was harming their bodies and threatening to kill them."[9] Likewise, along with depriving poorer members, the fat-cats were foolishly damaging their own bodies, too, through glutting themselves on rich foods—literally eating and drinking themselves to sickness and death—to say nothing of desecrating their bodies, which are the temple of God's Spirit (see 1 Cor. 3:16–17; 6:19–20).[10]

While Paul ultimately speaks of the Lord's judgment (1 Cor. 11:32) against the Corinthians for grossly mismanaging the food crisis, he first attributes their rash of illnesses and deaths to their self-destructive inclination to "eat and drink judgment *against themselves*" (11:29–30). Self-judgment, self-discipline, personal responsibility (11:32) are critical to the body's health, the mind's peace, and the heart's ease. God's gift of salvation in Christ is not a blank check. It calls for faithful action as much as grateful acceptance, not least caring for fellow believers' physical and fiscal welfare.

Prison Woes

Paul wrote his Philippian letter from prison (1:7, 13–14). Much remains uncertain about this imprisonment: place (Ephesus, Corinth, Rome?), type (house arrest, military barracks, pit/dungeon?), charge (disturbing the peace, subverting the empire?), punishment (temporary confinement, whipping/beating, awaiting execution?).[11] But we should take seriously Paul's assessment of "*suffering* in [his] imprisonment" (1:17). Prisons were no picnics. As Matthew Skinner summarizes, "Although practices varied widely across time, geography, and social strata, prisons were known for inflicting severe hardship. . . . Overcrowding, darkness, psychological distress, and malnutrition characterized the incarceration experience. . . . In addition to physical and emotional distress, prison settings also brought social shame upon their inhabitants and associates."[12]

Although Paul was likely not on death row, he seems to think he might die in custody. Not that this bothers him much: he says he will happily "depart [this life] and be with Christ" in eternal fellowship, an experience "better by far" than lingering in this painful world (Phil. 1:23). But on further reflection, he believes the Philippians' prayers and Jesus's power will result in "deliverance/salvation" (*sōtērian*) from prison and continued "fruitful labor" in ministry, producing joy and hope for Paul and "progress and joy in faith" for the Philippians

9. Downs, "Physical Weakness," 587.
10. Downs, "Physical Weakness," 584–86.
11. Lewis, "Roman Imprisonment"; Schellenberg, "Paul's Imprisonments"; Skinner, "Prison."
12. Skinner, "Prison," 615.

St. Paul in Prison

(1:18–26). This letter shows Paul's most upbeat side. He's almost too upbeat, as if he's desperately trying to put on a brave face and positively spin his reeling life for his readers. Might Christ's saving work be better evidenced by keeping Paul out of prison in the first place?

Not in Paul's book. Remember Paul's happy identification with the weak-yet-strong, crucified Christ, discussed in challenge 3. He claims to be a "better" minister of Christ than his competitors because of his "far more imprisonments, with countless floggings, and often near death" (2 Cor. 11:23). But that doesn't mean Paul was indifferent to pain and sorrow.

In a touching snippet of the Philippian letter, Paul bears his heart about a beloved friend named Epaphroditus, his "brother and co-worker and fellow soldier" (Phil. 2:25). The Philippian assembly had sent Epaphroditus with "gifts" for Paul (4:15–18), a care package for his support in prison. There was no prison cafeteria or infirmary to tend to inmates' basic needs. The incarcerated depended on family, friends, or volunteer social workers, like Epaphroditus and fellow Philippians in

Paul's case. No heaven-sent ravens fed Paul (1 Kings 17:1–7); no miracles cured his injuries or illnesses.

This was likewise the case for Epaphroditus, who became gravely ill, which in turn caused no end of "sorrow" for Paul, as he feared that his friend might die. Thankfully, mercifully (Phil. 2:27), Epaphroditus recovered. Now Paul "may be less anxious," not only for himself but for the Philippians who would have suffered great loss with Epaphroditus's death. Now Paul can send his ministerial friend back to Philippi for a joyous reception (2:27–30).[13]

What a flood of cognitive and emotional upheaval in such a short text! Distress, sorrow, anxiety, longing, joy—all swirling around Paul, Epaphroditus, and the Philippians. And all worked out in the rough-and-tumble of life, sustained by Christ-centered hope, joy, grace, and mercy without dramatic miraculous intervention. This is salvation worked out by struggling followers of Christ in collaborative partnership with God: "Work out your own salvation with fear and trembling; for it is God who is at work in you, enabling you to will and to work for his good pleasure" (Phil. 2:12–13; cf. 1:7; 4:15–20).

For Richer, for Poorer

We've already considered some ways the New Testament wrestles with economic disparities within local congregations and the wider society, including Jesus's "blessed are the poor" statements in Matthew/Luke and the close link between physical and fiscal elements of the Lord's Supper in 1 Corinthians. We now examine other cases simmering with socioeconomic tension.

While Jesus proclaims "good news to the poor" (Luke 4:18; 7:22) and promises the poor a "blessed" stake in God's realm (Matt. 5:3; Luke 6:20), he does not pledge to make them millionaires or eradicate poverty. He himself owned nothing and died penniless, with no financial legacy.

So is this blessed good news to be realized only in *spiritual* terms on earth and/or in *supernatural* conditions in heaven? Such an otherworldly perspective seems out of sync with God's incarnation *in the world* in Jesus Christ, who teaches his followers to pray, "Your kingdom come. Your will be done, on earth as it is in

---

13. Hicks ("Moral Progress") argues that Epaphroditus was not so much physically "ill/weak" (*astheneō*) as morally, emotionally, and "metaphorically" paralyzed by fear of persecution for associating with Paul. What distresses Paul is Epaphroditus's immature emotional and spiritual state. Yet, if fear were in the mix, it does not seem primary in Paul's dealings with Epaphroditus in a swirling complex of physical, emotional, mental, and social strains.

heaven" (Matt. 6:10; cf. Luke 11:2). If Christ does not guarantee prosperity for his people, surely he at least provides sufficient sustenance, as Paul's high-note ending to Philippians claims: "My God will fully satisfy every need of yours according to his riches in glory in Christ Jesus" (4:19).

Yet plenty of believers surely begged to differ about how "fully" their basic needs were being met. Some may have resorted to literal begging to survive. What gives here? Or rather, what's *not* being given, and why?

A Waste of Money

The story of a woman's extravagant pre-anointing of Jesus's body for burial is filled with cognitive-emotive tension—but not primarily because of Jesus's looming demise. Witnesses to this act express anger at Jesus for allowing this egregious waste of money that could have been used to aid the poor. Mark's version values the perfume at three hundred denarii, almost a full year's wages for a common laborer (14:4–5; cf. Matt. 26:8–9). The critics have a point, which they expect Jesus to agree with, given the Torah's explicit command to "liberally . . . open your hand to the poor and needy" (Deut. 15:10–11). This is reinforced throughout the Bible, including in Jesus's example of aiding the poor, keeping no personal money or goods, and insisting that a wealthy would-be follower "sell what [he] own[s], and give the money to the poor" (Mark 10:21). Many poorer folk no doubt resonated with Jesus's angry challengers, even as their dissonance compounded with his apparent complicity in the problem: Why should one person enjoy expensive salon treatment when the money could be used to help the rest of us?

Of course, this is not just anyone but rather the Lord and Savior Jesus, who justifiably receives this anointing fit for a king. Why should believers object to this act of honor and devotion? Is this one who gave his life for us not worthy of giving our whole lives and livelihoods in return (see Rom. 12:1)? Yes, in principle, but in practical terms, Jesus never asks his disciples to give any material goods to him, for his consumption. Rather, Jesus calls disciples to follow him as he pours himself out to serve them (Luke 22:24–27; John 13:1–17). Although anointed by God's Spirit to embody God's reign, Jesus never dons regal robes or otherwise flaunts his regal status. He eschews the accoutrements and appropriations of worldly rulers in favor of aiding the destitute (see Matt. 11:2–19; Luke 7:18–35). His earthly throne becomes a cross on which he exemplifies God's solidarity with the least and lowliest, those crushed by an exploitative empire.

On some level, the anointing woman senses that Jesus's impending death signals his sympathy with poor victims, which somehow works for their good. Her gesture prompts Jesus to honor her in a remarkable way: "Truly, I tell you, wherever the good news is proclaimed in the whole world, what she has done will be told in remembrance of her" (Mark 14:8).

But before this concluding commendation of the woman's act, Jesus has something else to say about the "good service [she has performed] for me," starting with, "For you always have the poor with you" (Mark 14:6–7). On the surface and out of context, this statement appears to trivialize the poor as a nagging component of earthly life, like a persisting swarm of gnats. Unfortunately, inexcusably, such a reading has roosted in some modern Christian circles to justify blaming and shaming the poor for being irresponsible and to decry a "social gospel" that values caring for the poor as supposedly perverting the "true" gospel, despite the Bible's broad-based support for such ministry.[14] As a prop for his public talks, the Christian social activist Jim Wallis holds up an old Bible with all passages dealing with social and economic justice cut out; this Bible "full of holes" barely holds together![15]

Putting the rest of the Bible and Jesus's overall mission aside, simply notice the rest of Jesus's sentence in Mark: "and you *can show kindness to [the poor] whenever you wish*; but you will not always have me" (14:7). There is ample time and opportunity to help the poor, which Jesus's followers "can"—and should—do normally. But these are not normal times. Time and opportunity to show physical affection for *poor* Jesus is rapidly ticking down. The woman did what "she could" for Jesus in this pregnant moment (14:8). Her perfuming won't keep him from suffering and dying. But it still represents "good news" for the poor because it represents "good service," "good work," even "*beautiful [kalon]* work"[16]—a work of art in a slum of poverty to remind us of the good goal of God's beautiful creation and to motivate working with God and Christ toward that goal, not least through material service. The story suggests that the woman uses her resources to aid the poor when she can because she loves the poor-loving Jesus.

The modern American "rugged individualist" interpretation of Jesus's present comment about the poor would never have occurred to him, the Gospel writers, or their first readers, especially those familiar with the Torah. The Deuteronomy text mentioned above regards persisting poverty as God's call to bless the poor

14. Pregeant, *For the Healing*, 113: "To use either Deut 15:11 or Jesus's statements on the poor 'always' being available *for help* in order to oppose antipoverty measures is to contradict the main emphases of biblical economics. It is Bible abuse of the first order" (emphasis original).

15. Wallis, *God's Politics*, 209–20.

16. Carter, *Mark*, 383, 386; cf. Spencer, *Reading Mark*, 243–47.

with tangible aid, not blame them: "Since there will never cease to be some in need on the earth, I therefore command you, 'Open your hand to the poor and needy neighbor in your land'" (Deut. 15:11). The plight of the poor would still pose an acute challenge to Gospel authors and audiences, prompting them to query why material conditions of poor disciples had not improved sufficiently after Jesus's resurrection. But only the most cynical and calculating would blame the anointing woman or Jesus for perpetuating poverty through wasteful self-indulgence.

Tax Dodges and Fishy Business

Dissonance and discontent about paying taxes were hardly unique experiences for Christ's followers. Benjamin Franklin's famous adage, "Nothing is certain in this world but death and taxes," applies across world history. Rich and poor alike chafe under government taxation, although the poor pay the greater price in health and well-being, virtually being taxed to death in imperial regimes.

BEFRIENDING TAXMEN "SINNERS"

The Synoptic Jesus is notorious for fraternizing with government revenue workers who collect annual head taxes for Rome and various tolls and tariffs on commercial goods, including fish caught in the Sea of Galilee and fish products ferried across it. Herodian client-agents of Rome controlled this inland sea and ringed it with tollbooths.[17] From one station Jesus recruited the tax officer Matthew to his mission (Matt. 9:9; 10:2–3).[18] Many tax/toll collectors, like Matthew, were Jews and thus despised by their countrymen as enemy collaborators. Some further tarnished their reputations by self-dealing profiteering (Luke 3:12–13). While Matthew left his business to follow Jesus, most other taxmen Jesus associated with—including guests at Matthew's party (Matt. 9:10–11)—did not join Jesus's movement. But a few did, like the "chief tax collector" Zacchaeus, who hosted Jesus, received his "salvation," and promised to repay those he had bilked four times over and redistribute half of his wealth to the poor (Luke 19:1–10).

Jesus followed John the Baptizer in challenging people to change their sinful ways (Matt. 4:12–17; Mark 1:14–15; Luke 5:32; 13:3–5). But only Luke's Jesus explicitly calls tax collectors "to repentance" (Luke 5:30–32), and even then, he does not make repentance a *prerequisite* of fellowship with "sinners," as John did

17. Hanson, "Galilean Fishing"; Sawicki, *Crossing Galilee*, 27–30.
18. This tax collector is named Levi in Mark 2:14–17 and Luke 5:27–32, though both Gospels list Matthew, not Levi, among the twelve apostles.

(3:7–14). Jesus seeks to save lost "sinners" by befriend-
ing and dining with them (5:29–32; 7:33–35; 15:1–2;
19:5, 9–10).

But while Jesus was becoming a "friend
of tax collectors and sinners" (Matt.
11:19; Luke 7:34), he was alienating
others—and not just more strait-
laced religious teachers like John
and some Pharisees (Matt. 9:10–11;
Mark 2:15–16; Luke 5:29–30; 15:2).

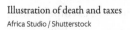

Illustration of death and taxes
Africa Studio / Shutterstock

A Jericho crowd "began to grumble" when they saw
Jesus heading to Zacchaeus's house, "He has gone to be the guest of one who is a
sinner" (Luke 19:7). And it's hard to imagine the four fishermen-disciples being
thrilled with Jesus's enlisting a shoreline toll collector. Was Matthew expected
to make reparations to fishermen he had exploited, on top of helping the poor?
The Gospels dodge that question, but it's not unreasonable to imagine economic
tensions among Jesus's first followers.

PAYING TAXES TO ROME

Legal and theological interests related to God's kingdom set the social and
economic problems of taxation in a wider frame. Is it lawful for God's people to
pay financial tribute to anyone but God to support God's work? Some Pharisees
and Herodians pose this precise question to Jesus in the temple: "Is it lawful to
pay taxes to the emperor, or not?" (Mark 12:14). In the Synoptic accounts, these
interrogators do not engage with Jesus in honest debate but rather seek to entrap
him into making a seditious proclamation (Matt. 22:15–22; Mark 12:13–17;
Luke 20:20–26). In recent memory, a pair of scholar-teachers—a Galilean named
Judas (not Iscariot) and a Pharisee named Saddok—promoted a vigorous but
nonviolent protest movement against Roman taxation on grounds that only God
had rightful claim to such tribute. Josephus reports that they were willing to
suffer torturous deaths for their beliefs and that Judas's sons, James and Simon,
were in fact later crucified by the Roman governor of Judea, Tiberius Alexander
(46–48 CE).[19] Maybe opponents of the Galilean Jesus could get rid of him by
association with tax rebels.

19. Josephus, *Antiquities* 18.3–9, 23–25; 20.100–102; Josephus, *Jewish War* 2.118; Horsley, *Jesus*,
77–89; Horsley and Hanson, *Bandits*, 190–92. Though Josephus does not report Judas's fate, Acts 5:37
claims that "Judas the Galilean . . . perished, and all who followed him were scattered."

Whatever their motivations, Jesus's questioners raise a valid stewardship issue. "The earth is the LORD's and all that is in it," Psalm 24:1 declares. In royal terms, God is sovereign king over the universe. Caesar and other monarchs usurp God's rightful rule by serving their own imperial interests rather than God's. This theological worldview does not demand anarchic repudiation of all taxes (with or without representation) or even theocratic administration of taxes by priestly agents. Various forms of government come and go, none perfect. But worldly powers exercise legitimate rule only as they implement God's aims of justice, righteousness, and mercy—not least in tax codes and policies.

In the Roman world, local Christ communities had no "tax exempt" status, and their poor majority members struggled under the onerous tax burden not just financially but cognitively and emotionally. Where is the relief, the salvation, from oppressive taxation we might expect as members of *God's* benevolent kingdom established in Christ?

What did Jesus say and do about taxes?[20] His famous pronouncement "Give to the emperor the things that are the emperor's, and to God the things that are God's" (Mark 12:17) doesn't settle the matter as neatly as sometimes assumed. No one pretended to separate religion and politics in the New Testament world, and though Jesus deftly avoids blatantly denouncing Caesar, he does not blithely endorse paying taxes as part of one's "civic duty." Giving Caesar his due may suggest giving him *back* his dirty money and having nothing to do with it! Carrying no money, Jesus has to borrow a coin—engraved with Caesar's image—to make his visual point. "Give Caesar everything he has coming to him!" On the flip side, "the things that are God's" are *everything* in Jesus's Jewish worldview. Jesus does not so much resolve the question as ratchet up the tension.

PAYING THE JERUSALEM TEMPLE TAX

So much for the Roman tax. But a strange story in Matthew raises another tax issue: paying the annual Jewish tax to support the Jerusalem temple (Matt. 17:24–27). All adult Jewish males (priests exempted) were required to pay this *half-shekel* tribute (m. Šeqal. 1), equivalent to two denarii, on top of Rome's one-denarius head tax. The temple tax represented a key "symbol of religious unity and Jewish identity."[21] Accordingly, when collectors ask Peter if his "teacher" Jesus pays this tax, Peter blurts out, "Yes [of course], he does" (17:24–25).

---

20. See Spencer, *What Did Jesus Do?*, 142–45.
21. Harb, "Matthew 17.24–37," 258.

But later, in Peter's home, Jesus presses him further, getting to the root of fiscal obligation: "From whom do kings of the earth take toll or tribute? From their children or from others?" Peter gives the obvious "others" answer, prompting Jesus's assessment from this "other" side, "Then the children are free" (Matt. 17:25–26)—tax free. Matthew's Jesus cares nothing about Caesar's or Herod's family fortunes or any earthly kingdom's revenue stream. Jesus advances God's benevolent kingdom on earth (4:27; 6:10) for God's "children" (6:32–33; 7:9–11; 10:29–31), heirs with Jesus the Son of the Creator's royal bounty by grace—with no imposed inheritance tax!

Wonderful news to everyone but the current temple leadership! The temple is God's house on earth, worthy of support. But the temple system (structures, administrators, operations) is not sacrosanct. The temple is not God and does not contain God. As with kings, so with priests: they must prove themselves to be worthy servants of God. When they fail, God sends prophets to challenge their authority and actions. Here Jesus echoes the critiques of his scriptural prophetic forebears: "'My house shall be called a house of prayer' [Isa. 56:7]; but you are making it a den of robbers [Jer. 7:11]" (Matt. 21:13). Why pay tribute to a failed system that robs God's people?

The temple's degradation worsened by Matthew's time. Rome destroyed the temple in 70 CE and replaced it with a pagan shrine to Jupiter. To pay for it, Emperor Vespasian imposed the *Fiscus Judaicus*, the same Jewish half-shekel tax now diverted to honor the chief Roman god![22] Matthew 17:24–27 thus bites on two levels: relative, first, to the impious temple establishment in Jesus's day and, second, to the blasphemous Roman sanctuary in Matthew's time. Neither aligned with the values of God's kingdom; neither merited financial support from God's children.

And yet, after touting the freedom of God's household, Jesus advises Peter to pay the temple tax for himself and Jesus. *And beyond that*, Jesus provides a weird means to pay it: a coin in the first fish's mouth that Peter hooks and pulls from the sea! The coin just happens to be a silver stater, worth two didrachmas (= four denarii), the exact amount of Jesus and Peter's "joint" tax bill (Matt. 17:27). What's going on here? This is hardly a call for Christ followers to plan a fishing trip just before taxes are due. Jesus uses fish to feed hungry people (14:13–34; 15:32–39), not as props for magic coin tricks. This story is obviously symbolic, but of what?

---

22. See Carter, *Matthew and Empire*, 130–44; Foster, "Vespasian."

It may be regarded as a "pre-vision of God's provision"[23] in God's restored realm, at last relieving the taxing burdens of this evil age on God's "free" children. In the meantime, however, Jesus and company must not rock the boat or "give offense to" the tax powers that be (Matt. 17:27), kingly or priestly, righteous or not. Does this mean Jesus advocates his people's continued oppression so as not to offend their oppressors? That would trigger cognitive dissonance and emotional upheaval if anything would.

Illustration of Peter paying the temple tax

Though Jesus will die for standing up against oppressive authorities, tax policy is not a hill worth dying on. But neither should it be blithely accepted as the cost of doing business in the world. The fish tale is as much about protest as provision: protesting earthly religious-political powers that usurp the Creator God, who made the primordial chaotic waters into a livable habitat for "the great sea monsters and every living creature that moves . . . with which the waters swarm" (Gen. 1:21). God's children enjoy—freely and responsibly—"dominion over the fish of the sea" (1:28) and all that is God's, *not* Annas's or Caiaphas's (high priests), not Tiberius's or Domitian's (Caesars), not Antipas's or Agrippa's (Herodian client-kings).[24] Catching a fish without running it through the toll checkpoint and finding a coin in its mouth to pay taxes may not topple the system, but it certainly tweaks it and points to the destiny of freedom for God's children.

Pass the Plate

Many modern-day worship services include a time of passing a platelike container among congregants to collect cash and checks to fund the church's work, including its charitable ministries. In lieu of passing plates, collection boxes may

23. Garland, "Temple Tax," 94.
24. Carter, *Matthew and Empire*, 140–42.

be set up in sanctuary foyers, or online contributions may be made through church websites. The image of the "plate," however, remains useful for conveying the missional aim of *feeding* and meeting other needs of poor members. That's the ideal at least. Unfortunately, it rubs against an inconvenient reality that a big chunk of solicited funds goes to maintaining institutional structures or, in its worst forms, feeding the greed of opportunistic leaders.

This is not a new problem: the ancient world had its share of hucksters and charlatans, who collected money from gullible fans on false pretenses, including supposed concern for the poor. Thus in Paul's one major fundraising campaign (he was no professional financier)—in which he solicits offerings from wealthier Gentile-majority congregations to support the Jewish "mother church" in Jerusalem, which has fallen on hard times[25]—he takes great pains to show that this "collection" is not a scam.[26]

Fundamentally, Paul grounds his fundraising for relief of the poor on Jesus's example of self-giving: "For you know the generous acts of our Lord Jesus Christ, that though he was rich, yet for your sakes he became poor, so that by his poverty you might become rich" (2 Cor. 8:8–9). Though rightful heir to all the Creator God's resources, Jesus divested himself of worldly goods for the good of the poor—that they "might become rich," not just spiritually but rich enough to sustain their lives through mutual giving and receiving.

Paul further roots his charity appeals in ethics, emotions, and economics: helping the poor is the "right" thing to do (2 Cor. 8:21); it marks tangible "proof of . . . love" for Paul and for the needy (8:24); and it aptly addresses the spiritual debt that Gentiles "owe" their Jewish gospel pioneers (Rom. 15:25–27). In truth, it does not seem right for the "first church" to languish in poverty. Its lacking basic provisions could hardly help but provoke dissonance and distress among other Jesus groups, to say nothing of doubts and derisions among outsiders. Tell us again: how exactly is this *good news*?

Can we really trust Paul? The issue of trust is a recurring problem for the persecutor turned proclaimer and now fundraiser. Is his pious rhetoric just a fancy cover-up to enhance his power and pocketbook? He makes every effort to back up his words with action, to put his money where his mouth is—or, rather, to show it's *not his money* at all. He refuses to take any money for his own support, except in extraordinary situations like imprisonment, where he gratefully accepts the Philippians' financial aid (see above). Otherwise, though claiming

25. Rom. 15:25–33; 1 Cor. 16:1–4; 2 Cor. 8–9; Gal. 2:9; see Downs, *Offering of the Gentiles*.
26. See Stenschke, "Obstacles on All Sides" (parts 1 and 2).

as much right as any apostle to basic material benefits for spiritual service, Paul declines to exercise this right so as not to put any "obstacle in the way of the gospel of Christ" (1 Cor. 9:8–12). He and his fellow workers work "night and day, so that we might not burden any of you [financially] while we proclaimed to you the gospel of God" (1 Thess. 2:9). Acts reports that Paul plied his trade as a tentmaker (leatherworker) in the workshop of fellow ministers Aquila and Priscilla, a married couple in Corinth (Acts 18:1–4).[27]

Still, just because Paul opted to be self-employed and not solicit funds for himself didn't mean he couldn't run a collection scheme. Charity drives always face the challenge of assuring donors that offerings will go directly to help the needy, not the greedy. Lest there be any question about Paul's interest, he proposes to send letters with anyone the church approves to take their gift to Jerusalem; he will only accompany the gift-bearers "if [they] think it is best that [he] go along" (1 Cor. 16:1–4 Message; cf. 2 Cor. 8:16–24; 9:1–5).

Further, collecting and managing funds inevitably raises equity concerns. On the cost side: Are all members contributing their fair share, or are some carrying heavy loads while others are freeloading? Paul encourages maximum participation by "each of you" (1 Cor. 16:2) in proportional giving, "according to what one has—not according to what one does not have" (2 Cor. 8:12). He also applies this principle to congregations. The wealthier Corinthians should give more than poorer Thessalonians and Philippians in Macedonia. But according to 2 Corinthians 8–9, the Macedonian assemblies gave magnanimously, "even beyond their means" (8:3), while the Corinthians made "bountiful" pledges but have not fulfilled them. Paul calls on them to pay up, lest they (and he) be "humiliated" by underperformance (8:6, 11; 9:1–5).

On the benefit side: Will this collection support local interests or siphon hard-earned monies to other places and peoples? In Paul's time, Greek cities and private organizations raised funds for various projects via subscriptions (*epidoseis*) from citizens and members. Usually these projects enhanced the local civic environment. Paul's collection disrupted this pattern by soliciting funds from believers in Corinth and other Greek cities for a foreign ethnic group (Jerusalem Jews) commonly considered inferior. As John Kloppenborg comments, "Paul's collection crossed ethnic and political boundaries that were in the first century well guarded and fraught with tensions. His *epidosis* constructed a polity that bridged a conspicuous ethnic and political chasm ... between free Greek cities of Asia, Macedonia, and Achaia and the non-Greek ('Eastern') inhabitants of

---

27. See Hock, *Social Context*.

Roman Palestine."[28] Paul was well aware of these ethnic-political tensions. But those adhering to the Jewish scriptures and the "gospel of Christ" (2 Cor. 9:13) covenant together with God and Christ in solidarity with the poor, irrespective of identity politics. Paul quotes the psalmist, "As it is written, '[God] scatters abroad, he gives to the poor; his righteousness endures forever'" (2 Cor. 9:9, quoting Ps. 112:9).

Finally, as Paul faced obstacles from the Gentile givers, he also fretted about the targeted Judean receivers of the collection. In Romans, Paul makes an impassioned plea to believers: "Join me in earnest prayer to God on my behalf, that I may be rescued from the unbelievers in Judea, and that my ministry [or offering] to Jerusalem *may be acceptable to the saints* [i.e., Christ believers]" (Rom. 15:30–31). Why wouldn't this gift be acceptable? Would the poor Jerusalem congregation turn down much-needed funds? The fact is, we don't know whether Paul's offering was delivered or received. But prejudices between Jews and Greeks ran both ways. Perhaps Jerusalem believers did not want to be indebted to Gentile benefactors.

Sadly, providing relief for the poor too often becomes a political hornet's nest. Despite their common allegiance to Christ, his followers have struggled to find a "fair balance" (2 Cor. 8:13–14) between giving and taking, being self-sufficient and other-dependent.

The Gap of Luxury

The so-called prosperity gospel peddled by some American evangelists—and swallowed by myriad followers—proclaims that the "abundant life" Jesus came to provide (John 10:10) includes material abundance. Baldly put, Jesus wants his people to be rich: the more money and possessions, the better, as glitzy signs of God's favor. Of course, these wealthy blessings are not purely divine gifts. They come at a price of contributions, typically demanding at least 10 percent of one's income (tithe). But why stop there? The more you give, the more you get back, right?

Jesus and his early followers would be shocked, and not a little saddened, at such a distortion of the self-sacrificing, other-serving gospel. As already mentioned, Jesus never promised earthly riches, and his adherents did not expect to revel in the lap of luxury. But they did advocate meeting people's basic needs in God's gracious realm. Accordingly, along with confronting the gap of luxury among richer (minority) and poorer (majority) members, Christ believers were

28. Kloppenborg, *Christ's Associations*, 263; cf. 245–64.

acutely aware of the chasm between their modest-to-meager modes of living and the opulent lifestyles of Roman plutocrats. Without aspiring to become super-elite enclaves, Christ groups still struggled with social inequality. Why should the very few luxuriate while the rest of us languish? Where's the saving justice in that arrangement?

Especially nettled by this economic disparity, the author of Revelation deals with this dissonance by blasting the imperial mercantile system and predicting its crashing demise. In sharp, vivid fashion, the author glosses Rome as Babylon and images the empire as a luxuriating, licentious whore and dominatrix of greedy worldly rulers seeking to monopolize global trade of precious gems and the finest construction materials, clothes, foodstuffs, animals, vehicles, "and human lives" (Rev. 18:13): "The kings of the earth have committed fornication with her, and the merchants of the earth have grown rich from the power of her luxury" (18:3; cf. vv. 7, 9).

A small religious sect cannot do much to challenge this Roman economic colossus, except pray and protest. Revelation does just that with boldness and flourish, adding a final doomsday prophecy: this new Babylon will *fall*, just like its ancient prototype (18:2). It will not just suffer a temporary recession, but all its trading ships will be burned, its ill-gotten wealth will be "laid waste," and its "merchants [or magnates] of the earth" will become bankrupt (18:17–19, 23) in advance of the coming city of God and the Lamb, the new Jerusalem, coursing with a crystal river generating abundant life, fruit, and "healing of the nations [or peoples]" (22:1–2).

The Roman Empire eventually did fall—four centuries after Revelation's writing, a bit late for the original audience. In a little over two centuries, however, Roman rule and the Christian church merged under Emperor Constantine. Then at least, Christians would benefit from Rome's wealth, yes? To some degree, but mostly it was still the elite economic powerbrokers who benefited, not the poor. The imperialization of the church certainly gilded its cathedrals, padded its treasury, and rewarded its chief officers. Yet what trickled down to the poor often passed through a tight sieve. Thus tensions between rich and poor have persisted in Christian social practice through various nationalizations of the church and idolizations of self-dealing Christian leaders.

5

One and All

The Social Challenge of Particularity and Partisanship

Make every effort to maintain the unity of the Spirit in the bond of peace. There is one body and one Spirit . . . one Lord, one faith, one baptism, one God and Father of all. (Eph. 4:3–5)

Tenet	Jesus Christ is the "one Lord" in perfect loving union with the "one God and Father of all," who incorporates people into "one body and one Spirit," irrespective of social distinctions.
Tension	How do followers of the loving, unifying Christ confront persisting strife and division among various identity groups, and how do they attempt to balance individual particularity with communal solidarity?

The famous Lord's Prayer, which Jesus taught his disciples and which Christians continue to recite (Matt. 6:9–13; cf. Luke 11:2–4), while suitable for private devotions, assumes corporate fellowship—individuals in solidarity with other petitioners of "*our* Father" for "*our* daily bread" and forgiveness of "*our* debts" as *we* forgive one another.

The Johannine Jesus also offers a longer prayer to his divine Father *for* his followers, present and future (John 17:1–25). In full awareness of his imminent death, Jesus pleads for the unity of all who carry on his work, mirroring his oneness with his Father: "I ask not only on behalf of these, but also on behalf of those who will believe in me through their word, that they may all be one. As you, Father, are in me and I am in you, may they also be in us, so that the world may believe that you have sent me. The glory that you have given me I have given them, so that they may be one, I in them and you in me, that they may become completely one" (John 17:20–23).

As Christ's followers matured, they increasingly appreciated the intimate, interpersonal bond of love between God and Jesus, based not primarily on philosophical reasoning but on experiential relating with Father and Son (and Spirit) in dynamic fellowship (*koinōnia*). By God's gracious love, they felt drawn into the divine circle of love and compelled to live in the Spirit of love (see Eph. 4:1–6; 1 John 1:3–4; 4:7–16). However, as we've seen in previous chapters, congregations struggled to live and work with one another in this loving spirit. Calls to unity were demanded because of the disunity and divisiveness that plagued Christ communities. The challenge to "maintain unity" (Eph. 4:3) was high-maintenance business.

The problem did not just revolve around issues and practices, like eating meat offered to idols and sharing food at the Lord's Supper in Corinth, or doctrinal disputes about perfectionism and Christ's incarnation in Johannine circles.[1] Conflict was also sparked by different identities and personalities. Groups consist of individuals; even more group-oriented societies must contend with particularity and partisanship. New Testament scholarship has rightly cautioned against overreading modern Western individualistic values into ancient Mediterranean communitarian contexts.[2] Yet it skews the picture to deny formative concepts of individual identity in antiquity.

In Paul's dynamic image of the believing community as the body of Christ (developed below), many members with various functions work together as one, "activated by one and the same Spirit, who allots to each one individually just as the Spirit chooses" (1 Cor. 12:11; cf. vv. 4–10). Unity and diversity must be held in creative tension. Easier said than done. As the New Testament writings attest, diversity can generate considerable tension without much creative resolution.

This chapter focuses on three large-scale New Testament symbols of believers' social identity: *people* of God, *body* of Christ, and *family* of God. Big images fund big ideas that profoundly shape communal experience. But before delving into these primary associational images, I briefly consider a secondary "church" (ecclesial) concept in Matthew.

1. See challenges 2, 3, and 4.
2. See Stendahl's classic study "Apostle Paul."

One Noninstitutional "Church" Assembling in Christ's Name

We've referred before to two levels of Gospel presentation: the primary level of Jesus's story and the secondary level of post-Easter experience of Christ through the Spirit. While reflecting on Jesus's past life, ministry, death, and resurrection profoundly shaped the Christ groups that were developing, the foundational Jesus stories chart an itinerant movement more than an institutional organization; hence, it's not surprising to find scant uses of *ekklēsia* (commonly rendered "church" elsewhere in the New Testament) in the Gospels. Among the Gospels, only Matthew uses *ekklēsia* and then only twice:

> And I tell you, you are Peter, and on this rock I will build my church [*ekklēsian*], and the gates of Hades will not prevail against it." (Matt. 16:18)

> If the offender refuses to listen even to the church [*ekklēsias*], let such a one be to you as a Gentile and a tax collector. (18:17)

While these references imply some form of settled association, they should not be equated with modern understandings of the "church" as physical building or Christian religious center separate from Jewish synagogues.

Ekklēsia designated any group "called together." It was "the standard term for the political assembly in a Greek city" and applied to various religious groups.[3] *Synagōgē* ("synagogue" or "gathering/meeting place") is a close synonym. In Matthew's context, while Jewish believers in Christ may have begun to feel alienated from other Jews (note *"their* synagogues," 4:23; 9:35), it pushes the evidence to assume a hard-and-fast church/synagogue split at this time. Like many religious, social, and political assemblies, early Christ followers used various available meeting sites (especially homes), without having their own purpose-built facilities. The promise of Matthew's Jesus to "build my church" is metaphorical (cf. 1 Cor. 3:9–17).

Matthew's "church" texts reflect security concerns: the first text deals with diabolical forces unleashed from the "gates of Hades"; the second with personal disputes among "church" members. In this second case, Matthew's Jesus advocates a progressive process of reconciliation, starting with the offended party reaching out to the offender; then taking along two or three allies if the offender remains unrepentant; and finally, if the problem persists, taking the matter to the whole congregation. Only as a last resort should the offender be removed from "church" rolls (18:15).[4]

---

3. Kloppenborg, *Christ's Associations*, 19–20, 104–6.

4. Throughout *Christ's Associations*, Kloppenborg examines membership rosters and requirements published by ancient guilds and associations.

In both "church" passages, Jesus reinforces his followers' ability to survive threats through their shared authority with him to bind and loosen, tighten and relax, procedures and practices in given situations (Matt. 16:19; 18:18). This binding/loosening applies to a dynamic process of holding dissonant biblical teachings in tension, interpreting them critically and compassionately in light of Christ's conduct and ongoing Spirit-presence in the assembly (18:20).[5] The case of disputing "church" members demands negotiating tensions between forgiveness and judgment, though biased toward the former (18:21–35).

One Nonnational "Nation" under God

I grew up reciting the pledge of allegiance every morning in my public grade school, along with millions of other American kids in the 1960s. But I had no idea until years later that the "under God" part of "one nation, under God, indivisible" had been recently added in 1954 at President Eisenhower's urging to "strengthen those spiritual weapons which will forever be our country's most powerful resource, in peace or in war."[6] He particularly had in mind the Cold War with the Soviet Union.

Various notions of America as God's chosen nation trade on, and to some extent displace, biblical images of Israel as God's chosen people. Ironically, professing allegiance to "one nation under God" aims to promote national unity (indivisibility) as it limits the constitutional right to freedom of religion, including the right to practice different religions or none at all. Dissonance and tension are never far from social and political experience.

Whatever one's viewpoint about the US or any other modern nation, the use of "nation" in English Bibles is problematic. The modern concept of nation-states with defined geographical boundaries and governmental structures does not map neatly onto the ancient Mediterranean world. For periods of time, city-states like Athens, Rome, and Carthage extended to empires through conquest. But there was little sense of a global "league of nations," let alone "united nations," or of "world wars" between independent nation-states.

The biblical Greek term *ethnos*, commonly rendered "nation," more accurately denotes a particular ethnic people sharing social, cultural, and religious histories, values, and practices.[7] Though Israel approximated a nation-state during its monarchic period, the biblical *ethnos* of Israel primarily identifies a people chosen

5. Powell, *Introducing the New Testament*, 134–35.
6. PBS, "God in the White House."
7. See J. Collins, "Transformation of Aseneth," 93–94.

Reverend George Docherty (left) and President Eisenhower (second from left) on the morning of February 7, 1954, at New York Avenue Presbyterian Church, the morning that Eisenhower was persuaded by Docherty that the pledge of allegiance must be amended to include the words "under God."

by God: "The Lord said to [Abraham], 'Go forth from your country and from your kindred and from your father's house to the land that I will show you. And I will make you into a great nation [or people, *ethnos*]'" (Gen. 12:1–2 NETS). This "promised land" proves to be more target area than demarcated territory. Abraham migrates in and out and scarcely owns "a foot's length" at the end of his life (Acts 7:5). His descendants largely follow this itinerant pattern with intermittent periods of conquest and settlement.

The plural "nations" (*ethnē*) often designates all non-Israelite/Judean peoples— the Gentiles—distinguished from the covenant *ethnos* and *laos* ("people") of Israel. This ethnic distinction embeds a difficult tension in biblical literature; campaigns of "ethnic cleansing" sometimes erupted between ethnic groups, but the Bible ideally envisions peaceful relations. The foundational Abrahamic covenant includes the universal goal that "all the tribes [*phylai*] of the earth shall be blessed" (Gen. 12:3 NETS; cf. Gal. 3:8–9). Or in Isaiah's updated version, "I have given you as a covenant [and] as a light to the nations [*ethnōn*]" (Isa. 42:6 NETS; cf. 49:6; Luke 2:31–32; Acts 13:47). Election and initial favoritism need not entail isolation and inimical protectionism.

But the challenge of making and maintaining peace among disparate peoples persists. The New Testament writers struggle with this issue in various ways, complicated by an influx of ethnic Gentile believers in congregations in Syria, Asia Minor, Greece, and Italy. In challenge 2, I discussed some aspects of Jewish-Gentile relations in the New Testament. We now explore these relations more fully.

God Does Not Play Favorites

Peter testifies at the Jerusalem Conference that "God made a choice among you that I should be the one through whom the Gentiles would hear the message of the good news," certified by the Holy Spirit's "cleansing [Gentiles'] hearts by faith ... ma[king] no distinction between them [Gentiles] and us [Jews]" (Acts 15:7–9). Thus Peter summarizes the remarkable events narrated in Acts 10:1–11:18, when he and six Jewish believers from Joppa (10:23; 11:12) visited the centurion Cornelius and his household in Caesarea, the Roman provincial capital. Not a normal social affair for either party! But this rendezvous was prearranged by coordinated instructions from the Lord ("double visions").[8]

Though a Roman officer, Cornelius was a devout, charitable man and worshiper of Israel's God, but he was not a full convert, as he opted to remain uncircumcised and unbound to Jewish rituals. The Lord's angel instructed him to dispatch men to find Peter at Simon the tanner's home in Joppa and bring him to Caesarea (Acts 10:1–8).[9] Just before these messengers arrive, Peter heads to Simon's rooftop for noontime prayer and lunch. But Christ interrupts, playing the surprising role of a table-waiter who projects a menu on a white screen lowered from heaven, featuring numerous "unclean" (nonkosher) animals.[10] Instead of taking Peter's order, Christ gives the order "Get up Peter; kill and eat" three times, each over Peter's strong objection, which Christ justifies by the principle "What God has made clean, you must not call profane [or common]" (10:9–16).

The overriding issue has less to do with food than fellowship, with *what* one eats than with *whom* one eats. Peter starts getting the point when the Spirit tells him that messengers are waiting below to take him to their master. Being summoned to a Roman officer's home in a city named after Caesar would have earlier

---

8. Tannehill, *Narrative Unity*, 116.

9. Tanning or leather processing was a dirty, smelly, low-class profession in the Jewish world but not specifically marked as ritually "unclean"; see Oliver, "Simon Peter."

10. Peter addresses the heavenly speaker as "Lord" (*Kyrios*), which could refer to either God or Christ. But the speaker's third-person reference to "what *God* has cleansed" points to the Lord Jesus Christ as speaker. Wilson, *Embodied God*, 87–88; cf. Spencer, *Journeying through Acts*, 120–21.

scared Peter to denial! But no longer. Peter keeps adapting, converting. Unlike the stubborn prophet Jonah, who fled *from Joppa* in a futile attempt to avoid God's call to preach to the Ninevites, Peter accedes to God's Gentile mission.[11]

Upon arriving in Cornelius's house, Peter opens with a confession, "I truly understand that God shows no partiality, but in every nation [*ethnei*] anyone who fears him and does what is right is acceptable to him" (Acts 10:34–35). There is no "most favored nation" status in God's world, including the *ethnos* of Israel, which is not to relegate all peoples to subordinate status but to elevate them to potential covenant fellowship with God.[12] This multiethnic scriptural strain counterpointing more "nationalist" anthems peaks to crescendo in the word God "sent to the people of Israel, preaching peace *by Jesus Christ—he is Lord of all*" (10:36–37). As Peter continues to unpack this inclusive gospel, God's Spirit interrupts mid-sermon, inspiring all uncircumcised hearers in Cornelius's home to praise God in "tongues"—just as Peter and company did at Pentecost (2:1–11)! Again, Peter gets the message: "Can anyone withhold [*kōlysai*] the water for baptizing these people who have received the Holy Spirit just as we have?" (10:47). "If then God gave them the same [Spirit] gift that he gave us when we believed in the Lord Jesus Christ, who was I that I could hinder [*kōlysai*] God?" (11:17).

Who can argue with that? With God! Well, as it happens, some Judean believers hold the circumcision line. They aren't anti-Gentile, but they think that Gentiles must keep the Jewish law to be saved members of the covenant community. This circumcision party eventually agrees with the "whole church" (Acts 15:22) on a compromise: no circumcision will be required for Gentiles' salvation, but Gentiles will be encouraged to concede to Jewish taboos against immorality and some food practices, particularly those tied to idolatrous worship (15:19–21, 28–29; 21:25). However, as I discussed in challenges 2 and 3, this purportedly "unanimous" decision (15:25) did not always guarantee harmony in mixed Jewish-Gentile Christ assemblies in Antioch, Corinth, and Rome, at least from Paul's perspective. Recall that Paul even called Peter to task for waffling on his acceptance of uncircumcised, nonkosher Gentile believers (Gal. 2:11–14).

On the one hand, we have Acts' more idealistic, optimistic portrayal of church unity and Peter's leading role in that drama; on the other hand, Paul's more realistic, antagonistic perspective. Like Acts, Paul embraces the oneness of Jewish and Greek devotees of Christ (1 Cor. 1:12–13; Gal. 3:27–28). But in the rough-and-tumble of congregational life, much work remains to be done in forging peaceful ethnic

11. See Wall, "Simon 'Son' of Jonah"; Spencer, *Journeying through Acts*, 122–23.
12. Cf. World Trade Organization, "General Agreement."

relations, and in the heat of debate Paul's incisive ("cutting") rhetoric could make matters worse (Gal. 5:12). Of course, it would be nice to have Peter's firsthand accounts of events (2:11–14). Regardless, Acts' triple accounts of Peter's acceptance of all ethnicities among God's people (10:1–48; 11:1–18; 15:7–11) trumpet strong calls to unity.[13]

Not My People, Now My People

The letter known as 1 Peter is a circular correspondence to associated congregations in northern and central provinces of Roman Asia Minor. The writer, either the apostle Peter or a devotee writing in his name,[14] addresses Christ believers as "aliens and exiles" (1:1; 2:11)—that is, moral and cultural strangers to dominant "Gentiles" (ethnē, 2:12; 4:3). Though these congregations include Jews and Gentiles (they're majority Gentile), these "Christians" (4:16) suffered on the margins of mainstream "Gentile" life.[15] The letter-writer shares this alien-exile identity, writing from a sister congregation in "Babylon" (as he glosses Rome, 5:13) and thus connecting the old exiling Mesopotamian power with the current oppressive Roman Empire.[16]

The threat to community life in 1 Peter comes from without, not within. As Donald Senior comments, "Through[out] the letter, the author . . . reflects none of the [internal] Jewish-Gentile polarity that is a dominant concern in other New Testament literature."[17] Accordingly, 1 Peter makes no mention of Peter's encounter with Cornelius or the Jerusalem Conference reported in Acts 15 and Galatians 2.

Survival as a harassed minority group demands a strong sense of internal unity. Christ adherents—Jew and Gentile—must pull together in this agonistic environment. Fighting each other is self-defeating: "Above all, maintain constant love for one another" (1 Pet. 4:8). Such communal love flows out of God's "great mercy" shown to sufferers, which gives them "a new birth into a living hope" of safety, including eternal "salvation" (1:3). This affective dynamic of God's merciful and hopeful love calls for the ebullient emotional response of rejoicing (agalliaō), "even if now for a little while you have had to suffer various trials" (1:6).[18]

13. See Spencer, Gospel of Luke and Acts, 223–27.

14. See Powell, Introducing the New Testament, 480–86.

15. First Pet. 4:16 represents one of only three uses of "Christian/s" (Christianoi, "Christ-ones") in the New Testament, along with Acts 11:26 and 26:28. All three reflect a label used by outsiders, not a self-designation used by Christ believers.

16. Senior, "1 Peter," 4–7.

17. Senior, "1 Peter," 62.

18. Hockey (Role of Emotion) notes that agalliaō "can express exuberant, even vocalized, joy" (117) and interprets the second-person plural form (agalliasthe) in 1 Pet 1:6, 8 as present indicative, suggesting "you are continuing to rejoice" amid intense suffering (120–21; cf. 105–41).

Facing societal rejection, as Jesus did, his followers must also reject outside opinion and rejoice in their God-ordained identity as "a chosen race, a royal priesthood, a holy nation, God's own people" (1 Pet. 2:9), echoing the covenantal status God conferred on the Israelites at Mount Sinai in contradistinction to their former status as enslaved persons in Egypt (Exod. 19:3–6). Now Jewish and Gentile believers in Christ have been joyously (re)joined by God's "mercy" into one "nation" (*ethnos*). The chosen/elected (*eklekton*) element emphasizes God's gracious formation of a new people. This people was formerly unchosen/unelected; now they are transformed from outsiders to insiders, from foreigners to fellow citizens.

There are two sides, however, to covenantal relations. While God's love and mercy remain steadfast in a volatile world, the people's faithfulness to God is more prone to fearful flight and fickleness. Before leaving Mount Sinai, the Israelites already reneged on the covenant deal. Anxious over Moses's delayed return from the mountaintop, the people crafted a golden calf to worship (Exod. 32). So began a fraught history of struggle between God and Israel,[19] of God's warning the people about the severe consequences of their waywardness and wooing them back to faithful fellowship—a cycle of reclaiming, rechoosing, and re-creating God's "nation."

Walter Brueggemann states, "Israel in the Old Testament is endlessly self-conscious about its own identity and continually reflects on its distinctive role as a historical people. . . . Israel continually negotiates its theological and historical destiny." Israel must navigate its ongoing transformation from "not a people" to "God's people," as the prophet Hosea demonstrated in his precarious eighth-century BCE context.[20] Strange as it seems, God calls Hosea to marry a prostitute, who bears him three children, the last two a daughter named Lo-ruhamah ("Not shown mercy") and a son named Lo-ammi ("Not my people"). Hosea's family embodies God's redemptive love toward rebellious Israel and a renewed covenant with a reclaimed—and renamed—people: "I will have pity [or mercy, *ruhamah*] on Lo-ruhamah, and I will say to Lo-ammi, 'You are my people [*ammi*]'; and he shall say, 'You are my God'" (Hosea 2:23; cf. 1:6–2:1).

After designating Christ believers as God's chosen *ethnos*, 1 Peter amplifies this identity by direct appeal to Hosea: "Once you were not a people, but now you are God's people; once you had not received mercy, but now you have received mercy" (1 Pet. 2:10). What Brueggemann says about Israel in the Old Testament

19. The name "Israel" can be interpreted as meaning "struggler with God" (see Gen. 32:27–28).
20. Brueggemann, *Sabbath as Resistance*, 46.

Olive tree in Hebron

applies to Jewish and Gentile followers of Christ in the New Testament: "The identity of Israel as YHWH's people is a treasured claim, but one permeated with risk. For that reason, Israel always contested its identity, its destiny, and consequently, its membership."[21] In other words, God's people remain vulnerable to cognitive dissonance and emotional upheaval requiring negotiation and renewal in challenging situations.

The people's faithful commitment to God predicates on their humble gratitude to God (1 Pet. 5:5–6), who alone graciously creates and covenants with God's people, leaving no space for "nationalistic" pride and superiority. While continuing to have their cultural distinctions, Jewish and Gentile believers in Christ have no warrant for divisive ethnic partisanship and identity politics.

While 1 Peter tags the outside world opposed to Christians as "Gentile," Paul's letters confront Jewish-Gentile tensions *within* congregations. In Romans, Paul affirms God's merciful formation and reclamation via the same Hosea text 1 Peter uses (Rom. 9:25–26; cf. 9:14–24). Paul particularly drives this point home to Gentile believers in the wake of the Jews' expulsion from Rome in 49 CE by Emperor Claudius (cf. Acts 18:2). When Jews returned after Claudius's death in 54 CE, they were not always welcomed back with open arms, even within the

21. Brueggemann, *Sabbath as Resistance*, 48.

Christ community. In the face of this prejudice, Paul reminds Gentile believers that they have no basis for lording themselves over their Jewish brothers and sisters who *first* accepted Jesus Messiah. Paul aims to nip Gentile anti-Judaism in the bud—specifically, the olive bud. The Gentiles are "wild shoots" that God graciously grafted into Israel's "natural" family (olive) tree generated from the "rich root" of Christ (Rom. 11:17–24).

And what about *unbelieving Jews* who reject God's Messiah and appear "broken off" from the Christ-tree? This causes the Jewish Paul no end of cognitive dissonance and emotional distress (Rom. 9:1–3). He also worries that widespread Jewish spurning of Christ might be taken as a sign that Christ's mission has failed. But he counters this angst with a particular distinction and a universal vision: first, "It is not as though the word of God has failed. For not all [ethnic] Israelites truly belong to [faithful] Israel" (9:6–7); yet finally, Paul hopes that "all Israel will be saved," all those broken off will be *regrafted* through God's unfailing mercy (11:26).[22]

Tear Down This Wall!

At West Berlin's Brandenburg Gate in the summer of 1987, President Ronald Reagan delivered a speech urging Soviet leader Mikhail Gorbachev, "Tear down this wall!"—the infamous wall dividing not only Berlin but Western and Eastern Europe. Two years later, the wall was dismantled. Walls, gates, fences, and other barricades have long demarcated insiders and outsiders, favored people and dangerous foes. Such borders must be policed, and trespassers punished. Breached and broken walls signal either conquest or conciliation, war or peace.

In Ephesians, the Pauline writer[23] triumphantly proclaims that Christ "is our peace; in his flesh he had made both groups into one and has broken down the *dividing wall*, that is, the hostility between us" (Eph. 2:14). The author then underscores Christ's peacemaking role three more times (2:15, 17 [twice]). Who are the "both groups" Christ reconciles? Again, Jews and Gentiles: covenantal Israelites, on the one hand, and "far off aliens and strangers," on the other hand (2:12–13). While the language echoes 1 Peter, the focus is distinct. Remember that 1 Peter addresses Jewish and Gentile believers *together* as "aliens and exiles" counterpoised to the outside "Gentile" world; Ephesians reserves "alien" status for Gentile converts *before*

22. See Spencer, "Metaphor, Mystery, and the Salvation of Israel."

23. As with 1 Peter, many scholars regard Ephesians as a pseudonymous circular letter—in this case, composed by devotees of Paul for congregations in western Asia Minor; see Powell, *Introducing the New Testament*, 341–48.

they were "brought near" by Christ (2:13). While Ephesians also "insists" that Gentile Christ followers "must no longer live as [outsider] Gentiles live, in the futility of their minds" (4:17), primary emphasis falls on boundary-breaking Jewish-Gentile oneness *within* the close-knit "household of God" (2:19)—an open house without dividing walls.

Walls segregating Jews and Gentiles evoke Torah and temple boundaries. God's "law with its commandments and ordinances" (Eph. 2:15) was given to Israel to delineate God's blessed way of life, set apart from others' adverse ways. But Jewish law also advocated considerate treatment of aliens/immigrants on a par with neighbors: "You must love [immigrants] as yourself, because you were immigrants in the land of Egypt"

People atop the Berlin Wall near the Brandenburg Gate on November 9, 1989. The text on the sign ("Notice! You are now leaving West Berlin") has been modified with "*Wie denn?*" ("How?").

(Lev. 19:34 CEB; cf. 19:18). Unfortunately, however, at vulnerable times in Israel's history, some groups regarded the law as mounting a "national" security blockade against foreign contamination. For example, the Hellenistic-Jewish Letter of Aristeas avers, "In his wisdom [God's] legislator . . . surrounded us with *unbroken palisades and iron walls* to prevent our mixing with any of the other peoples in any matter. . . . He hedged us in on all sides with strict observances connected with meat and drink and touch and hearing and sight, after the manner of the Law."[24]

Reinforcing these legal "iron walls"[25] were actual stone walls around Jerusalem and within the temple compound. From 520 to 515 BCE returnees from exile built a second temple to replace the one destroyed by the Babylonians. In the next century, Nehemiah, Judah's governor, constructed a security wall around the entire city. Herod the Great's major temple renovation project, beginning toward the

24. Letter of Aristeas 139, 142 (see Shutt, "Letter of Aristeas," 22; Perkins, "Letter to Ephesians," 399).
25. Twentieth-century Christians used similar "Iron Curtain" imagery to divide the Western world from the supposedly "godless" Soviet Union.

The Wailing Wall in Jerusalem

close of the first century BCE, included building a massive retaining wall made of boulders around the temple mount. The temple complex was bordered by pillared walkways (colonnades) for the general public. Beyond these porticoes, however, were lower stone-post railings (balustrades) *separating* the court of Gentiles from inner sanctuary spaces. Josephus reports that signs were posted on these barriers warning Gentiles not to trespass—on pain of death![26] Acts reports that some worshipers accused Paul of bringing a missionary companion, Trophimus—an *Ephesian* Gentile—into the Jews-only sector of the temple, beyond the posted barricade. Paul had done no such thing, but his accusers stirred up a mob that might have killed him if Roman soldiers had not intervened (Acts 21:27–36).

Sacred boundaries are serious business. The letter to the Ephesians' claim that Christ *broke down* ("destroyed," 2:14 NIV) the "dividing wall" of "hostility" between Jews and Gentiles is a serious claim, eerily reminiscent of Babylon's demolition of Solomon's temple and Rome's leveling of Herod's temple (70 CE). Only a small segment of the retaining wall remains standing to this day, the Wailing Wall, where Jews—and Gentiles—still come to pray and mourn.

But Jesus was no iconoclastic temple destroyer. He was a temple reformer and transformer—a greater-than-Herod renovator—reconstructing "the whole

26. Josephus, *Jewish War* 5.193–94; 6.124–26.

structure ... into a holy temple in the Lord ... built together spiritually into a dwelling place for God" (Eph. 2:21–22). Jesus broke down the ethnic dividing wall spiritually and physically, "in his flesh," bringing Jews and Gentiles together into "one body" (2:14, 16). Christ's cross crosses out ethnic enmity by "putting to death that hostility" embedded in dividing walls (2:16).

We're back to the paradox of the cross that both precipitates dissonance and presses through it to peaceful resolution. How can one innocent Jewish man's torturous Roman execution eradicate Jewish-Gentile enmity? Only by God's unbounded grace mediated "by the Spirit: that is, the Gentiles have become fellow heirs, members of the same body, and sharers in the promise in Christ Jesus through the gospel" (Eph. 3:5–7). Exactly how the cross works in this reconciling operation remains a profound "mystery" (3:4). But somehow in God's redemptive "plan" (1:10), Christ absorbed in his broken body the brunt of human hostility once for all—*one* for all.

One Nondenominational "Religious" Body in Christ

The body of Christ represents a major image of communal life in Pauline literature. We have touched on "body" language in Ephesians 2 (above) and in 1 Corinthians 8–10 and Romans 14–15 (see challenge 2; cf. 1 Cor. 12:1–31; Rom. 12:1–7). No concept of the Christ community more intentionally balances members' individual and interconnected roles as integral working parts of one body—without partisanship.

Blessed Be the Ligaments That Link

In 1782 English Baptist pastor John Fawcett published a hymn collection that included "Brotherly Love." It remains popular today, often sung after Communion as "Blessed Be the Ties that Bind" (the opening line). While "ties that bind" evoke images of restraining ropes, these are "blessed" ties of fellowship that "bind our hearts in Christian love," that forge a "bond of peace" in Christ's "one body," as Ephesians envisions the ecumenical community and Colossians applies to a local congregation (Eph. 4:3–4; Col. 3:14–15).

These closely related Pauline writings also use an anatomical analogy to describe the ties that bind as *ligaments* linking the various people-parts to the *head* controller, Christ:

> We must grow up in every way into him who is the head, into Christ, from whom the whole body, joined and knit together by every *ligament* with which it is equipped ... promotes the body's growth in building itself up in love. (Eph. 4:15–16)

[Hold] fast to [Christ] the head, from whom the whole body, nourished and held together by its *ligaments* and sinews, grows with a growth that is from God. (Col. 2:19)

The English "ligament" derives from the Latin *ligamentum*, related to *ligatio* ("tie/ bond"), *ligare* ("join/bind"), and, yes, *religio* ("religion"). A "religious" body constitutes members joined together in a covenantal bond with divine and human beings.

The Greek term for "ligament" is *haphē*, related to *haptomai*, "touch." Aristotle correlates functions of "contact" (*haphē*) with "action-passion" (*poiein-paschein*): "But if we must investigate 'action-passion' . . . we must also investigate 'contact.' For action and passion . . . can only occur between things which are such as to touch [*hapsasthai*] one another; nor can things enter into combination at all unless they have come into a certain kind of contact [*hapsamena*]."[27]

As J. B. Lightfoot comments on this passage, Aristotle "lays great stress on the mutual sympathy and influence of the parts in contact."[28] Physical, social, emotional, and behavioral dynamics of "touch" work together for the whole body's benefit. Each individual part is vital to the body's healthy function, provided it is "working properly" in loving tandem with other parts (Eph. 4:16). Detached, "out of touch" parts impair the entire body's ability to operate. To use a sports analogy, tearing ligaments in one's knee hampers not only the individual player but the whole team's performance.

Moreover, the Ephesians and Colossians texts emphasize the primary connection of all linked parts to Christ, the head of the body, who orchestrates the "whole body" to carry out its love-centered ministry (Eph. 4:15; Col. 2:8–10, 19). In colloquial language that happens to fit modern neuroscience, we might say that Christ is the "brains of the operation." No part of the body and no-body can live without vital connection to the brain. In Colossians, Christ's dynamic headship in the communal body is challenged by independent, headstrong, head-swollen philosophers "puffed up without cause by a [limited] human way of thinking" (Col. 2:18–19; cf. 2:8).[29] In their bloated conceit, these teachers snapped the creative tension between "one and all" and broke the bond of love sustaining Christ's body.

Building Up the Body without Boasting

Anatomy and architecture converge in the image of bodybuilding. As we've seen, Ephesians applies this metaphor to "building up the body of Christ . . .

---

27. Aristotle, *On Generation and Corruption* 1.6.
28. Lightfoot, *Saint Paul's Epistles*, 199.
29. See Sumney, *Colossians*, 156–57.

in love" (Eph. 4:12, 16), with special emphasis on breaking down the "dividing wall" between Jews and Gentiles (2:14) and building up "the whole structure" on "the foundation of the apostles and prophets, with Christ Jesus himself as the cornerstone" (2:20–22; cf. 1 Pet. 2:4–6).

If Ephesians presents a vision of Christ's collective body as a sturdy-jointed, holy-purposed building of God, 1 Corinthians shows Paul struggling to realize this vision in the construction zone of a highly gifted—and hotly conflicted—congregation. He writes this letter in response to a disturbing report about quarrels or rivalries among them. Hence he writes, "I appeal to you, brothers and sisters, by the name of Lord Jesus Christ, that all of you be in agreement and that there be no divisions (*schismata*) among you, but that you be united in the same mind and the same purpose" (1 Cor. 1:10).

Paul especially frets about factions rallied around popular ministerial figures: leaders of political parties that were rooted in personality cults. Note that the ministers themselves did not promote these parties; rather, others appropriated their names for political aims. Paul's name was among those co-opted and pitted against supposed rivals, such as Apollos, Cephas (Peter), and even Christ (1 Cor. 1:12)! While Paul does not detail these parties' policies and platforms, we may chart possible labels and slogans drawn from hints in 1 Corinthians and elsewhere (see table below). In any case, Paul seeks to abolish these parties, not least those associated with him and Christ: "Has Christ been divided? Was Paul crucified for you? Or were you baptized in the name of Paul? I thank God . . . that no one can say that you were baptized in my name" (1:13–15).

Party Politics in Corinth

Party Favorites	Party Labels	Party Slogans
Paul	• "Founders": charter members devoted to founder Paul • "Libertarians": Gentile members attracted to Paul's law-free message, narrowly interpreted	"All things are lawful" (1 Cor. 6:12; 10:23)
Apollos	• "Sophisticates": enamored with "eloquent wisdom [*sophia*]" (1:17; cf. Acts 18:24) • "Charismatics": attracted to super-gifted, spellbinding ministers • "Baptists": valued Apollos's ties to John the Baptizer (Acts 18:25; 19:1–7)	"Wisdom and power" (cf. 1:17–2:4; 3:18–20)

Party Favorites	Party Labels	Party Slogans
Cephas (Peter)	• "Traditionalists": remained faithful to Jewish law and the Jerusalem "mother church" • "Apostolics": preferred Jesus's tradition delivered to the twelve apostles over Paul's "untimely" commission (15:8) • "Rockies": exalted the apostle whom Jesus called "Rock" (Cephas/Peter)	"Law and order" (cf. 14:40)
Christ	• "Independents": rejected all ministers and submitted to no one but Christ • "Jesus People": claimed to walk in perfect step with Jesus • "Super-Spiritualists": lorded their spiritual closeness to Jesus over their inferiors	"All you need is Jesus" (cf. 12:3, 18–24)

Whatever the disputed fine points on various matters of faith and practice, Paul subordinates these to the collaborative body of Christ, built on the one "foundation [that] is Jesus Christ" (1 Cor. 3:11). As with physically building a healthy body or sturdy house, the body/house of Christ thrives as individual parts work together for common cause and mutual benefit (10:31–33). The energy for such a holy project comes from the Holy Spirit operating within "your body"—that is, "the [one] body of you [all]": "Do you not know that your body is a temple of the Holy Spirit within you, which you have from God, and that you are not your own?" (6:19–20; cf. 3:16–17).[30]

Dissonance between individual and communal concerns dissolves in the flourishing body of Christ, which values each person's contribution as vital to the body's well-being. No one is independent or unnecessary; indeed, "the members of the body that seem to be weaker are indispensable" (1 Cor. 12:22). No one has the right to trumpet their abilities over another's; blowing one's own horn only creates grating dissonance. There's no room for flexing bodybuilders or fawning hero-worshipers. Again, Paul includes himself in this deal: "Let no one boast about human leaders. For all things are yours, whether Paul or Apollos or Cephas or the world or life or death or the present or the future—all belong to you, and you belong to Christ, and Christ belongs to God" (3:21–23).

This sense of humility and unity does not stop Paul from claiming the Lord's authority when warranted. But as we saw in challenge 1, Paul also acknowledges

---

30. All the second-person pronouns in 1 Cor. 6:19–20 are plural.

he doesn't have clear commands from the Lord on every matter; in such cases he offers his best spiritual opinion (1 Cor. 7:6–7, 10–12). "I think that I too have the Spirit of God" (7:40), which is to say, "I have as much right as any other leader, if not more, to share what *I think* about the Spirit's guidance, but I may still be misguided. I may need more insight. I may need to change my mind to conform more fully to the 'mind of Christ'" (2:16; cf. Rom. 12:2).

One Nonhereditary, Nonhierarchical Household of God

Overlapping images of one nation/people and one body/building also hint at one family/household. Caesars fancied themselves as fathers, even divine fathers, of one big happy family of subjects,[31] and houses provided the main constructed environments for family life. When this concept is applied to Christ believers, "Through [Christ] both [Jews and Gentiles] have access in one Spirit to the *Father*. . . . [You are] also members of the *household of God*, built upon the foundation of the apostles and prophets, with Christ Jesus himself as the cornerstone" (Eph. 2:18–20; cf. 1 Pet. 2:4–10).

The dominant notion of kinship in the ancient world, however, undercut ideals of unity and universality with realities of heredity and hierarchy. As Jonathan Sacks notes, "The worldview of antiquity . . . was built on the belief that differences in power, wealth and status were part of the ordained order. Status was a given of birth. Hierarchy was written into the fabric of the universe. Some, said Aristotle, are born to be free, while others are born to be slaves." Likewise, as Sacks's characterizes Plato's view, "People must be trained to believe that differences in fate are preordained, if societies are to defend themselves against unrest: inequalities can be lamented but they cannot be changed."[32]

The prevailing Jewish view, however, regards "God [as] the parent of humanity" and all persons as "members of a single extended family" with special concern to care for each other as "brothers and sisters . . . something we feel in our bones." Festivals of Passover and Booths (Tents) stress compassionate feeling and action toward enslaved and homeless persons, reminiscent of the Israelites' travails in Egyptian work camps and wanderings in the Sinai wilderness.[33] The Hebrew Bible moderates distinctions in birth and rank, pedigree and status, but it does not eradicate them. Genealogies and hierarchies favoring patriarchs, monarchs, and

31. See Peppard, *Son of God*, 60–67.
32. Sacks, *Dignity of Difference*, 108.
33. Sacks, *Dignity of Difference*, 112.

chief priests are also prominent, reflecting persisting tensions between egalitarian ideals and stratified realities.

New Testament narratives envision the covenantal family of God drawn from all families of the earth. Jesus's forerunner John announces to some smug teachers, "Do not presume to say, 'We have Abraham as our ancestor [or father]'; for I tell you, God is able from these stones to raise up children to Abraham" (Matt. 3:9; Luke 3:8). Jesus relativizes biological kinship in favor of spiritual-moral ties: "Here are my mother my brothers! Whoever does the will of God is my brother and sister and mother" (Mark 3:35; cf. Luke 8:19–21; 11:27–28). Matthew's Jesus resists ranking titles among religious teachers and family heads: "But you are not to be called rabbi, for you have one teacher, and you are all students. And call no one your father on earth, for you have one Father—the one in heaven" (Matt. 23:8–9). In Acts, Peter interprets the Spirit's Pentecost outpouring by quoting the prophet Joel: "I will pour out my Spirit upon all flesh," all types of people—young/old, sons/daughters, enslaved/free persons—cutting across social and familial distinctions (Acts 2:17–21; Joel 2:28–32).

But that's not the whole picture. Some ancestral and authority lines still divide the family album. Matthew and Luke certify Jesus's messianic pedigree back to Patriarch Abraham and King David (Matt. 1:1–17; Luke 3:31, 34), though Luke traces Jesus's line further back, to the first human, Adam (3:38), in solidarity with all people. Though Jesus has various followers, including women (Mark 15:40–41; Luke 8:1–3; 10:1–12), the Gospels prioritize twelve male apostles destined to "sit on twelve thrones, judging the twelve tribes of Israel" as patriarchs in Christ's kingdom (Matt. 19:28; cf. Luke 22:28–30). While Acts allows for some women ministers, the primary preachers, teachers, and leaders are all men;[34] and while Paul and other men play key parts, the twelve Jerusalem apostles lead the way (see 1:15–26).

The Pauline writings also reflect tensions in God's Christ-knit family. On the one hand, Paul envisions an inclusive, mutually supporting community. As a late and unlikely choice to be Christ's special emissary to Gentiles, he revels in the magnanimity of God's grace in Christ (1 Cor. 15:8–11; Gal. 1:11–17) across stratifications of genealogy, ethnicity, class, and gender: "In Christ Jesus you are all children of God through faith. . . . There is no longer Jew or Greek, there is no longer slave or free, there is no longer male and female. . . . And if you belong to Christ, then you are Abraham's offspring, heirs according to the promise" (Gal. 3:26–29; cf. 1 Cor. 12:12–13; Col. 3:11). One and all are children of God, heirs of God's promise.

34. See Spencer, *Dancing Girls*, 144–65.

On the other hand, Paul stops short of dismantling standard family systems dominated by patresfamilias who rule over subordinate household members, including wives and enslaved persons (male and female) as well as children. Though believers are "one in Christ" and in ecclesial life, such unity does not necessarily obtain in domestic matters and certainly not in the wider society. Later Pauline texts in Ephesians-Colossians and the Pastoral Letters affirm common "household codes" (Eph. 5:21–6:9; Col. 3:18–4:1; 1 Tim. 2:9–15; 6:1–2; Titus 2:1–10; cf. 1 Pet. 2:18–3:7), and 1 Corinthians sends mixed messages about the freedom of women and slaves (see below). Whatever liberative seeds Paul may have sown, they would take centuries to sprout into movements for women's liberation, emancipation from slavery, and advocacy of equal rights. Paul was no first-century feminist, abolitionist, or democrat; and if he were, he would have been executed as a social and political rebel earlier than he was.

Paul and associates wrestled with tensions in the Christ family between inclusive, egalitarian ideals and constrictive, authoritarian realities. They negotiated these tensions in various ways, including adopting a major image of family relations and adapting traditional household hierarchies.

Adopted Heirs

The key metaphor Paul adopted for kinship was in fact adoption.[35] This analogy envisages reversing humanity's alienation from God's household through (re-) adoption by the will of the Father, embodied in the life of Jesus Christ the Son and enacted through the agency of the Holy Spirit. By adoption, the Father, Son, and Spirit graciously incorporate human beings into their beloved "trinitarian" family circle (see Rom. 8:14–17; Gal. 4:3–6).[36]

The Greek word for "son" (*huios*) is embedded in the term for "adoption" (*huiothesia*). This linguistic link fits the Greco-Roman cultural pattern of male family heads adopting adult sons to carry on the family line in the absence or incompetence of natural sons. The paterfamilias adopted his successor to secure his political and economic legacy, not out of charity toward an orphan-adoptee. Julius Caesar, for example, adopted Octavian to inherit his eternal imperial authority under the title of Caesar Augustus.[37]

The Jewish biblical picture both mirrors and modifies this pattern. God, Israel's true Sovereign, adopts David and descendants as God's viceregent: "I will establish

---

35. See Burke, *Adopted into God's Family*; Heim, *Adoption in Galatians and Romans*.
36. See Heim, "In Him and through Him."
37. See Peppard, *Son of God*, 46–48.

the throne of his kingdom forever. I will be a father to him, and he shall be a son to me" (2 Sam. 7:13–14; cf. Ps. 2:6–7).[38] In this royal family arrangement, God remains responsible for disciplining the human king when he abuses his power, as often happens with Israel's rulers.

The New Testament writings consistently identify Jesus as the messianic son of David but also as transcending that lineage by his intimate union with God and perfect modeling of God's character. Yet among the "mélange of metaphors"[39] used to understand Jesus's unique person and work, divine adoption has its place, particularly associated with his resurrection (Rom. 1:1–4) and baptism—"You are my Son, the Beloved; with you I am well pleased," or "I am pleased to *choose* you" (Mark 1:11).[40] Jesus's "beloved" relationship with the Father adds an emotive-relational dimension not assumed in ancient adoptive arrangements.[41]

While Jesus's filial relationship to God is exceptional, it is not exclusive: it includes not only Davidic kings but also the people of Israel (see below) and all believers in Christ, Jewish or Gentile, male or female. Although focusing on sons, given the cultural milieu and Jesus's maleness, Paul easily elides in Romans 8 from masculine *huios*/*huiothesias* ("son/adoption as sons") terminology (8:14–15) to the neutral *tekna* ("children"), applied to both sons and daughters (8:16–17).[42] Even more remarkably, Paul declares all these "children" to be "heirs of God" and "joint heirs with Christ," with just as much right and privilege to call God "Abba! Father!" as Jesus himself (8:16; Gal. 4:6).

But there's a caveat: abundant life in God's adoptive family is no mere transactional legal right but rather flows out of a deep experiential interpersonal relationship with Christ, including suffering and dying in Christ as well as rising "with him" in "newness of life" (Rom. 6:1–4; 8:17). Such dissonant experience marks believers' lives in this "present time" while spurring them to persevere in their hope of full and final "adoption, the redemption of our bodies" (8:23). In the meantime, we both glory in the present "first fruits of the Spirit" and groan with all creation and the sympathetic Spirit, yearning for the consummation of God's adoptive/redemptive work (8:19–28).[43]

---

38. See Scott, "Adoption," 16–18.
39. Bartlett, "Adoption in the Bible," 388.
40. Peppard, *Son of God*, 106–12.
41. In antiquity, "adoption was not nearly so much a matter of affection as it was of pragmatic distribution of wealth and power." Bartlett, "Adoption in the Bible," 384.
42. Scott, "Adoption," 18.
43. See Heim, "Inward Groaning."

By connecting family adoption with bodily redemption in Romans 8:23, Paul evokes related images of release (freedom, salvation) from lethal forms of bondage, such as "sin" (6:6), "decay" (8:21), and evil "spirits of the world" (Gal. 4:6; cf. 4:8; Col. 2:8, 20). Again, spiritual metaphors trade on social realities, in this case the status not of hereditary sons (and daughters) but of enslaved persons in masters' households.

Some slaves in the ancient world rose to management positions within the household and partially shared the status of prominent masters.[44] Yet many others either suffered under abusive masters or were condemned to harsh labor as state prisoners. Likewise, some wives (especially upper-class) and independent women (single, divorced, widowed) had considerable influence in households. Among believers in Christ, businesswomen like Lydia and Priscilla (with husband Aquila) led "churches" in their homes, as did Nympha in Colossae (Acts 16:14–16; Rom. 16:3–5; 1 Cor. 16:19; Col. 4:15). Yet standard familial order kept wives, daughters, and female slaves subordinated to male authorities and subject to mistreatment. Slave girls were especially vulnerable to exploitation sexually by household heads and economically by businessmen (Acts 16:16–19).[45]

Imaging Christ's family members as both adopted children and redeemed chattel reinforces the expansive, inclusive, and unitive spirit of God's household. Yet the Pauline tradition also develops "son" and "slave" metaphors in distinctive ways. In Roman society, adopted "sons," as we've seen, could become full heirs of the household head in lieu of absent or inept natural sons. In God's household, however, adopted children of faith did not replace anyone but rather joined the brother-/sisterhood as *joint heirs with Christ*, God's "firstborn" Son (Rom. 8:29; Col. 1:15).

But whether natural or adopted, heirs to the paterfamilias ranked above enslaved persons and hired hands (cf. Luke 15:17–24, 29–32). If freed, however, slaves had more opportunities for advancement, including gaining citizenship. And so, Paul can place metaphorical adopted children and emancipated persons on the same honored level in Christ.

But Paul also complicates the slave analogy by referring to freed/redeemed believers, including himself, as metaphorical *slaves of God, Christ, and other*

44. Dale Martin argues that one dimension of "Paul's rhetoric" trades on "status improvement aspects of slavery to an important master," thus using "slavery as a positive metaphor for Christian salvation by upward mobility." Martin, *Slavery as Salvation*, 65.

45. See Glancy, *Slavery as Moral Problem*; Glancy, *Slavery in Early Christianity*; Spencer, *Dancing Girls*, 144–66.

people (Rom. 6:18–22; 1 Cor. 7:22; 9:19; Phil. 1:1 ["servants" = "slaves," *dou-loi*]) and by proclaiming that *Christ* "emptied himself, taking the form of a slave [*doulou*]" in his life and "death on a cross" (Phil. 2:7).[46] Moreover, later writings by Paul or someone using his name insist that literal slaves who fol-low Christ still submit *as slaves* to their masters (Eph. 6:5–8; Col. 3:22–24; 1 Tim. 6:1).

And what was Paul's personal experience? According to Acts, he was born a citizen of Tarsus (his hometown) and of Rome at large (Acts 16:36–38; 21:39; 22:25–29). We might fairly wonder, then, if Paul's family owned slaves. In prison, he received service from slaves such as Onesimus (Philem. 10–13) and Epaph-roditus (Phil. 2:25–30).[47] Strange, then, that he would embrace "slave" status, even to God and Christ.

Likewise, we have no record that Paul ever had children. Yet he regarded himself as a spiritual "father" and "mother" to his "children" in Christ (1 Cor. 3:1–2; 4:15; Gal. 4:19; 1 Thess. 2:7–11; Philem. 10). And he combines parent-child-slave language in depicting his close relationship with Timothy: "But Timothy's work you know, how like a son [or child, *teknon*] with a father [*patri*] he has served [or slaved, *edouleusen*] with me in the work of the gospel" (Phil. 2:22).

Adapted Hierarchies

It's easy to get confused in this metaphorical thicket. By juxtaposing figura-tions of hierarchy and slavery with declarations of equality and freedom, on the one hand, and demands for submission and service, on the other, does Paul not risk doublespeak, urging redeemed believers to live double lives? They are "no longer slaves" in Christ (Gal. 3:28; Col. 3:11; cf. 1 Cor. 12:13; Philem. 16), and yet they are to take on slave duty to God/Christ and to maintain slaves' servile obligations to earthly masters?

This also applies to women—single or married, free or enslaved—whom Paul regards as collaborative sisters in faith and ministry (Rom. 16:1–7, 12–15; Gal. 3:28), even as he (or an associate) exhorts "wives to [be] subject to your husbands" (Col. 3:18; cf. Eph. 5:24).

Again, do faithful wives, along with believing slaves, operate as double agents, as it were, in a house divided into spiritual ("in the Lord") and domestic

46. In a stunning paradoxical statement, Mark's Jesus identifies himself as a servant/slave (*diakonos/doulos*) who offers his life-and-death as "ransom [or redemption] for many" (Mark 10:43–45).

47. On Epaphroditus as a "likely (freed) slave sent by the Philippians," see Marchal, "Slaves," 173.

compartments? Or do they somehow shift between two houses, one in which
they have joint heirship with Christ and the other in which they serve patriarchs?
How can that household arrangement "stand"—as Jesus challenged critics of his
liberative ministry (Mark 3:25) and as Lincoln echoed to Americans bitterly
divided over slavery?[48]

While these critical questions clearly shape Pauline writings, the letters reach
no clear resolution. Paul and company show their work as they wrestle with
multiple metaphors and situations to formulate a delicate balance of aims for
God's household:

1. *Maintaining* the status quo of conventional society (not rocking the boat)
2. *Mitigating* the harshest aspects of standard family systems in favor of loving
   service "as to the Lord" (Eph. 6:7)
3. *Mutualizing* family relations in Christ, thus weakening patriarchal domi-
   nance

The final product is a tapestry in progress in which three distinctive strands are
being woven together while some threads are left dangling.[49]

Text	Maintenance	Mitigation	Mutualization
1 Corinthians 7	*Slaves*: "Were you a slave when called [to Christ]? Do not be concerned about it. Even if you can gain your freedom, make use of your present condition more than ever." (7:20–21)	*Slaves*: "Whoever was called in the Lord as a slave is a freed person belonging to the Lord, just as whoever was free when called is a slave of Christ." (7:22–23)	*Women*: "The husband should give to his wife her conjugal rights, and likewise the wife to her husband." (7:3)
1 Corinthians 11	*Women*: "Christ is the head of every man, and the husband is the head of his wife. . . . Man was not made from woman, but woman from man." (11:3, 8)	*Women*: permitted to pray and prophesy in worship—provided they wear head coverings (11:4–7).	*Women*: "Nevertheless, in the Lord woman is not independent of man or man independent of woman. For just as woman came from man, so man comes through woman." (11:11–12)

48. Lincoln, "House Divided."
49. I chart a sample of Pauline texts, including 1 Pet. 2–3 (the Petrine writers show affinity with
Pauline thought; cf. 2 Pet. 3:15–16). Other relevant passages in the Pauline orbit include 1 Cor. 14:33–36;
1 Tim. 2:8–15; 5:3–16. For excellent treatments of these texts, see Gench, *Encountering God*.

Text	Maintenance	Mitigation	Mutualization
Ephesians 5–6	*Women*: "Wives, be subject to your husbands. . . . For the husband is the head of the wife, just as Christ is the head of the church." (5:22–23) *Slaves*: "Slaves, obey your earthly masters with fear and trembling, in singleness of heart." (6:5–6)	*Women*: "Husbands, love your wives, just as Christ loved the church. . . . Husbands should love their wives as they do their own bodies." (5:25) *Slaves*: "Obey your earthly masters . . . as slaves of Christ, doing the will of God from the heart." (6:5–6)	*Women*: "Be subject to one another out of reverence for Christ. . . . Each of you, however, should love his wife as himself, and a wife should respect her husband." (5:21, 33) *Slaves*: "Whatever good we do, we will receive again from the Lord, whether we are slaves or free. And, masters, do the same to them, for you know that both of you have the same Master in heaven." (6:8–9)
Colossians 3–4	*Women*: "Wives, be subject to your husbands." (3:18) *Slaves*: "Slaves, obey your earthly masters in everything." (3:22)	*Women*: "Husbands, love your wives and never treat them harshly." (3:19) *Slaves*: "Masters, treat your slaves justly and fairly." (4:1)	*Women*: "Christ is all and in all. Clothe yourselves with love, which binds everything together in perfect harmony." (3:11, 14) *Slaves*: "There is no partiality. Masters . . . know that you also have a Master in heaven." (3:25–4:1)
1 Peter 2–3	*Women*: "Wives . . . accept the authority of your husbands, so that . . . they may be won over without a word by their wives' conduct." (3:1) *Slaves*: "Slaves, accept the authority of your masters with all deference, not only those who are kind and gentle but also those who are harsh." (2:18)	*Women*: "Husbands . . . paying honor to the woman as the weaker sex [or vessel]." (3:7) *Slaves*: "Christ also suffered for you, leaving you an example. . . . When he was abused, he did not return abuse; when he suffered, he did not threaten; but he entrusted himself to the one who judges justly." (2:21, 23)	*Women*: "Husbands . . . show consideration for your wives in your life together . . . since they too are also heirs of the gracious gift of life." (3:7) *Slaves* (implied): "Finally, all of you, have unity of spirit, sympathy, love for one another, a tender heart, and a humble mind." (3:8)

The New Testament forges no perfect union of thought and practice on household issues, reminding us again of Lincoln's words, this time from his Second Inaugural Address (March 4, 1865), uttered thirty-five days before the armistice at Appomattox, which in turn was just six days before his assassination at Ford's theater: "Both [sides] read the same Bible and pray to the same God, and each invokes His aid against the other.... The prayers of both could not be answered. That of neither has been answered fully."[50]

While the preceding table's selected texts provide a basic, self-explanatory sampling of New Testament household codes, an extra word is in order concerning the 1 Peter texts, which remain an outlier in one respect, pushing from awkward to plain awful. In exhorting enslaved believers to "accept the authority of [their] masters with all deference," the writer mandates submission not only to "kind and gentle" masters but also to "those who are harsh"—without providing any countervailing charge to masters not to mistreat their slaves (cf. Eph. 6:9; Col. 4:1). In fact, suffering at the hands of abusive taskmasters merits "God's approval" and fits the pattern of Christ's passive suffering on the cross, as he "entrusted himself to [God,] who judges justly" (1 Pet. 2:23). Some comfort is afforded by affirming that the letter's addressees "have been healed" by Christ's "wounds" or "welts" (*mōlōpi*) (2:24), an experience with which slaves were all too familiar (cf. Sir. 23:10 CEB: "a household slave who is constantly examined won't be lacking bruises [*mōlōpos*]"; 28:17 CEB: "The blow of a whip raises a welt [*mōlōpa*]"). But bruising beatings still hurt, and healed wounds keep reopening with repeated whippings.

This basic line of household submission to the paterfamilias extends to "wives," who "*in the same way* [must] accept the authority of your husbands," including unbelieving husbands (1 Pet. 3:1). Here the model is not Christ's subjection to Roman authorities but Sarah's obedience to Abraham, her "lord" (3:5–6). That may seem like a more congenial comparison, until one remembers that, to save his own neck, Abraham handed over Sarah to a foreign ruler's harem—twice (Gen. 12:10–20; 20:1–18)! This is to say nothing of Abraham's near sacrifice of his son Isaac without breathing a word to Sarah (22:1–14). To be sure, unlike with the advice to slaves, 1 Peter adds a mitigating and mutualizing word to husbands: "In the same way, show consideration for your wives in your life together ... since they too are also heirs of the gracious gift of life." But even this more egalitarian perspective is undercut by patronizing women "as the weaker sex [or vessel]" (3:7).

Clearly, in many New Testament congregations, all was not bliss on the home front. When Christ groups gathered in homes of prominent members with their larger houses and households, including slaves (see Philemon), tensions between ethical ideals and social realities simmered below the surface, threatening to erupt into more open conflict. No wonder the writer of Ephesians urged readers to maintain "the bond of peace" (Eph. 4:3).

50. Lincoln, "Second Inaugural."

6

Seen and Secret

The Perceptual Challenge of Skepticism and Gnosticism

	Have you believed because you have seen me? Blessed are those who have not seen and yet have come to believe. (John 20:29)
Tenet	Jesus Christ came to earth as the incarnate Revealer of God—"the reflection of God's glory and the exact imprint of God's very being" (Heb. 1:3)—in plain sight to anyone with "eyes to see."
Tension	If Jesus so brilliantly revealed God, why did so many, including his disciples at times, misperceive his identity and mission? How could Jesus's first followers still "see" him after his departure from earth? How could others believe in Jesus, whom they had never seen?

Is seeing believing, or is it deceiving? Depends on how long you stay chained in Plato's cave. In the famous scenario Plato's Socrates sketched for his student Glaucon, unenlightened people are like locked prisoners facing the back wall of a dark cave with their backs against an internal wall blocking any light except from a fireplace set near the cave's ceiling. These prisoners have no capacity to view or envision "real" events outside the cave. Their reality consists of darkness or delusion, the latter represented in shadow-puppet forms projected on the cave wall, backlit by the fire. They have no clue about their condition, however, unless someone manages to escape outside, see "true" live figures, and return inside to reveal the "truth" to other prisoners.

But even then true knowledge and (in)sight are hard to come by, since the released prisoner, accustomed only to dark, shadowy vision—which he assumes discloses reality—will have a difficult time discerning what's "really" there. More distortion results from eye-squinting and -shielding from bright sunlight and then reverting to murky images cast by moon and starlight. Confusion only compounds when this venturer returns and tries to explain what he has only seen and understood darkly to cave-mates who have no idea what he's talking about.

Drawing of Plato's allegory of the cave

Humanity is thus beset by "two kinds of disturbances of the eyes, stemming from two sources—when they have been transferred from light to darkness and when they have been transferred from darkness to light."[1] Only enlightened philosophers can hope to "see" the world rightly and clearly, to distinguish the real and ideal from shifting forms and shadows, to gain extrasensory vision into divine, heavenly realities beyond the mundane and superficial.

We need not spelunk through Plato's cave to get the point. We know about optical illusions, how our eyes can play tricks even in plain daylight. More critically, we know about the vagaries of spiritual perception, which calls us to "see" the apparently invisible world of "spirit(s)," including the invisible (to the natural eye) God-Spirit. More specifically, how do Christ followers "walk by faith, not by sight" (2 Cor. 5:7), without stumbling and straying? How do we experience faith as "the conviction of things not seen" (Heb. 11:1) without fabrication and delusion? The twentieth-century French philosopher and mystic Simone Weil incisively adapted Plato's cave to contemporary moral and spiritual life: "The image of the cave refers to values. We only possess shadowy imitations of good. . . . There is a distinction between those who remain inside the cave, shutting

1. Plato, *Republic* 518a; cf. 514–18, 532.

their eyes and imagining the journey, and those who really take it. How can we distinguish the imaginary from the real in the spiritual realm? We must prefer real hell to an imaginary paradise."[2]

Like Weil, the New Testament writers were no armchair thinkers musing about mystical matters: they truly took the Christ journey on earth, however hellish and dimly lit the path might be. Though staunchly "hoping against hope" (Rom. 4:18), believing against dominant cultural values that Jesus Christ truly revealed God—such that "all of us, with unveiled faces, [are] seeing the glory of the Lord" through the Spirit (2 Cor. 3:18)—the New Testament authors were not naive about the challenges of spiritual perception. Seeing Christ is believing, if Christ *clearly* makes himself known, which is not always the case during his earthly life, much less afterward.

How do believers "see" an absent, ascended Lord? How in the world do they catch glimpses of God in Christ and keep growing "with knowledge and full insight" (Phil. 1:9)? Is such spiritual insight only for the special few who excel in wisdom (Plato's philosopher) or decode some secret knowledge (*gnōsis*)? Or can "all of us" see the glorious Lord (2 Cor. 3:18)?

The Cryptic Christ in the Gospels

Jesus as a Traveler on the Road in Luke

Luke's Jesus "rejoice[s] in the Holy Spirit" and praises the Father for revealing spiritual wisdom and knowledge to him, the Son (Luke 10:21–22). The divine will is most intimately known in the dynamic, triadic relationship among Father-Son-Spirit. But it is not hoarded; knowledge of the Father is made available to "anyone to whom the Son chooses to reveal him" (10:22). "Anyone" is not everyone, however; for some, it will remain *hidden* knowledge but not randomly so. Those who think they are "wise and intelligent" on their own merit block themselves from true insight, while those with childlike, even "infant"-like, openness to Jesus will be blessed with growing understanding of "these things" concerning God and the cosmos ("heaven and earth," 10:21).

Luke's Jesus subverts elitist Platonic and Gnostic epistemologies (approaches to perceiving/knowing). The philosopher-guru who thinks he's forged the golden keys to knowledge has only managed to lock himself in his own study—his man cave! The decoder-gnostic who claims to have top-secret information straight

2. Weil, *Gravity and Grace*, 99, 101.

from Christ beyond the ken of most mortals only reveals his pathetic conceit. Jesus's primary aim is to disclose, not conceal—except from self-selected, wise-in-their-own-eyes know-it-alls. Jesus chooses a motley crew of twelve apostles and other disciples, male and female (Luke 6:12–16; 8:1–3)—no sophisticated philosopher or secret agent in the bunch—to grow progressively in wisdom, as Jesus did from childhood (2:40, 52). There is also no conquering king or court prophet in the group: "Blessed are the eyes that see what you [disciples] see! For I tell you that many kings and prophets desired to see what you see, but did not see it, and to hear what you hear, but did not hear it" (10:23–24).[3]

Blessed indeed, *except* when they do not see or hear what Jesus shows and tells in clearly painted signs and plainspoken parables. Even for commonsense, no-nonsense folk, like the disciples and crowds, these signs and parables can become "secrets" or "mysteries" (*mystēria*, Luke 8:10), not because of their obscurity but because of seers'/hearers' obstinacy, because they do not develop their perceptive capacities. "Let anyone with ears to hear listen!" (8:8). "Pay attention to how you listen"—literally, "*Look/See* [*blepete*] how you *listen/hear* [*akouete*]!" (8:18). Jesus's words and deeds are accessible to all but are not automatically intelligible by the ear at first sound or by the eye at first glance. They can thereby seem "hidden/encrypted" (*apokryptō*, 8:17) to imperceptive respondents, including disciples (18:34). The situation is ripe for cognitive distortion between shallow and deep knowledge of the earthly Jesus—a problem that only worsens after Jesus's resurrection, when he appears only spasmodically in different forms.

Luke reports a remarkable case of two disciples' limited sight shortly after Jesus's resurrection. Though not part of the twelve, Cleopas and an unnamed companion (his wife?) were dedicated followers of Jesus. They had pinned their messianic hopes on Jesus, only to have them dashed with his crucifixion. As they trudged along the seven-mile journey from Jerusalem to their home in Emmaus, the couple tried to make sense of Jesus's tragic end—to little avail. They'd heard Mary Magdalene and other women's astonishing testimony that Jesus "was alive" and had vacated the tomb (24:22–23), but they didn't know what to make of this news. In many ways, it just added to their confusion and depression. "We had [so] hoped that he was the one to redeem Israel" (24:21). Little chance of that now.

Along their dejected walk to Emmaus with "sadness" written all over their faces,[4] another traveler joins the pair and asks, "What are you discussing [lit.

---

3. See Wilson, *Embodied God*, 208–14.
4. "Sadness" (*skythrōpia*)—"sorrow that gives a gloomy aspect to one's face." BDAG, s.v. "σκυθρωπός," 932–33.

throwing back and forth, *antiballete*] with each other?" (Luke 24:17).[5] They tell him about Jesus's crucifixion and wild reports of his empty tomb (24:19–24). The "stranger" (24:18) listens at first without offering any response—and without revealing that *he is the very Jesus* they're talking about, walking alongside them, alive and well! It's strange enough that the risen Jesus appears here but stranger still that these disciples do not recognize him, and he seems in no rush to make himself known, even though it would lift their spirits—and raise more questions but with the prospect of happy answers.

Why do Cleopas and partner not "see" Jesus? We're only told that "their eyes were kept from recognizing him" (Luke 24:16). By God? By Jesus? Is he wearing some disguise, modifying his voice, appearing in a different form? More likely, the couple's overwhelming cognitive and emotional distress prevents their sensing Jesus's presence. They are bound in the shadows of distorted thinking and feeling. Whatever Jesus's appearance in his new risen state, he's still the "real" embodied Jesus. He's no phantom, no ghost, and no figment of imagination, as he soon makes clear when he pops in on other disciples: "Look at my hands and my feet; see that it is I myself. Touch me and see; for a ghost does not have flesh and bones as you see that I have" (24:39–40).

But Jesus takes a different tack with Cleopas and companion, remaining incognito for the entire journey to Emmaus. And along the way, he's not a particularly sympathetic or reassuring listener. After the two have unburdened their hearts, Jesus, still unknown to them, chides them, saying, "How foolish you are, and how slow of heart to believe all that the prophets have declared!" (Luke 24:25). He then lectures them about how the Jewish scriptures anticipated a suffering Messiah, though he cites no specific texts (24:25–27). Later the couple recalls how this traveler had sparked their interest with his teaching (24:32). But for now, they're still not ready to "see" and "hear" him. Jesus doesn't make it easy. When they approached the village, he "walked ahead as if he were going on" (24:28), and presumably he would have done just that, if the pair had not "urged him strongly" to stay the night (24:29).

Jesus agrees to stay—but not for long, as it happens. At dinner, the stranger-guest turns revealer-host, as Jesus "took bread, blessed and broke it, and gave it to them" (Luke 24:30), reminiscent of the Last Supper (22:19). "Then"—at this signal moment of table service—the couple's "eyes were opened, and they recognized" their Lord Jesus. Yet no sooner did they "see" him than he "vanished from

5. Spencer, *Luke*, 618.

their sight" (24:31). Now you see him, now you don't!

Though the risen Jesus is visible in the same flesh-and-bone body in which he lived and died (Luke 24:37–40), his body has also been upgraded, as it were, with supernatural abilities of appearing, disappearing, and transporting from place to place, ultimately, after forty days, to the heavenly sphere (Acts 1:1–3). Why does Jesus act this way, playing hard to get on the road and hard to keep in the house? It seems that he's training his followers to sustain their spiritual fellowship with him in

Jesus and the Disciples on the Road to Emmaus

his physical absence. The Emmaus story showcases two vital means of ongoing communion with Christ: through *word* and *food*, *Scripture* and *table*, the latter commemorating Jesus's death "until he comes" (1 Cor. 11:26; cf. Luke 22:14–20) in the ritual variously known as the Lord's Supper, Holy Communion, Eucharist, or Mass. Thereby the unseen Christ via natural lenses may be seen through spiritual senses.

Jesus as a Gardener near the Tomb in John

No New Testament book declares more emphatically than John's Gospel that the embodied, flesh-and-blood Jesus revealed the glorious fullness of God. To see Jesus is to see God; to hear Jesus is to hear God: "Truth came through Jesus Christ. No one has ever seen God. It is God the only Son, who is close to the Father's heart, who has made him known" (John 1:17–18).

As brilliantly, however, as God's light shone through the human Jesus (John 1:4–9; 8:12; 9:5; 12:35–36), several characters in this Gospel do not see Jesus for who he "truly" (*alēthōs*) is. They remain blind to the "truth" (*alētheia*) that Jesus reveals in word, deed, and person (14:6). These "sight"-challenged people include Jewish leaders, teachers, and Jesus's own disciples from time to time,[6] as

---

6. See John 3:1–12; 8:12–20; 9:13–34, 41; 12:37–43; 14:8–10; 20:11–16, 24–29.

if they are unable to emerge from their gloomy tunnel (cave) vision and adjust their focus to the divine glory radiating through Jesus. Like the literal blind man in John 9, they need Jesus's help to "see" Jesus.

Again, this spiritual myopia becomes more acute after Jesus's death and resurrection, this time focalized through one of Jesus's closest followers, Mary Magdalene. Mary sticks with Jesus to the end, "standing near the cross" with his mother, her sister, and "the disciple whom he loved" (John 19:25–26). And she stands out as the first to visit Jesus's tomb early Sunday morning and see, even "while it was still dark," that the tomb was open and empty (20:1–2). Yet she's naturally perplexed by this discovery. Seeing into the tomb's dark abyss is not believing. After reporting the spooky scene to Peter and another disciple, all Mary can do is go back to the tomb, weep about her Lord's missing body, and peer inside the vacuous space. Then she suddenly finds herself sandwiched between a pair of white-clad angels sitting inside the tomb on the vacant slab and a man she takes to be the area gardener standing a few paces outside the tomb, each posing the same question, "Woman, why are you weeping?" (20:15).

Here the story takes a turn similar to that in the Emmaus Road incident, because this supposed gardener is in fact the *risen Jesus*, whom Mary Magdalene does not yet recognize through her veil of tears. Again, seeing Jesus in his risen body is not believing, and speculating about some disguised appearance of Jesus (gardener's clothes, wide-brimmed hat pulled down across his face) is beside the point. The story features a disciple who knows Jesus well. Yet even her spiritual vision is momentarily distorted, and Jesus does not immediately correct it. He plays along for a while, asking her somewhat cheekily, "Whom are you looking for?" (John 20:15). It makes us readers chuckle a bit while Mary cries!

Fortunately, Jesus doesn't make Mary wait as long as the Emmaus couple before revealing his identity. His urgent calling of her name "Mary/*Mariam*!" triggers her recognition (John 20:16). His personal voice opens her clouded eyes and moves her to embrace him. But Jesus pushes back, resisting her "hold" on him because he knows he will soon leave this earth, "ascending to my Father and your Father, to my God and your God" (20:17). While affirming the intimate fellowship between him, his divine Father, and faithful followers like Mary, Jesus knows that, in his physical absence, this will primarily be a spiritual communion.

Mary's encounter with the risen Jesus is *not*, mind you, an out-of-body (even less an anti-body) experience but a palpably physical one. With unabashed assurance, she tells her brothers in Christ, "I have seen the Lord" (John 20:18). She can also claim to have touched Jesus's live body before he pulled away.[7] Likewise, the male disciples receive two visits from the embodied risen Christ. Although he drops in on them in their locked quarters, his space-defying resurrected body still bears the marks of his crucified body. In the first scene, Jesus shows "his hands and his side" to ten disciples (the Twelve minus Judas and Thomas), and they rejoice once they have *seen* him (20:20); in the second incident, with Thomas now present, Jesus gives this invitation: "Put your finger here and *see* my hands. Reach out your hand and put it in my side" (20:27). That invitation is enough to prompt Thomas's confession, "My Lord and my God" (20:28). Seeing the risen Jesus's scarred hands and pierced side *is* believing.

Good for Mary Magdalene, the male apostles, and for other firsthand eyewitnesses of the risen Jesus (cf. 1 Cor. 15:1–7). But what then, after his ascension? Must writers and readers of the New Testament rely exclusively on selective testimonies of post-resurrection visual encounters with Jesus? The Johannine Jesus pronounces, "Blessed are those who *have not seen* and yet have come to believe" (John 20:29). It's nice to be blessed, but how exactly does this non-seeing faith work? How can one come *to* faith in unseen reality *through* faith? What inspires faith *in* Christ, not merely as a set of beliefs *about* Christ but as a warm, trusting relationship *with* Christ?

The role of the Holy Spirit becomes critical. In his second post-resurrection appearance in John 20, Jesus commissions his followers by breathing on them and saying to them, "Receive the Holy Spirit" (20:22). Thus inaugurates the unseen Spirit's vital work of sustaining Jesus's presence and influence across time and space within and among believers. It will be this very Spirit, the "Spirit of truth," as Jesus promised, who "abides with you" (14:17), who "will teach you everything, and remind you of all that I have said to you" (14:25), who "will testify on my behalf" (15:26). In sum, this Holy Spirit represents "another Advocate" like Jesus (14:16), the spitting image and breath of Jesus, flowing in continuous fellowship with the Father and Son—sight unseen to the natural eye but ablaze to the spiritual eye of faith.[8]

The Mystic Paul in Acts and Letters

Saul/Paul was not an eyewitness to Jesus's earthly life, as far as we know. When he became aware of the early Jesus movement, he wanted to eradicate it, violently

7. The Greek construction of John 20:17 suggests, "Do not *keep holding* on to me."
8. On the role of the Spirit in John, see Burge, *Anointed Community*; Levison, *Unconventional God*, 133–69.

(Acts 8:3; 9:1–2; 1 Cor. 15:9; Gal. 1:13; Phil. 3:6; 1 Tim. 1:13).[9] Although Paul's reasons for pursuing Christ believers remain uncertain, it's clear that he perceived the Jesus sect as a serious threat to his people's faith and way of life. To be clearer, Paul's persecutorial animus against the Jesus "Way" was a radical-extremist position among Jews who did not accept Jesus as Messiah, including among Pharisees with whom Paul identified (Acts 23:6; Phil. 3:5)—which makes it more incredible that he becomes a leading apostle of the risen Christ and author of numerous letters included in Christian Scripture. As I've mentioned before, Paul himself represents a major cognitive-dissonant conundrum.

What accounts for Paul's about-face view of Jesus, which amounts to an apocalyptic change of worldview? How does Paul come to see Jesus in a different light during Jesus's (mostly) unseen post-ascension life, during which Paul is awaiting Jesus's climactic reappearing (*parousia*) on earth? How does Paul's personal conversion[10] translate to others' experiences of Christ in the New Testament? Exceptional, prototypical, or something in between?

At base, Paul's re-visioning of Christ is visionary, mystical, spiritual, supernatural (which is *not* to say it is anti-material or unnatural).[11] This re-visioning runs back and forth on dual-lane tracks, which we may mark as (1) personal confrontation *by* God and (2) prayerful contemplation *of* God.[12] The seeking, seizing God makes the first move (track 1): Paul is hell-bent on going his own way and must be stopped in his tracks and shown the light. Once his spiritual eyes begin to open, Paul seeks after God more keenly (track 2) as God continues to reach out and reveal. Paul thus enters a dynamic formative process of confrontation and contemplation in the mystic light of God in Christ through the Spirit.

Another way to chart the double optics of Paul's spiritual journey is to say that (1) seeing is discovering and that (2) seeing is loving.

9. The term for "violently" in Gal. 1:13 (*kath' hyperbolēn*) may be rendered "severely" (CEB) or "intensely" (NIV). Paula Fredriksen suggests that it refers to exacting the maximum Jewish punishment of thirty-nine lashes (which Paul himself received after converting to Christ [2 Cor. 11:24; cf. Deut. 24:3]), not to the "lurid violence [of execution] depicted in Acts" (Fredriksen, *Paul*, 82–83; "Paul," 127–28). Even so, we must still contend with Paul's stark admission that he aimed to "destroy/kill" (*eporthoun*, Gal. 1:13) the Christ movement.

10. Paul's "conversion" was not from one religion (Judaism) to another (Christianity) but a dramatic reorientation *within* Paul's Jewish mindset, now oriented around the crucified-risen Jesus Messiah. See Thiessen, *Jewish Paul*, 40–42, 55–57.

11. I use "mystic" and "spiritual" language as loose descriptors of hidden, less-than-obvious, unseen (to the naked eye) experience, not as technical metaphysical, philosophical, or psychological categories and certainly not as antithetical or alternative to material, embodied reality. Thiessen provides a more nuanced assessment of Pauline spirituality in the framework of material concepts of *pneuma* ("spirit"). In brief, "for Paul and for his initial readers, *pneuma* was material—the best material available because it was unchanging and eternal" (*Jewish Paul*, 117; see 113–22).

12. Cf. Caputo, *Specters of God*, 199–203; Tillich, *Courage to Be*, 177–78.

Seeing Is Discovering

Paul's coming to faith in Jesus Messiah was not the result of careful research and deliberative thought. From Acts' perspective, Paul had his mind made up, set like stone against the Jesus movement and backed up by stones hurled at Stephen, one of Christ's boldest witnesses (Acts 7:58–8:1). Paul was not looking to change. He had one-track tunnel vision aimed at tracking down believers in Christ (9:1–2). But one bright noonday (22:6) he is suddenly hit by the blazing Christ-train barreling down the track from outside the tunnel—*at him*! The risen-ascended Jesus comes down and personally stops Paul in his tracks: "I am Jesus, whom you are persecuting" (9:5). Aptly, this dramatic Christ appearance leaves Paul blinded for three days while he prays, fasts, and receives instruction, commission, and baptism from the Lord's messenger, Ananias (9:9–18).

Paul must first *unsee* before gaining new *(in)sight*; he must endure three dark days in his private unlit cave, his sealed tomb, until he can break into the light of the risen Christ, who himself was resurrected on the third day. Paul's three-day liminal period takes place in a Damascus house, but the address just happens to be on Straight Street (Acts 9:11)—a fitting location for "straightening" out Paul's life and setting him on a new course.

Paul experiences a fundamental *discovering* of Christ: *un*covering truth he had missed that now completely *dis*rupts his worldview and *re*orients his life around the lodestar of the crucified-risen Christ. Thereon, as Paul says, in his own words now, "I decided to know nothing among you except Jesus Christ, and him crucified" (1 Cor. 2:2). But again, Paul's decision is not determinative; it is decided *for him* by Christ. Paul does not opt for Christ's way as much as he is co-opted by Christ through a stunning vision—a Christophany, as scholars call it.

Or to use another scholarly term, Paul's encounter with Christ is nothing less than an *apocalyptic* event, based on his own testimony: "I did not receive [the gospel] from a human source, nor was I taught it, but I received it through a *revelation* [*apokalypseōs*] of Jesus Christ. When God, who . . . called me through his grace, was pleased *to reveal* [*apokalypsai*] his Son to me, so that I might proclaim him among the Gentiles, I did not confer with any human being" (Gal. 1:11–12, 15–16).

Paul offers no details matching Acts' Damascus Road narrative. One word encapsulates Paul's transformative episode: *revelation* [or *apocalypse*]. Its root sense suggests decrypting (*apokalyptō*), discovering, or unveiling the true, God's-eye perspective on the world through the lens of the cosmic Christ-event, which proves world-shaking, world-remaking, world-righting to those bound in their shadowy caves. Although changed in the blinding blink of an eye, Paul will "work out [this] salvation with fear and trembling" (Phil. 2:12) the rest of his life—and then "dimly [enigmatically, *ainigmati*] . . . only in part," awaiting when "we will see face to face . . . [when] I will know fully, even as I have been fully known" (1 Cor. 13:11–12). Paul's letters document this working/writing out his evolving understanding of Christ's revelation of God, especially through his death, "even death on a cross" (Phil. 2:8).[13]

Furthermore, Paul does not live on the strength of one big-bang revelation. Defending himself against those who question his apostolic authority, he poses the rhetorical question, "Have I not seen Jesus our Lord?" (1 Cor. 9:1). Here he uses a perfective verb form, which suggests prominent ongoing effects: "Have I not seen and do I not continue to see Jesus?" In another letter to the Corinthians, who seem enamored with ecstatic-mystical experiences, Paul claims to have had numerous "visions and revelations" (*apokalypseis*), including "revelations" (*apokalypseōn*) of "exceptional [or superlative] character" (2 Cor. 12:1, 7). Paul obliquely references one mysterious tour of "Paradise" at a top "third heaven" security level that he experienced some fourteen years ago—"whether in the body or out of the body I do not know" (12:3). Dramatic accounts of premortem transports to heaven were common in ancient literary apocalypses composed by inspired "seers" (200 BCE–200 CE), like John in the book of Revelation (see below).[14]

Paul, however, offers no extended report of his celestial vision and would rather not mention it at all, since nothing would be gained except boosting his spiritual cred to impress others. Yet he deems "it is necessary to boast" enough to put his meddlesome rivals and detractors in their place (2 Cor. 12:1; see challenge 2). Boast enough, but not too much. More importantly, Paul flips the whole strutting contest on its head, "boast[ing] all the more gladly of *my weaknesses*, so that the power of Christ may dwell in me" (12:9). Among a general catalog of "weaknesses, insults, hardships, persecutions, and calamities for the sake of Christ," Paul highlights a chronic "thorn in the flesh" he suffers (12:7, 10). Whatever affliction this "thorn" represents, it is no nagging little barb or splinter but is more like a "spike" or "stake" (*skolops*) with deadly potential to "torment" (12:7).[15] It more closely associates Paul with Christ's crucifixion on Skull Hill than with grand excursions to heavenly heights.

13. On the mystical-apocalyptic dimensions of Paul's Christ-centered experience and teaching, see Segal, *Paul the Convert*, 34–71; Blackwell, Goodrich, and Matson, *Paul*.
14. See J. Collins, *Apocalyptic Imagination*; G. Carey, *Death*, 244–45; G. Carey, *Ultimate Things*; Morray-Jones, "Paradise" (parts 1 and 2).
15. See Sampley, "Second Letter," 164–65.

In visual-audio terms, Paul stresses objective, overt example—"what is seen in me or heard from me" (2 Cor. 12:6)—over his subjective, secret experience. The epiphanies of Christ that Paul touts most focus on Jesus's life and death—that is, his resurrection life issuing out of crucifixion and channeled through the mortal bodies of ministers like Paul who share in Christ's sufferings. Paul says we are "always carrying in the body the death of Jesus, so that the life of Jesus may also be *made visible* in our bodies. For while we live, we are always being given up to death for Jesus' sake, so that the life

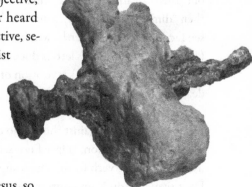

Heel bone of a man crucified in first-century Jerusalem
Larry Koester / flickr.com / CC BY 2.0

of Jesus may be *made visible* in our mortal flesh" (4:10–11). Christ continues to be incarnated in plain sight in the vulnerable bodies of his witnesses on earth.

Seeing Is Loving

But the suffering, "weak" Paul is by no means a passive vessel. He actively cultivates and participates in Christ's life-giving work, seeking to see and "know Christ" more clearly and fully, not in glitzy visions and flashy revelations but in "the power of his resurrection and the sharing of his sufferings [*pathēmatōn*], by becoming like him in his death" (Phil. 3:10). Everything else, visions included, is "sewer trash" (3:8 CEB).

This sympathizing with Christ reflects Paul's fellowship in Christ's painful "passions" (*pathē*), or we could say it reflects his *compassionate communion* with Christ and all fellow sufferers. In a word, it's about *love*, and not just in word but in deed, not just in feeling but in acting—mysticism and ministry mingled together. Love is the "most excellent" (*hyperbolēn*) vehicle (1 Cor. 12:31), greater than any "exceptional" (*hyperbolē*) revelation (2 Cor. 12:7) for seeing and serving Christ. Nothing else matters. Everything else must be suffused with love to be worth anything, including great (in)sights: "If I have prophetic powers, and understand all mysteries and all knowledge . . . but do not have love, I am nothing" (1 Cor. 13:2). Without love that "bears all things, believes all things, hopes all things, endures all things," any spiritual vision we might claim proves spurious (13:7).

Recall, too, that some influencers in the Colossian congregation also flaunted their visionary experiences and became "puffed up without cause by a human way of thinking" (Col. 2:18). As he did with the ersatz Corinthian "super-apostles" (2 Cor. 11:5; 12:11), Paul knocks down the high-flying Colossian mystics to humble ground from where love may rise to true spiritual heights. Love may be envisioned as the flight suit for trekking through God's vast realm with fellow voyagers in Christ: "As God's chosen ones, holy and beloved, clothe yourselves with compassion, kindness, humility, meekness, and patience.... Above all, clothe yourselves with love, which binds everything together in perfect harmony" (Col. 3:12, 14).

The Optimistic Believers in Hebrews

In challenge 2, we considered the repeated warnings in Hebrews against those being tempted to recant their faith and defect from the Christ community. We also observed, however, that Hebrews tempers these warnings with hopeful calls to "hold fast" and persevere in faith, as a host of faithful witnesses have done in Israel's past, culminating in "Jesus the pioneer and perfecter of our faith" (Heb. 12:2). Here we delve into the optics of this "Hall of Faith" (11:1–12:4), the seen and unseen dimensions of historic journeys of faith in quest of a "better" future (11:16, 40).

The seen world, past and present, is fraught with hardship, struggle, and the specter of death for God's people (Heb. 10:32–33; 11:35–38).[16] The eye of faith (*pistis*), however, sets this worldview in a wider frame, seeing "things not seen" with the naked eye (11:1), seeing the larger creational picture, the "universe . . . created by a word from God so that the visible came into existence from the invisible" (11:3 CEB). This does not mean that God made the world *ex nihilo*, out of nothing,[17] but that everything in the universe has been forming from interacting invisible elements, beyond our ability to scope out fully—an idea compatible with current theoretical physics. The ancient writer of Hebrews believed in unseen God-guided forces ever-making, remaking, and moving the world toward a "better" future. It was, ultimately, an optimistic worldview, employing a mystical optic (opti-mystic) through the lens of faith, seeking the "invisible" God and seeing into the gracious future for God's people (11:6). This "assurance of [unseen] things hoped for" (11:1), however, is not just pie-in-the-sky for Hebrews. It has been pulsing throughout biblical history since the beginning. Consider four exemplars of faith who have extraordinary spiritual perception and conviction.

---

16. See Dyer, "'All of These Died'"; Dyer, *Suffering*, 150–74.

17. Genesis 1:1–2 portrays God's creation of the world from chaotic, watery darkness—not from nothing.

Noah (11:7)

Noah undertook his arduous ark-building project on the sole basis of God's forecast of a terrible flood, of catastrophic "events *not yet seen*" (11:7 NIV), of unseen colliding elements and forces that would produce all-too-visible and all-too-palpable devastation, though too late for every creature except Noah, his immediate family, and representative animals through whom God would remake the world. Only by faith can Noah work, live, and survive in these volatile time-space dimensions, visible and invisible.

Abraham (11:8–19)

With God's promise to create a new people out of Abraham and his descendants rooted in a secure homeland (Gen. 12:1–3), God appeared to be moving in the solid realm of the seen. Nothing captures our senses more viscerally than offspring and landscape. Yet Abraham had to move for a long time and distance in the *unseen* realm of faith and hope—"not knowing where he was going"—and once he got to the promised land, still wandered and "liv[ed] in tents," not settling and putting down stakes (Heb. 11:8–9). "By faith" Abraham "looked forward" to permanent life in a "heavenly" realm "whose architect and builder is God" (11:8–15) and whose "earthly" counterpart is a Plato-like "sketch and shadow" of "heavenly" reality (8:5). Abraham "died in faith without having [fully] received [God's] promises," but he did not die hopeless. He embraced these promises beforehand via his far-sighted, macroscopic faith: he "saw and greeted" them "from a distance" (11:13).

But what about the promise of innumerable descendants, which looked very unpromising since the elderly Abraham and his "barren" wife Sarah had no children when they followed God's call? The likelihood of producing offspring seemed "as good as dead" until God blessed the couple with a son, Isaac. Yet Abraham's faith was pushed further, as he later believed that God commanded him to offer Isaac's life as a sacrifice! According to Hebrews, Abraham "was ready" to carry out this incredible act because he believed God would raise Isaac from the dead, if it came to that. It didn't, as it turned out, but "figuratively speaking"—and faithfully seeing the unseen future—Abraham "did receive [Isaac] back" from the dead (11:17, 19).

Moses (11:23–29)

During Pharaoh's campaign to kill all Israelite baby boys, his daughter rescued the infant Moses and raised him as her own. Yet "by faith Moses, when he was grown up, refused to be called a son of Pharaoh's daughter, choosing rather to share ill-treatment with the people of God" (Heb. 11:24–25). Hebrews omits the part of the story where Moses's fellow Israelites resent and reject his initial attempts to help them (Exod. 2:11–14; Acts 7:23–29) and, more oddly, adds that Moses "considered abuse suffered *for Christ* [or *the Messiah*] to be greater wealth than the treasures of Egypt" (Heb. 11:26). How does Christ figure *back* into Moses's story?

Pamela Eisenbaum comments, "It is unlikely the [Hebrews] author means that Moses envisioned Christ; rather he projects the current situation onto the past."[18] Perhaps, but more likely Hebrews suggests that Moses envisioned Christ through extrasensory insight into the unseen future, "*looking ahead* [by faith] to the reward" of God's redemptive purpose in Christ (Heb. 11:26). Moreover, Moses endured Pharaoh's opposition and eventually led the Israelites to freedom "as though he *saw him who is invisible*" (11:27); thus the writer of Hebrews recalls Moses's momentous glimpses of God's "face" normally veiled from human sight (Exod. 33:11, 17–23; Num. 12:8; Deut. 34:10).

Jesus (12:1–3)

As we saw in challenge 2, Hebrews regards Jesus as the prototypical, consummate faithful Son of God, the starter and finisher of the marathon "race" of faith. This implies that at the cross—the most excruciating juncture of Jesus's journey—Jesus was able to persevere by sensing "the joy that was set before him," by seeing and feeling his anticipated resurrection and exaltation with God beyond crucifixion (12:2). But the primary emphasis falls not on Jesus as the subject of forward-looking faith but as the object: "looking *to*/fixing eyes *upon*" Jesus as forerunner of the faith-race. He ran a short but significant leg on earth in solidarity with suffering humanity. By the time Hebrews was written, however, that era was past, accessible by memory and testimony, not by sight; and the risen Jesus was now stationed at God's heavenly right hand, out of earthly sight (12:2; cf. 1:3, 13; 4:14; 8:1; 10:12). Nevertheless, faith opens access to the unseen "cloud"-sphere—the great "cloud of witnesses" to faith's journey (12:1)—and to the gracious God via prayer offered in Jesus's name, even as Jesus himself "offered up prayers and supplications" to God during the difficult "days of his flesh" (4:14–16; 5:7–10).

18. Eisenbaum, "Letter to the Hebrews," 483.

The Kaleidoscopic John in Revelation

The book of Revelation opens by disclosing its visionary thrust: "The revelation of Jesus Christ, which God gave him to *show* his servants . . . he *made it known* by sending his angel to his servant John, who testified to the word of God and to the testimony of Jesus Christ, even to all that he *saw*" (Rev. 1:1–2). This introduction tracks the transmitted insight concerning Jesus Christ from God to Jesus to an angel to John to readers. While the text contains oral/aural elements (word, testimony), visual media predominate: unveiling, showing, manifesting, seeing. The final written product reflects John's virtual synesthetic experience— *seeing sounds and words*. While John is "in the spirit on the Lord's day," he hears a trumpeted command, "Write in a book *what you see*" (1:10–11).

John receives his vision at the island of Patmos in the Aegean Sea. He's not there on vacation, however. Quite the contrary, he seems to have been banished to Patmos by Roman authorities for his vigorous witness to Christ. We don't know the precise conditions of John's exile, but he associates the experience with "persecution" that he "share[s] with [*synkoinōnos*]" seven congregations on the western Asia Minor mainland (Rev. 1:9). Likewise, we don't know many details about these communities' hardships. One reported case of execution stands out ("Antipas my witness [*martys*], my faithful one, who was killed among you," 2:13), but this may have been exceptional rather than normative (though see 17:6; 20:4). Still, John and fellow believers were living at a time of intense suffering. They saw and felt their pain acutely.

But John sees much more. He sees through and beyond the present pain and suffering to the overarching reality breaking in now and consummating soon. We will explore this "now and near" tension in challenge 7. Here we focus on the content and impact of John's revelation for his beleaguered friends in Christ.

First and foremost, John sees a dramatic picture of the risen Christ "like the Son of Man," the same title Jesus uses for himself in the Gospels. But Revelation's portrait explodes with pyrotechnic imagery rarely seen in the Gospel narratives, including eyes blazing "like a flame of fire" and feet "like burnished bronze, refined as in a furnace" (1:12–16). Revelation does coordinate, however, with the Synoptic Gospels' apocalyptic expectation (drawn from Daniel) of seeing "'the Son of Man coming on the clouds of heaven' with power and great glory" to rescue God's suffering people (Matt. 24:30, quoting Dan. 7:13; cf. Mark 14:26; Luke 21:27). Adding bold brushstrokes from the prophet Zechariah, John highlights the universal perception of this climactic coming: "*Look!* He is coming with the clouds; *every eye will see him*, even those who pierced him" (Rev. 1:7; cf. Zech. 12:10).

Revelation's depiction of dazzling kaleidoscopic images of mythic proportions drawn from heavenly, earthly, human, animal (lamb, lion, dragon, beast), and material (scrolls, seals, trumpets, gates, jewels) spheres—designed to flood the visual-perceptual zone—is characteristic of apocalyptic literature. A key purpose of such phantasmagoric writing is to expand a troubled people's historical perspective around, above, and beyond the mundane, constrictive, enervating view of immediate crises. *Look* in all directions, back and forth, up and down. Immerse yourself in the vast vision of God's overarching, inexorable creative and re-creative work across space and time.[19] Demonic domains and evil empires will come and go, but the good and gracious purpose of God will ultimately come to full flower in the new heaven and earth (Rev. 21:1–7).

The apocalyptic book that caps off the New Testament canon stands out for focalizing God's cosmic-historic mission through the living Christ: "the Alpha and the Omega, the first and the last, the beginning and the end" (Rev. 22:12; cf. 1:8, 17–18; 21:6). John's visions spiral out toward the climactic "Omega point,"[20] where pure divine light radiates from the shared "throne of God and of the Lamb," which is openly revealed to God's people: "They will see [God's] face. . . . There will be no more night; they need no light of lamp or sun, for the Lord God will be their light, and they will reign forever and ever" (22:4–5). No filter or shadow, no veil or cave, no delusion or pretense.

So Revelation's congregations are buoyed in their present turmoil by the glorious picture John paints of Christ's coming to consummate God's just and peaceful reign in heaven and earth. At the end, Revelation resounds with the antiphonal voiceover of Christ and his people: "'Surely I am coming soon.' Amen. Come, Lord Jesus!" (22:20).

Yet John's kaleidoscopic vision, for all its fantastic projections of a future wonderworld, is no escapist fantasy. It is anchored in what is "trustworthy and true" (Rev. 21:5; 22:6)—more specifically *who* is trustworthy and true, the "True One" (3:7), the all-seeing Christ, who may be seen here and now, amid the current crisis. Before John sees the living Christ in the heavenly throne room (4:1–2, 9–11;

---

19. Cf. Keller, *Facing Apocalypse*, 51: "Every glimpse or word of God gets diffracted—through the multiplicity of messengers, the facets of gems, the polymorphism of imagery."

20. A key concept of Teilhard de Chardin, the Catholic paleontologist, philosopher, and mystic: the "'Omega point' [is] where the individual and collective adventure of humanity finds its end and fulfillment." Delio, *Unbearable Wholeness*, 78.

5:5–6) or riding to earth with "armies of heaven" in a climactic D-Day (21:11–16), John first sees the dramatic image of Jesus "like the Son of Man" positioned "*in the midst of* the lampstands"—specifically, "seven golden lampstands" representing the seven Asia Minor congregations (1:10–13, 19–20). John does not image Jesus as an ornate, static statue, like the numerous monuments to Caesar displayed in temples and city squares across the Roman Empire. Rather, John sees the living, dynamic presence of Christ actively embedded with his people.

In the letters, John links key features of the opening Christ-vision and channels Christ's voice to each church. For example, "To the angel of the church in Ephesus write: These are the words of him who holds the seven stars in his right hand [see Rev. 1:16], who walks among the seven golden lampstands [see 1:13]" (Rev. 2:1). Notice, too, the adaptation from Christ's being "in the midst of the lampstands" (1:13) to *walking among* them—a further distinction from inanimate statues, emphasizing Christ's active fellowship with believers in their present environments.

The first word Christ says to each church is *Oida*, "I know" (Rev. 2:2, 9, 13, 19; 3:1, 8, 15). It's as if he says, "I know—see, feel, hear, perceive, experience—firsthand all you're going through, the bad and the good, and how you're responding in various ways, bad, good, and indifferent." Christ is no silent, passive observer but an involved pastor and teacher, offering support and encouragement, on the one hand, and rebuke and challenge, on the other hand, to *his* congregations.

Accordingly, every congregant must heed Christ's Spirit-inspired message. Christ's opening "I know" is framed by the same closing exhortation, "Let anyone who has an ear listen to what the Spirit is saying to the churches" (Rev. 2:7, 11, 17, 29; 3:6, 13, 22). Here the primary solicited response is aural; but remember that this book closely intertwines audio and visual components of revelation. The Christ who speaks personally to the seven churches is seen as much as heard "in the midst" of his people.

And Christ himself sees his followers with penetrating sympathy and solidarity. He "loves us" (Rev. 1:4) as one of us. He "knows" our situations because he *sees* us with piercing "eyes like a flame of fire" (1:14; 2:18). He sees us as "a Lamb standing as if it had been slaughtered, having seven horns and seven eyes" (5:6). John sees this Lamb-Christ in the heavenly realm as one who bears the marks of death, knows evil's death-dealing power, and yet now stands on the other side of death, raised to new life and equipped with consummate power (seven horns) and perception (seven eyes) to reveal and realize God's unfolding plan (seven-sealed scroll) to redeem all creation (5:1–10). Note well, however, that the Lamb-Christ does not look on the world from a distant gilded throne or mountain lion perch (5:5): his all-seeing seven eyes are *mobile* and *missional*—"the seven spirits of God *sent out into all the earth*"—ever guiding and guarding his people (5:6).

On the island of Patmos, John, the fellow sufferer "in Jesus" (Rev. 1:9), is blessed with a moving picture of God's right-making rule on earth as it is in heaven through the dying-and-living Christ—"moving" in both affective (emotive) and narrative (movie) senses. For a time, John looks through the lenses of Christ's panoramic eyes. At Christ's command, John produces the movie script of his vision, unveiling the Christ "who is and who was and who is to come" (1:4) for those with eyes to see beyond the cave in faithful and true communities lighted here and now by the fiery-eyed slain and raised Lamb.

7

Now and Near

The Temporal Challenge of Delay and Deferment

	"Lord, is this the time when you will restore the kingdom to Israel?" He replied, "It is not for you to know the times or periods that the Father has set by his own authority." (Acts 1:6–7)
Tenet	As the Son of Humankind, Jesus Christ promised to return to earth to culminate the restoration of God's realm. His earliest followers expected this climactic "appearance" (*parousia*) within their lifetimes.
Tension	As decades passed after Jesus's resurrection and believers continued to die, doubts and questions increased about when he would return and about his followers' fates in the meantime.

While adapting past scriptural images of God's faithful deliverance of persecuted people and affirming Christ's supportive presence here and now "in the midst of" his congregations, Revelation tilts toward a grand finale of God's cosmic purpose for the universe at Christ's (re)appearance (*parousia*) on earth. And it expects that consummation to be *soon/near* (Rev. 1:3; 3:11; 22:6–7, 10, 20). John and his first readers likely expected Christ's climactic coming within their lifetimes, though they did not pinpoint dates.

Of course, history has proven them wrong—for two millennia and counting. This delay has led to no end of apologies, projecting John's vision into a distant future conveniently relevant to interpreters' current events, sometimes marked on the calendar, notwithstanding Jesus's self-admitted ignorance of "that day or hour" (Mark 13:32).[1] When the magic date passed, die-hard believers would re-calibrate Revelation's supposed code and reschedule the big event until eventually giving up in abject disappointment or even suicide (self-martyrdom). Adjusting end-time expectations represents a textbook example of cognitive dissonance (see prologue).

By and large, however, *within* Revelation there is little dissonance about time delays. It trumpets a strong note of assurance that Christ is coming soon to rescue God's distressed people and renew the world. To be sure, Revelation provides time notes marking short and long periods of significant events, both catastrophic and triumphal, before the "end." On the devastating side: "half an hour" of heavenly silence before earthly disasters erupt (8:1); "the hour, the day, the month, and the year" of assaults from evil spirit/angel forces against humanity (9:15); "forty-two months" (11:2; 13:5), "one thousand two-hundred sixty days" (11:3), "three and a half days" (11:9, 11; 12:6), and "a time, and times, and half a time" (12:14) of mass calamities. On the deliverance side: a "thousand years" (20:4–7) of God's people reigning with Christ. But these temporal figures, like so much of Revelation's language, are *figurative*, not literal. The point is that everything unfolds "in God's time."[2] The time is "at hand" because God has everything well in hand. In the meantime, God's people are called to hold on—though not much longer and not in fear and anxiety, but rather living confidently in God's eternal now, forever and ever, amen.

One verse addresses a possible time-lag problem by dismissing it: "There will be no more delay" (Rev. 10:6). This "no delay" language may echo what Habakkuk says in the context of the Babylonians' siege of Jerusalem in the late sixth century BCE: "There is still a vision for an appointed time; it speaks of the end, and does not lie. If it seems to tarry, wait for it; it will surely come; *it will not delay*" (Hab. 2:3). Unlike Revelation's John, however, Habakkuk prophesies in a mode of "complaint" over God's tardiness to help his assaulted people and halt their "proud" attackers: "O LORD, how long shall I cry for help, and you will not listen? Or cry to you, 'Violence!' and you will not save?" (1:2). "I will keep watch to see what he will say to me, and what he will answer concerning my complaint.... Look at the proud!" (2:1, 4). In the venerable scriptural tradition of lament, Habakkuk pushes through his angst to hope in God's salvation, which "will surely come" and "not delay" unduly. He just needs to hold on a while longer.

1. See Beal, *Book of Revelation.*
2. Hill, *In God's Time.*

Commentary on the Habakkuk Scroll from Qumran

Yet such waiting is no walk in the park. The prophet's protest of God's seemingly dilatory response is serious and heartfelt, precisely because he trusts God's covenantal commitment.[3] "We're hurting here, Lord! How much longer will you let your people suffer? Surely not much longer! Your steadfast love demands swift action." Thus, we imagine, Habakkuk wrestles with cognitive dissonance and emotional upheaval.

Nearer the time of Revelation, a group of separatist Jewish priests, encamped by the Dead Sea, anticipated God's imminent apocalyptic defeat of the "Kittim" (Romans)—"the last gentile world power to oppress the people of God"[4]—and purification of the covenant community. This worldview was inspired in part, according to the sect's Teacher of Righteousness, by Habakkuk's prophecy: "God told Habakkuk to write down that which would happen to the final generation, but He did not make known to him when time would come to an end. *For there shall be yet another vision concerning the appointed times. It shall tell of the end and shall not lie* (2:3). Interpreted, this means that the final age shall be prolonged and shall exceed all that the prophets have said; for the mysteries of God are astounding. *If it tarries, wait for it, for it shall surely come and shall not be late* (2:3b)" (1QpHab 7.1–10).[5] This interpretation sees Habakkuk predicting "the end" of the age beyond the prophet's own time, extending to the Teacher's present era. Yet the Teacher expects further delay. Rest assured, however, the end

3. See Eklund, *Practicing Lament*; Ferber and Schwebel, *Lament*.
4. Gitay, "Kittim," 522; cf. Dan. 11:30.
5. Vermes, *Complete Dead Sea Scrolls*, 511–13 (emphasis original).

"shall surely come and shall not be late." Hope may be delayed but not belatedly. The Teacher and his fellow Covenanters expected to share in God's final victory.[6]

Again, however, whereas Habakkuk lamented God's tardiness and the Teacher of Righteousness appropriated Habakkuk to assure his community that God will come right on time ("not be late"), Revelation's John does not seem bothered by temporal tensions. There will be no more delay. Period. Christ is coming soon. The Spirit and Christ's people are ready for the great consummation of the universe (Rev. 10:6; 19:1–8; 22:7, 12, 17, 20). Hallelujah! John is an eternal optimist—just like the writer of Hebrews, as discussed in challenge 6.

And in challenge 2 we noted that Hebrews also exhorts would-be defectors from the faith not to "shrink back" but to "live by faith" in hard times, which will end "in a very little while" with the Lord's "coming" (Heb. 10:36–39). This language echoes the Greek version of Habakkuk 2:3–4. Like Revelation, Hebrews projects confidence about the future, "assurance of things hoped for" (11:1), resolving tensions and anxieties, temporal and otherwise, by *dissolving* them in bold affirmations of faith.

Other parts of the New Testament, however, while sharing the hope of Christ's imminent return and "the time of universal restoration" (Acts 3:21), address the problem of delay in Christ's *parousia* more deliberately and sympathetically toward those beset by worry and confusion over God's timing. Waiting for relief from intense suffering, even in the short run, can be excruciating. "Hope deferred makes the heart sick" (Prov. 13:12). Luke and Acts, Pauline literature, and the letters of James and 2 Peter treat this heartsickness of delay and deferral concerning Christ's reappearance in various ways.

Watch and Work: Jesus's Challenge in Luke and Acts

The Gospels and Acts were written a generation or two (65–100 CE) after Jesus's ascension and predicted return.[7] This gap began to stretch expectation of Jesus's imminent *parousia* to the breaking point. "How long, O Lord?" pressed in with increasing urgency.

In the mid-twentieth century, Hans Conzelmann argued that Luke managed the problem of Christ's delayed *parousia* by expanding the arc of salvation history over three periods, with Christ-events at the midpoint, preceded by the "old" age of God's dealings with Israel and succeeded by the "new" age after Christ's

---

6. See Mermelstein, *Power and Emotion*, 214–19.
7. Possibly later with Acts; see Pervo, *Dating Acts*.

ascension, destined to culminate in his return at an unknown time.[8] The temporal problem Conzelmann highlighted remains a critical issue, although most recent interpreters view his three-part schema as too rigid for Luke's nuanced narrative.

Jesus's Parables and Prophecies

As Luke's Jesus forecasts his return to earth, he also acknowledges its open timetable and the nagging problems its delay might pose for his followers. We may reasonably assume both that Jesus had prescient insight into future trends (we have serious "futurist" thinkers today) and that Luke shaped his report of Jesus's prediction to address concerns in Luke's own generation. Luke especially casts Jesus's parables and prophecies as challenges to watch and work in the *meantime* between his departure and return.[9]

PARABLES OF FAITHFUL AND UNFAITHFUL SERVANTS (LUKE 12:35–48)

Jesus assumes common household social structures in the ancient world with dominant masters/lords and subordinate slaves/servants, without explicitly affirming or critiquing the system.[10] Though he promotes freedom from sin, sickness, and satanic oppression and may be fairly said to destabilize hierarchical norms, Jesus was not a crusading abolitionist.

In short compass, Luke's Jesus sketches three household management scenarios concerning various indefinite "comings" in order to ready his servant-followers for his future coming "at an unexpected hour" (12:40).[11]

Wedding Banquet (12:35–38). Jesus exhorts disciples to "be dressed for action and have [their] lamps lit" for his (implied) return to earth, as household slaves should be poised to serve their master when he returns from a wedding banquet at an inconvenient hour "during the middle of the night, or near dawn" (12:38). But Jesus also flips hierarchical labor on its head. Finding his slaves watching and waiting to serve him, the master cinches his belt and caters to their needs: "He will come and serve them" (12:37). Thus Luke's Jesus helps his disciples cope with his uncertain return schedule by combining a call to vigilant duty with the hope of his benevolent ministry—an economy of mutual service.

---

8. Conzelmann, *Theology of St. Luke.*

9. See Spencer, *Gospel of Luke and Acts*, 65–68.

10. Spencer, *Luke*, 337–43.

11. Other relevant parables include the parable of the widow and the unjust judge (Luke 18:1–8; see Spencer, *Salty Wives*, 264–314) and the parable of the ten minas (19:11–27; see Spencer, *Luke*, 485–90).

Thief Break-In (12:39–40). Jesus abruptly shifts metaphorical characters, with his followers now cast in the householder role and himself in the villainous guise of a night-thief! At a base level, Jesus makes the obvious point that thieves do not let homeowners know when they're planning to break in. Since householders remain in the dark about thieves' timetables, they must always remain alert (or, to update the scenario, install a twenty-four-hour security system). Just so, Jesus's disciples must stay ever watchful for his coming "at an unexpected hour" (12:40).

On another level, however, the metaphor breaks down, this time with jarring effect in portraying the coming Son of Humankind as a sneaky night-thief aiming to steal from his own people. Though not the story's primary thrust, this sinister element marks an undercurrent of *warning* that even Jesus's closest followers might cling so tightly to worldly concerns (cf. 8:14) as to regard Jesus's climactic coming as an unwelcome interruption. Just before speaking these parables, Jesus challenges his "little flock" to give their earthly goods to the poor and thus invest in God's heavenly realm—on earth!—"where *no thief comes near*" to steal (12:32–33).

Landlord Absence (12:41–48). Peter seems shaken by Jesus's thief image, querying, "Lord, are you telling this parable for us or for everyone?" (12:41). Both, really, as Jesus offers a stewardship lesson for "everyone" (12:48), even as the disciples remain his primary audience.

In the present parable, an estate owner takes an extended business or leisure trip with an uncertain return date. Before departing, he designates one of his slaves as foreman over the others, with responsibility to be a "faithful and prudent manager" (12:42) for the good of the master's enterprise. But if the master's protracted absence prompts the slave manager to exploit the other slaves for his own benefit, he can expect a rude awakening and harsh accounting when the master finally returns at an unexpected hour. The master's surprise arrival will feel like a burglar attack!

As in the first scene, the householder represents the coming Jesus at an uncertain, unexpected time. What, then, should Jesus's servant-followers be doing in his absence, whatever its duration? Contrary to the parable's slave manager, faithful disciples must persevere in the ministry Jesus has entrusted to them: "Blessed is that slave whom his master will find at work when he arrives" (12:43).

Prophecies of the Coming Son of Humankind (Luke 17:20–21:36)

Hard and Ho-Hum Times (17:20–37). One time some Pharisees ask Jesus about "when the kingdom of God" is coming—that is, "When will God's saving rule culminate on earth?" (17:20). A reasonable question for serious God-seekers. But Jesus disqualifies the question on grounds that God's redemptive rule is already evident here and now "among [or within, *entos*] you," though not (yet) showing the most explosive apocalyptic signs many expected (17:21). No need to track the skies for meteoric phenomena or excite people with flashes in the pan: "Look, here it is!" No, no, "There it is!" (17:21).

Jesus overstates the case by saying, "The kingdom of God is not coming with things that can be observed" (17:20). He means, "not observed" (yet) in epic, cosmic events. In line with previous statements, Luke's Jesus means that God's kingdom partly operates underground, progressing little by little (see 13:18–21) but also occasionally breaking out in dramatic demonstrations. For instance, regarding his exorcism ministry, Jesus announces, "If it is by the finger of God that I cast out the demons, then the kingdom of God *has come to you*" (11:20).

But that's not the whole story. Jesus's present saving work makes a good start in realizing God's right-making rule on earth, but it is not the end, as he explains to his disciples, knowing the difficult challenges they will face after his death. After he's gone, they "will long to see *one of the days* of the Son of Man, and [they] will not see it" (17:22)—either past days of Jesus's liberating ministry or future days reprising that ministry and presaging *the day* of his climactic return (17:24, 30).

In the meantime—which, remember, has extended for decades by the time Luke writes—Jesus offers no false illusions of bliss. Times will be hard for his followers, just as he "first must endure much suffering and be rejected by this generation" before rising from the dead, ascending to heaven, and returning in glory someday (17:25). Ironically, however, the interim period will be not just hard but also *ho-hum* in many respects. It will be business as usual, one blessed (or not) bland day after another, "eating and drinking, buying and selling, planting and building," sleeping and rising—then repeat over and over again—oblivious to the coming day of reckoning and restoration (17:28). In such a persisting daily grind, Jesus's disciples could easily become complacent about remaining faithful (what difference does it make?) or despondent about his return (why should today be any different?).

Jesus urges two key dispositions. First, quit flitting about and pining for some big-bang heavenly deliverance; the Son of Humankind will come when he comes, and you'll know it when he comes—you can't miss it (17:23–24). In the meantime, stay focused on the present hour/day—God's urgent, pregnant "today."[12] Second, quit looking back and longing for the good old days; they weren't that good anyway—they had plenty of their own problems. In the meantime, keep forging ahead, right up to "the day that the Son of Man is revealed" (17:30); keep your "hand to the plow" in faithful cultivation of God's field (9:62).

Destructive and Deceptive Times (21:5–36). In typical apocalyptic perspective, Luke's Jesus expects things to get worse before they get better, to devolve into more chaos before the Son of Humankind irrupts to make all things right at last. In this fraught environment, Jesus's followers naturally want to know, "When will this be, and what will be the sign[s] that this is about to take place?" (21:7)—this turmoil before the final turnaround, this end-time madness before the End, God's ultimate makeover? How long, O Lord?

Jesus offers no quick, cheap panacea. He candidly predicts that "the generation" after his departure will be inundated with military conflicts, political uprisings, and natural disasters. The desire for rescue will become intense, with no end of pseudo-saviors ready to take advantage. Jesus warns his disciples not to fall prey to messianic pretenders who claim, "'I am he!' and, 'The time is near!'" (21:8) The tough times will roll for a while: "These things must take place first, but the end will *not follow immediately*" (21:9). Jesus's final advent will be delayed, and the waiting period will not be pleasant.

But it will not extend indefinitely. Jesus envisions a cataclysmic assault against Jerusalem "by the Gentiles" (21:24) as the banner sign that his redemptive return "is drawing near" (21:28; cf. vv. 20, 30–31). As it happens, the First Jewish–Roman War (66–73 CE) resulted in Rome's destruction of Jerusalem around forty years after Jesus's death. As prescient Jewish prophets of old anticipated Jerusalem's fall to Babylon centuries before, so Jesus expects Jerusalem's assault by Rome on the not-too-distant horizon.

At the time of Luke's writing (80–90 CE), Jerusalem's fateful demise was a fait accompli. Luke's dual-level narrative of history both remembered and interpreted vindicates part of Jesus's forecast: Jerusalem had been "surrounded by [Roman] armies" who inflicted "desolation" and "great distress" (21:20, 23). But at the same time, another part of Jesus's projection remained unfulfilled. His claim that the catastrophic events of the Roman War would usher in the "near" cloud-riding *parousia* of the Son of Humankind had not yet been realized in Luke's day (and has not been since). Rome's power persisted. The generational delay in Jesus's return to a tumultuous earth from his death to Jerusalem's demise is one thing;

12. Luke highlights "today/this day" (*sēmeron*) as the ever-present time of salvation; see 2:11; 4:21; 5:26; 13:32–33; 19:5, 9; 22:34, 61; 23:43.

delaying an additional decade or two (or two hundred!) ratchets up cognitive and emotional tension. Will the Son of Humankind find faith on earth at his coming (18:8), God knows when? Good question—one that impinges not only on human faithfulness but on God's too. How long, O Lord?

Again, what should Jesus's followers do in the challenging meantime? How can they endure the present crises with confidence and courage (21:19)? Luke's Jesus provides another two-pronged answer. On the one hand, he assures his disciples of his continuing support. Though physically absent, he will be with them in mind and spirit, giving them "words and wisdom" to withstand hostile prosecutors and traitors, even within their families (21:12–19). Earlier Jesus had assured his associates that the Holy Spirit would come to their defense and "teach [them] at that very hour what [they] ought to say" (12:12). Now, he promises a more personal advocacy: *his Spirit* will inspire and fortify them (21:15). Jesus will be no absentee Lord. He will maintain a vital "virtual" presence.

On the other hand, Jesus expects his adherents to be watchful and prayerful—watchful so that "that day [of his return] does not catch [them] unexpectedly, like a trap," rather than a release; prayerful so that they "may have the strength . . . to stand before the Son of Man" with integrity, having remained faithful throughout rough periods preceding his coming (21:34, 36).

The Disciples' Qualms and Questions

While Luke's Jesus tries to prepare his followers for the rocky interim between his departure and return, they can hardly be expected to think clearly and calmly in the throes of his crucifixion, resurrection, and ascension. Across the forty-three days of these shocking events (Luke 24:21; Acts 1:3), they will inevitably have new doubts, questions, and anxieties regarding God's rule in Jesus Messiah, not least its timing. If not now, when?

Hopeless Disciples Three Days after Jesus's Crucifixion (Luke 24:1–49)

While Jesus's followers share widespread Jewish belief in a general, end-time resurrection (cf. John 11:23–34), they struggle to grasp his announcement that he would be resurrected "on the third day" (Luke 9:22; 18:33). At the dawn of the third day (Sunday) after his crucifixion, no one in Luke expects Jesus to be alive or expects his corpse to be anywhere but its tomb. When these expectations begin to be challenged, doubt and despair set in before hope can sprout.

Mary Magdalene and Companions (24:1–9). The women come to Jesus's tomb at daybreak Sunday with one intention: to anoint Jesus's dead body with spices. They are thoroughly "perplexed" when they find no body in the tomb. Confusion escalates to terror when "suddenly two men in dazzling clothes" inform them that Jesus "has risen" just as "he told [them]" (24:4, 6). Only then is their memory of Jesus's resurrection forecast jogged and their hope revitalized.

Peter and the Apostles (24:10–12). But that doesn't mean the women have all their doubts assuaged or that others believe their report. The male apostles dismiss their testimony as "an idle tale" (24:11). It doesn't fit their worldview, which includes stereotyping women as prone to hysterics. Peter at least thinks it is worth dashing to the tomb to see for himself. He is "amazed" at the empty burial cloths he sees, but amazement does not equal understanding.

Cleopas and Companion (24:13–35). Recall from the discussion of this passage in challenge 6 the hopelessness that overwhelms the two disciples as they trudge from Jerusalem to Emmaus on the "same day" (24:13) the women had reported Jesus's empty tomb. Neither the women's reports nor Peter's reports nor Jesus's actual, but unrecognized, presence alongside them alleviate their disappointment over Jesus's failed mission (24:15–24). When the Emmaus couple finally recognize Jesus as he breaks bread with them, he vanishes. Is it time for Jesus to mount a cloud and reappear on earth in "power and great glory" (21:27)? Who knows?

Wider Company of Disciples (24:36–49). The risen Jesus suddenly appears to a larger group in Jerusalem, including the eleven apostles. Though he greets them with "Peace be with you," they become "startled and terrified . . . frightened, and [riddled with] doubts," thinking they're being haunted by "a ghost" (24:37–38)! Even after Jesus invites them to "touch and see" his living flesh-and-bone body, their rejoicing remains mixed with "disbelieving and still wondering" (24:39, 41). Occasional post-resurrection reappearances of Jesus do not relieve all cognitive dissonance and emotional upheaval.

HOPEFUL DISCIPLES FORTY DAYS AFTER JESUS'S RESURRECTION
(ACTS 1:1–11)

Over the next forty days, the risen Jesus makes no public appearances but keeps visiting his apostles, eating with them (1:4; 10:41) and instructing them "through the Holy Spirit . . . about the kingdom of God" (1:2–3). No doubt easing some of their tension, Jesus also keeps them on edge by ordering them to wait in Jerusalem for the Holy Spirit's outpouring "not many days from now" (1:5). More mystery, more delay.

Enough already, the apostles seem to think. Can we get on with it? "Lord, is this the time when you will restore the kingdom to Israel?" (Acts 1:6). Now that Jesus has "endure[d] much suffering" (Luke 17:25), come through the ordeal of crucifixion, and risen to new life, what is the purpose of further death and suffering in the world? Is Jesus's resurrection not the pivotal, apocalyptic event signaling the triumph of good over evil, life over death, God over all? Why not go public now? What in the world are we waiting for? Hasn't the Divine Life-Spirit already been maximally manifest in God's Son Jesus from birth (Acts 1:35) to baptism (3:21–22) to transfiguration (9:28–36) to resurrection (1:2)? Perhaps the apostles envision a narrower, "nationalistic" kingdom *of* Israel, but that's not what they ask about. Jesus has been teaching them about God's kingdom (1:3), making it likely that their query about "the kingdom" is shorthand for God's realm, which they hope Jesus is about to "restore *to* Israel." The hope of Israel's restoration encompasses a broad vision of salvation, re-creation, and resurrection in which God's life flourishes in God's people Israel for the redemption of the world (see 23:6; 24:15; 26:6–8; 28:20).

Though the apostles ask a reasonable "when" question, it draws a dismissive response from Jesus: "It is not for you to know the times or periods that the Father has set by his own authority" (1:7). In other words: None of your business! All in due time, but in the meantime, Jesus commissions his delegates to bear Spirit-empowered witness "in Jerusalem, in all Judea and Samaria, and to the ends of the earth" (1:8), which of course will take some time, maybe a lot of time, to fulfill. In terms of end-time (eschatological) matters, Luke's Jesus focuses more on spatial-extensional aims—reaching the "ends [*eschatou*] of the earth"—than on temporal-existential concerns at the end of the age.

After instructing and commissioning his delegates, Jesus leaves them to their Spirit-inspired work as a cloud lifts him into heaven. As they gawk at Jesus's dramatic ascent, two white-clad messengers "suddenly" appear to redirect their focus—"Why do you stand looking up toward heaven?"—and to announce Jesus's return "in the same way as [they] saw him go into heaven" (1:10–11). This scenario parallels the dazzling duo who challenged the women's perception at the empty tomb—"Why do you look for the living among the dead?" (Luke 24:4)—and declared Jesus's resurrection (24:4–5). The drama of God's rule in Jesus Messiah keeps evolving through various times and places toward Jesus's consummative *parousia* (Acts 3:20–21).

The Ascension of Christ

Yet the date of Jesus's return is not fixed, except in God's mind, and God isn't telling, perhaps allowing God to grant more time—as long as it takes—to spread the gospel to the ends of the earth. Jesus has an "open return" ticket back to earth, which he uses for periodic visits (e.g., 9:3–6) in advance of his final advent. Given this unfixed schedule, Jesus's followers must not fix their attention on the skies, must not have their "head in the clouds," but must get on with the mission Jesus assigned them—as long as it takes.

Encourage and Endure: The Challenge of Paul and James

Paul and James[13] believed that Jesus's return was near. Their pastoral counsel via letters was more urgent than that conveyed in Luke's later narratives, more anchored in the actual *now* than in an eternal "today." Two key problems complicate

13. On authorship and date, see Hartin (*James*, 16–25), who concludes that James of Jerusalem, the brother of Jesus, most likely wrote (with secretarial help) the letter of James in the late 60s CE.

the interim between Jesus's resurrection and return: (1) the mortal problem of persisting death and dying (Paul) and (2) the material problem of poverty and suffering (James).

Paul: Dying and Delaying

Here I follow a generally accepted sequence of Paul's writings, with an eye to detecting variable views regarding the increasing delay of Christ's *parousia*. This is not to say, however, that we can precisely track developments in Paul's thinking on a timeline. He wrote letters for different reasons to different audiences at different times. His views modified and matured along the way but not always neatly and tidily. I focus here more on tensive than progressive relations among ideas of Christ's delayed coming in three "clusters" of Pauline letters.[14]

1–2 THESSALONIANS

First Thessalonians is likely the oldest New Testament writing (early 50s CE), composed about two decades after Jesus's death. Paul urges the Thessalonians "to wait for [God's] Son from heaven, whom [God] raised from the dead" (1:10)—that is, for the Lord Jesus's "coming" (*parousia*, 2:19; 3:13; 4:15; 5:23). Paul does not, however, expect to "wait" long. The benediction assumes the Thessalonian believers will be alive at Jesus's reappearing: "May your spirit and soul and body be kept sound [whole] and blameless at the coming of our Lord Jesus Christ" (5:23).

Still, this promising news is weakened by consternation over loved ones who have recently died. What would happen to them at Jesus's *parousia*? Would they miss out or be shortchanged on the culminating blessings of God's kingdom? Since Paul addresses a primarily Gentile congregation unschooled in the Jewish hope of general resurrection, they desperately need Paul's pastoral grief counsel. He offers words of hope and comfort (1 Thess. 4:18; 5:11) so that they might "not grieve as others do who have no hope" but rather rest assured that "Jesus died and rose again" and that "God will bring with [Jesus] those who have died" at the *parousia* (4:13–14). More specifically, the triple blare of the Lord's command, the archangel's shout, and God's trumpet-blast will rouse the dead from their graves and raise them up to meet Jesus in the air "first"—before those still alive ascend to join Jesus's return to earth to "be with [him] forever" (4:16–17).[15]

---

14. On "clusters" of Pauline letters, see L. Johnson, *Constructing Paul*, 74–92.

15. Analogous to people going outside the city to escort a visiting dignitary *into town*, believers in Christ (dead and living) will be raised up from earth to accompany his (re)entrance *to earth*. Contrary

The call to "encourage one another" (1 Thess. 4:18; 5:11) includes offering not only consolation and comfort but also exhortation and challenge. Hence, Paul also warns the Thessalonians to stay vigilant in the interim. "Concerning the times and the seasons" (5:1), Paul does not leave the matter as open-ended as Acts does (all in God's time, worldwide mission in the meantime) but rather invokes the "night-thief" image of Christ's any-moment invasion. Paul exhorts the Thessalonian "children of the light and day" to stay alert to the Lord's imminent coming. The challenge to "not fall asleep" plays on common associations of death and sleep (rest in peace) and hints that many of Paul's addressees will be alive when Jesus comes. In any case, "whether we are awake [i.e., alive] or asleep [i.e., dead]," we are ready to "live with [Christ]" (5:2–10).

Yet the times and seasons march on, prompting a second Thessalonian letter. We don't know how much later 2 Thessalonians comes along: perhaps weeks or months, if written by Paul; years, even decades, if written in Paul's name, as many scholars think. Whatever the delay between the two Thessalonian correspondences, the problem of Christ's delayed coming becomes even more acute if 2 Thessalonians was composed after Paul's death.

How does the second Thessalonian letter cope with the cognitive dissonance triggered by the first's shaky assumptions? Two strategies. One approach denies the problem by reconfiguring Christ's expected return on a decisive day—"the day of the Lord"—as *already realized*, not just in part but in toto (2 Thess. 2:1–3). The details remain fuzzy, but this belief seems to focus on Christ's kingdom as a dynamic spiritual presence here and now, within and among his followers (like in Luke 17:20–21), with nothing more to wait for, no grand consummative coming (*unlike* in Luke 17:22–27). All that's left is to live day by day into the full reality of Christ.

A second approach doubles down on belief in Christ's imminent *parousia* by ceasing earthly employment. Why should we pursue worldly wages when Christ's new world lies on the near horizon? Perhaps some think that such dedicated waiting, without working, would hasten the final day. At any rate, Paul is not impressed. Alertness is not idleness. As Paul manually "worked night and day" to support himself while ministering to the Thessalonians, they should do the same, "earn their own living" and "not be weary in doing what is right"—until Jesus comes (1 Thess. 2:9; 3:6–13).

---

to popular opinion, Paul envisions no "rapture" from earth to heaven. See Crossan and Reid, *In Search of Paul*, 165–77.

1–2 CORINTHIANS AND ROMANS

Paul writes 1 Corinthians a few years after 1 Thessalonians and continues encouraging his readers to "wait for the revealing [*apokalypsin*] of our Lord Jesus Christ," who "will also strengthen you to the end" (1 Cor. 1:7–8).[16] Again, Paul seems to expect Christ's reappearance within the Corinthians' lifetimes, in which they need Christ's fortification through hard times "to the end." Paul does not spell out the harsh conditions, simply referring to them as "the present [*enestōsan*] distress" (7:26 NASB) (the people know what they're going through). This struggle typifies "the present [*enestōtos*] evil age" (Gal. 1:4), from which Christ has begun to save us and which Christ will soon complete. While "the appointed time has grown short" (1 Cor. 7:29), that doesn't lessen the anguish of the current crisis.

For all of Paul's gritty perseverance through suffering, he's no masochist. Pastor Paul wants to spare his flock as much distress as possible, wants them "free from anxieties" (1 Cor. 7:32). That's a nice sentiment, but it may surprise us that Paul targets *family life* as the principal source of stress. While that is true to a point, it discounts the fact that many receive their surest comfort and support from their families. Though Paul would probably concede these basic family benefits, his main concern under the present pressure before Christ's return is that his spiritual children should not augment their distress by changing their family status, as in getting married and having children. He prefers they "remain as [they] are" (7:26) so they can give full attention to "the affairs of the [coming] Lord, how to please the Lord" (7:32). Paul pushes this "stay as you are" policy further, advising Christ-believing slaves *not* to "gain [their] freedom," "even if [they] can," but rather to "make use of [their] present condition now more than ever" to demonstrate their spiritual freedom in Christ, their true "belonging to the [coming] Lord" (7:21–22).

This counsel to freeze family plans and not change household positions flows from Paul's conviction that everything *will change* dramatically with Christ's return. As Christ himself was "first" raised to new life (1 Cor. 15:20–22), so at Christ's final appearing, "we will all be changed," even though "we will not all die" (15:51). As in 1 Thessalonians, Paul affirms that all believers, dead or alive, will be raised up with Christ. Here, however, Paul makes no temporal distinction (dead

16. L. Johnson (*Constructing Paul*) clusters Romans with Galatians on thematic grounds. But Romans also has affinities with the Corinthian letters. Paul likely wrote Romans from Corinth a year or so after writing 2 Corinthians. Two of Paul's most valued associates, Aquila and Priscilla, had close ties with both the Corinthian and the Roman congregations (Acts 18:1–3; Rom. 16:3–4; 1 Cor. 16:19).

rise first, then the living), even as he adds the transformational component that living believers will "put on" immortal bodies "in a moment, in the twinkling of any eye" (15:42–44, 50–54). At that moment, former earthly statuses will cease to matter (cf. Matt. 22:22–33; Mark 12:18–27; Luke 20:20–26).

In 2 Corinthians, written no more than a few years after 1 Corinthians,[17] Paul is preoccupied with his personal sufferings for Christ (2 Cor. 4:8–9; 6:4–10; 11:23–29; 12:6–10). Not that these knock him down; in fact, he boasts in his hardships as badges of identification with Christ on others' behalf, "always carrying in the body the death of Jesus, so that the life of Jesus may also be made visible in our bodies" (4:10; see challenge 6). Not only preaching about Christ crucified (1 Cor. 1:17–2:5) but effectively *participating* in Christ's death,[18] Paul now seems to be more aware that he might die before Christ's *parousia*.[19] But again, no worries, no reason to "lose heart," since "we know that the one [God] who raised the Lord Jesus will raise us also with Jesus, and will bring us with you into his presence" (2 Cor. 4:14–16).

Paul also announces his "confidence" that death will not interrupt his fellowship with Christ, even for a moment. Mixing building and clothing imagery, Paul envisions his mortal body as an "earthly tent" destined to be exchanged for an "eternal [house] in the heavens," or "swallowed up by [eternal] life" in an immortal body (2 Cor. 5:1–3). Here Paul does not directly address when this transformation will take place, but he raises the spooky possibility of some interim state of disembodied nakedness and homelessness between death and resurrection (5:3–4).[20] Even Jesus, remember, was not raised until the third day postmortem (cf. 1 Cor. 15:4). But however long the delay until final resurrection, Paul believes that his fellowship with Christ, consciously or unconsciously, will intensify at the moment of death: being "away from the body" means being "at home with the Lord"; exiting the earthly domicile (*ekdēmēsai*) means instantaneous entry into Christ's heavenly dwelling (*endēmēsai*) (2 Cor. 5:8). Although death may temporarily separate one's flesh and bones from the body's life-force (soul? spirit?), there will be *no effective separation from Christ's loving presence* (cf. Rom. 8:37–39).

---

17. On the historical background to 2 Corinthians, including the possibility that it contains multiple letters, see Powell, *Introducing the New Testament*, 310–14.

18. See Gorman, *Participating in Christ*.

19. Cf. Phil. 1:20–26; G. Carey, *Death*, 225–26.

20. G. Carey (*Death*, 223) notes that Paul's world entertained various notions concerning intermediate states of "disembodied souls" (see 1 En. 22:3) and righteous martyrs—in particular, "receiv[ing] immortal souls upon their deaths" (see 4 Macc. 17:12; 18:23).

So has Paul begun to waffle about his hope of Christ's imminent return? Is he hedging his bets in case he happens to die? Not necessarily. He concludes the discussion about earthly and heavenly life by declaring that "all of us must appear before the judgment seat of Christ" (2 Cor. 5:10). As Adela Yarbro Collins comments, "This statement suggests an imminent return of Christ as judge over his own, whether still alive or recently dead."[21] And, we might add, it remains consistent with Paul's teaching elsewhere regarding the resurrection of deceased *bodies* at this final reckoning day: we will all stand *bodily* before Christ's bench.

So much for what Paul thinks will happen *then*, at Christ's *parousia* or at moments of death before then. But what about *now*? Despite the bevy of present hardships besetting Paul (2 Cor. 6:4–5), he does not succumb to wistful longing for the "sweet by-and-by." And this is for good reason—namely, that he's already begun feasting on the sweet fruits of God's gracious salvation in Christ: "Look, now [*nyn*] is the right time! Look, now [*nyn*] is the day of salvation!" (6:2 CEB). Or "Now is the favorable time [*kairos euprosdektos*]" (ESV), the time "favorable for bringing God's grace to fruition."[22]

In Romans,[23] Paul's most "mature" and possibly last writing,[24] "now-time" becomes even more palpable, more encompassing, and nearer: "You know what time [*kairon*] it is, how it is now [or already] the moment for you to wake from sleep. For salvation is *nearer* to us now [*nyn*] than when we became believers" (Rom. 13:11). Paul's sense that "the day is near" has intensified existentially more than foreshortened extensionally.[25] Paul is more living the messianic life than longing for it. He's having the time (*kairos*) of his life in Christ now (*nyn*), we might say, more than pining for a future time (*chronos*) of relief. He's had a spiritual "awakening" and continues to live in the light of that experience guiding him through the "far gone" night (13:12), the darkest, direst phase before the dawn.[26]

Paul thus adapts earlier imagery of rising/awakening from sleep—which provided assurance that deceased believers would rise/awaken to meet Christ and prompted night-and-day alertness by those remaining alive to welcome him (1 Thess. 4:13–5:11; cf. 1 Cor. 15:12–22, 50–57)—to encourage maximal living

21. A. Collins, *Paul Transformed*, 13.
22. BDAG, s.v. "εὐπρόσδεκτος," 410–11.
23. L. Johnson (*Constructing Paul*) clusters Romans with Galatians on thematic grounds. But Romans also has affinities with the Corinthian letters. Paul likely wrote Romans from Corinth a year or so after writing 2 Corinthians. Two of Paul's most valued associates, Aquila and Priscilla, had close ties with both the Corinthian and the Roman congregations (Acts 18:1–3; Rom. 16:3–4; 1 Cor. 16:19).
24. Welborn, *Paul's Summons*, 68; this book provides a brilliant, provocative study of Rom. 13:8–14.
25. Welborn, *Paul's Summons*, 52, 69.
26. Welborn, *Paul's Summons*, 50.

in the present as Christ's representatives, who are veritably "clothed" with Christ (Rom. 13:14).[27] The primary Christ-life duty "owed" to the community is *love*, rippling out from "one another" (*allēlous*) to "neighbor" (*plēsion*) to "another/ the other" (*heteron*) (13:8–10), as "God's love has been poured into our hearts though the Holy Spirit" (5:5).[28]

COLOSSIANS–EPHESIANS

Many scholars classify Colossians and Ephesians as "deutero-Pauline" letters written in Paul's name by devotees after his death. One reason for distinguishing them from Paul's authentic writings is their conventional household codes, which are designed to maintain long-term family stability, in contrast to Paul's recommending in 1 Corinthians 7 a halt to marriage and childbearing in the present stormy period before the imminent dawn of Christ's world-changing return (see challenge 1). Whether or not different household structures demand different authorship, Colossians and Ephesians seem to reflect later stages of thought after further delay of the *parousia*.

Yet these letters still maintain vigorous hope that "God is coming" (Col. 3:6) to judge the world "when Christ . . . is revealed [and] then you will also be revealed with him in glory" (3:4), when God will "gather up all things in [Christ], things in heaven and things on earth" (Eph. 1:10). God's saving rule in Christ is "not only [being realized] in this age" but will culminate "in the age to come" (1:20–21; cf. 3:7), at "the day of redemption" (4:30). In other words, Colossians and Ephesians reflect a tensive already/not yet view of God's kingdom. Even so, they tilt toward the "already" and refrain from temporizing the "not yet" as imminent. Now and *always*, "forever and ever," yes (3:21); now and *finally* in "the fullness of time" (1:10), yes. Now and *near*, not so much.

Deferred future hope, short or long, becomes less of a problem the more palpably believers experience union with the exalted Christ now. Not that the writers of Colossians and Ephesians claim with 2 Thessalonians 2:2 that "the day of Lord is already here." But they do accentuate believers' current participation

---

27. Welborn (*Paul's Summons*, 49–53) argues for a marked contrast between Paul's early eschatology in 1 Thessalonians and later view in Romans. Dunn (*Theology of Paul*, 310–13), however, maintains "a striking consistency" in Paul's overall perspective, amid different emphases appropriate to different personal and congregational contexts. Neither Welborn nor Dunn, it must be said, regards the *parousia's* delay as causing much angst for Paul and his people, whereas I think it was a bigger problem requiring negotiation.

28. Welborn, *Paul's Summons*, 55–60. The "other" (*heteron*), distinguished from "'neighbor' or 'brother,'" opens the door to consider the obligation to love believers beyond one's small circle." Jewett, *Romans*, 808.

in the crucified-and-risen Christ—internally and celestially, in human hearts and in heavenly heights. Though there remains "the hope laid up for you in heaven" (Col. 1:5), the living presence of "Christ in you" realizes "the hope of glory" (1:27) now. Through baptism, believers have already "put off the body of the flesh" with Christ, been "buried with him [and] also raised with him through faith in the power of God, who raised him from the dead" (2:11–12; cf. Rom. 6:1–11). Presently, this experience of dying and rising with/in Christ remains cryptic: "Your life is *hidden* [*kekryptai*] with Christ in God," waiting to "be revealed with [Christ] in glory" at the *parousia* (Col. 3:3–4; cf. 2:2–3). But "hidden" experience is no less real for being more personal than public, more mystical than empirical—and for anticipating full disclosure at Christ's ultimate coming/revealing.[29]

While Colossians refers to being raised "above" with Christ (Col. 3:1–2), Ephesians declares that God "made us alive together with Christ . . . and raised us up with him and seated us with him in the *heavenly places* in Christ Jesus" (Eph. 2:4–6; cf. 1:3). Though biblical literature commonly partitions the universe into the "earth/world below" and the "heavens/skies above," these are not isolated sectors hermetically sealed off from one another. There is plenty of overlapping middle ground between up and down; there is no clean-break relocation from earth to heaven in Christ. We live day by day on earth even as we enjoy fellowship with Christ "in the heavenly places" and wait with/in Christ for his climactic appearing. At the same time, we struggle on earth, here and now, with "spiritual forces of evil *in the heavenly places*" as they wreak havoc in the universe (6:12). We live *in between* times and places, ages and atmospheres.

James: Suffering and Supplicating

The letter of James was written to "dispersed/scattered" believers (James 1:1) undergoing various trials and hardships. Framing passages call for poor members to patiently endure the predations of the rich and powerful (1:2–18; 5:1–18).[30] Such perseverance is fueled by (1) the promise of eschatological (final) blessing for poor sufferers and judgment on rich oppressors and (2) the practice of ecclesial (communal) prayer.

29. Dunn (*Theology of Paul*, 313) takes Colossians to be Paul's letter and notes that here Paul's "expectation of Christ's final 'appearing' is as calm and confident as it ever was (Col. 3.4)."

30. "Blessed is anyone who endures" (1:12); "We call blessed those who showed endurance" (5:11); L. Johnson, *Letter of James*, 323.

Eschatological Promise

James first images the fate of evil rich persons in terms of a natural floral cycle. As the flower's momentary splendor fades and falls under the rising sun's "scorching heat," so the rich "will wither away," beginning now "in the midst of a busy life" and, by implication, culminating in final judgment (1:10–11). By contrast, the poor and "lowly" can look forward to "being raised up" and awarded "the crown of life that the Lord has promised" (1:9, 12). This "raising" includes the dual prospect of present healing by the risen Jesus (5:15)[31] and future "crowning" with eternal life (cf. Rev. 2:8–11).

With the imperative "Look! [*idou*]" (obscured in the NRSV), James's last chapter draws on the work of field hands and farmers to characterize both the oppressors and the oppressed. Note my translations:

> Look! The wages you [rich people] withheld from the workers who mowed your fields cry out to the Lord. (5:4)

> Look! The farmer waits patiently for the earth's crop [produced by] the early and late rains. (5:7)

The first text establishes the evidential ground "for the miseries that are coming to you [rich people]" in "the last days" as reprisals for defrauding the poor, whose cries for justice the Lord will soon answer (James 5:1, 3; cf. Luke 18:6–8). The second reinforces the poor's ground for hope at "the coming [*parousias*] of the Lord" (James 5:7, 8). As surely as the farmer knows that his diligent planting and cultivating, nurtured by seasonal rains, will yield a good harvest, so poor laborers may be assured that their hard toil will give way to blessed care by the "compassionate and merciful" Lord, whose "coming [*parousia*] is near" (5:7–11).

But all will not be perfect bliss at the Lord's coming, as two more instances of "Look!" underscore (again in my translation):

> Look! The judge stands at the gates. (5:9)

> Look! We who endure are blessed. (5:11)

The judge represents the soon-coming Lord Jesus, who stands near ("at the doors"; cf. Matt. 24:30–33), ready to stand in judgment not only against rich exploiters, most certainly (James 5:1–5), but also against poor sufferers, *if* they

---

31. Cf. Acts 3:6, 16; 4:9–12; 9:34; Bauckham, "James," 134–35.

continue to "grumble against one another" (5:9). But why would they do that when they have common foes to grumble about? A prevailing sense of helplessness under powerful thumbs can lead the oppressed to take out their pent-up frustrations on one another and even turn against each other in scrabbling for scarce resources.

Beyond that, they might also be tempted to grumble *against the Lord* for delaying to come and alleviate their chronic suffering, "a suffering more intense, it should be said," according to Luke Timothy Johnson, "because of the *cognitive dissonance* between the conviction that 'God opposes the arrogant' [James 4:6] and the experience that the arrogant [rich and powerful] condemn and murder the righteous ones [5:5–6]."[32] How long, O Lord, will you let these tyrants get away with murder? We need help now! Near doesn't seem nearly enough.

Still maintaining that Christ's relief-bringing return is at hand, James bolsters the call for believers to endure a little longer. One might wonder, however, whether the biblical prophets and Job are the best examples of "patience" and "endurance" James could muster (5:10–11). Not if his main aim is to urge readers to suffer in silence and serenity. The prophets and Job rail against unjust afflictions perpetrated by malevolent forces, seemingly endorsed by God in some cases, especially Job's. At least in the canonical story, God ultimately restores Job's health and fortune (though not his original lost loved ones) in this life (Job 42:10–17).

Some commentators distinguish between two terms—*hypomonē* ("endurance") and *makrothymia* ("patience")—James uses for perseverance: the former connotes a more passive resignation by mistreated underlings (*hypo* [under] + *monē* [stay]); the latter a more active resistance of harmful people and situations for an extended time ("long [*makro*]-suffering").[33] If these different shades of meaning apply in James, they are both approved as means of handling present hardships until Jesus comes. Moreover, if *hypomonē* tilts toward a passive, stoic endurance of suffering,[34] it does not suggest hapless capitulation. In ancient Greek literature, it was often associated with steely courage (*andreia*) under fire that inspired robust pushback. In the Hellenistic-Jewish writing known as 4 Maccabees, as the Greek-Syrian tyrant Antiochus IV tried to torture Jews into denouncing their heritage, he "saw the courage [*andreian*] of their virtue and their endurance

32. L. Johnson, *Letter of James*, 323 (emphasis added).
33. Hartin, *James*, 247–49; L. Johnson, *Letter of James*, 312–13.
34. Though such "patience" ill fits the canonical Job, it better suits the Hellenistic Testament of Job (e.g., Testament of Job 4:5–6; 27:3–7; Hartin, *James*, 245).

[*hypomonēn*] under the tortures . . . as an example [for his own soldiers'] endurance" and bravery in battle (17:23–24).[35]

ECCLESIAL PRAYER

As the patient endurance James urges in the challenging meantime before Christ's *parousia* is not resigned nihilism, it is also not rugged individualism. One can only persevere with others' help. James would concur with the counsel of Hebrews amid the "hard struggle with sufferings . . . and persecution" (Heb. 10:32–33) about "not neglecting to meet together, as is the habit of some, but encouraging one another, and all the more, as you see the Day approaching" (10:25). James spurs readers to come together in supportive *prayers of faith* for God's guiding wisdom, healing power, forgiving grace, and sustaining care (James 1:5–8; 5:13–18).

As James singles out Job's model patient endurance, he appeals to Elijah's exemplary "powerful and effective" prayer (James 5:16). Elijah's expected role as advance man for God's restored realm (Mal. 3:1–2; 4:5–6; Mark 9:11–13) fits James's sense of eschatological urgency. Yet James emphasizes not so much Elijah's end-time starring role as his ordinary supporting role in the economic and political life of ninth-century BCE Israel. James commends Elijah's effectual prayer: first for famine-producing drought (as judgment on Ahab and Jezebel's wicked rule) and then for fertilizing rains on the harvest-yielding earth (James 5:17–18; cf. 1 Kings 17:1; 18:1–2, 41–45). Again, James grounds hope of flourishing life in agrarian processes.

But how exactly is Elijah's control of notoriously wild weather phenomena normative for ordinary, vulnerable people? While specific climate "acts of God" may be beside the point for James, the praying Elijah proves relevant as "a human being like us," someone "of like-suffering [*homoiopathēs*]" (James 5:17). No sooner has Elijah bested 450 prophets of Baal and restored rain to the land (1 Kings 18:20–45) than he flees from Queen Jezebel's vengeful wrath, hides in the wilderness, and sinks into a state of lonely despair bordering on the suicidal (19:1–4). Buoyed by the Lord's angel, however, who tends to the prophet's needs for food and rest, Elijah journeys farther to Mount Horeb, where God personally addresses him, recommissions him for service, and assures him that he is not at all alone but can count on seven thousand colleagues who "have not bowed down to Baal" (19:18).

35. See Spencer, "Beyond Trench's Study," 142–43.

The great prophet Elijah is as subject to human frailty as anyone. Whether in Elijah's historic past days or in the present last days of intense affliction before Christ's *parousia*, God's people can only survive and thrive in the strength God provides through faithful prayer *with* fellow sufferers. Don't try this on your own!

Reset and Repent: The Petrine Challenge

The letters of 1–2 Peter are not as closely related as their designations suggest. Their purported authorship by the apostle Peter is disputed by scholars. A stronger case can be made for Peter's endorsement, if not composition, of the first letter, even with its lofty Greek style, which is thought to be beyond the ability of the fisherman from Galilee. The literary polish may have been provided by Silvanus, a "faithful brother" in Christ who served as Peter's secretary and emissary of this "short letter" (1 Pet. 5:12).[36]

Second Peter, however, though presented as Peter's "second letter I am writing to you" (2 Pet. 3:1), is notably distinct from the first in style, themes, and chronological orientation. Formulated as Peter's last will and testament drafted shortly before his death, the letter targets the period *"after* [Peter's] departure" so that his audience "may be able *at any time* to recall these things" (1:14–15). The main audience is the generation(s) after the deaths of Peter and fellow apostles (3:2; cf. 3:4, taking "ancestors" as apostle-fathers). How long after remains uncertain—but long enough for serious concerns to mount regarding Christ's delayed coming (3:3–13).[37]

Hope Commended amid Suffering in 1 Peter

Like James, Peter addresses scattered groups ("exiles of the Dispersion") of Christ-believing sufferers "tested" by "various trials" (1 Pet. 1:1, 6–7; cf. 4:12–19; James 1:1–4, 12; 5:7–11). Also like James, Peter advocates patient endurance until Jesus's imminent return: "even if now *for a little while* you have had to suffer, ... the end of all things is *near*" (1 Pet. 1:6; 4:7). Peter uses different language, however, opting to speak of Jesus's being "revealed" (*apokalypsei*, 1:7, 13; 4:13; cf. 5:1) rather than "coming" (*parousia*). In any case, Peter instills in his readers

36. See Powell, *Introducing the New Testament*, 480–86.
37. Harrington, "2 Peter," 237: "The date of the composition of 2 Peter has been placed almost everywhere between 60 and 160 C.E."; L. Johnson, *Writings of the New Testament*, 439: "Certainly 2 Peter is one of the last NT writings to be composed, but it could well have been written before the end of the first century."

a vibrant "living hope" rooted in Jesus's resurrection and impending glorious revelation and realization of the final "outcome [end, *telos*] of [their] faith, the salvation of [their] souls" (1:3–9, 13; 3:21–22; 4:13).

Yet, more than James, Peter accentuates the tension between present suffering and future blessing. Together with fellow elder-overseers of "the flock of God," Peter assumes a hybrid identity as both "witness [*martys*] of the sufferings of Christ" and "as one who shares [*koinōnos*] in the glory to be revealed" (1 Pet. 5:1–2). More specifically, he counterweights the uplifting message of joy and hope with a mandate to submit to "the authority of every human institution" (2:12) and thereby "follow in [Christ's] steps" of humble suffering (2:21). Peter focuses on long-standing political and familial institutions ruled by emperors, governors, masters, and husbands, who may use their authority for good or ill, care or abuse, of their subjects (2:13–3:7).

In this social context (see challenge 5), Peter goes so far as to give extra credit to Christian slaves who respectfully take unjust beatings from cruel masters, as Christ himself did on the cross (1 Pet. 2:18–24). He further advises "wives, *in the same way*, [to] accept the authority of [their] husbands," including unbelieving husbands, with an aim to win them to Christ through wifely "purity and reverence" and a "gentle and quiet spirit" (3:1–4). Nothing is said about politely taking a beating from violent husbands, but the slave analogy implies such submission. To be sure, believing husbands should "show consideration for [their] wives in [their] life together" (3:7), but the need to spell out this counsel suggests all-too-common "fear"-inducing (3:6) abuse by husband-overlords.

The pastoral Peter seems less inclined than Paul to spare his people undue household suffering in the short, already stressful time before Christ's return (cf. 1 Cor. 7:26–39). Though expecting salvation for the righteous and judgment for the wicked when Christ is "revealed in the last time" (1 Pet. 1:5), Peter also contends that "the time has come for judgment *to begin with the household of God*" (4:17), judgment executed by "Jesus Christ, who has [already] gone into heaven and is at the right hand of God, with angels, authorities, and powers [already] made subject to him" (3:21–22)[38] and who "stands ready to judge the living and the dead," believer and unbeliever (4:5–6). Peter would agree with James that Jesus "the Judge is standing at the doors" to hold both followers and foes to account for how they treat one another (James 5:9; cf. 1 Pet. 3:8–16). But

---

38. Contrast Paul's sequence in 1 Cor. 15:23–24: "But each in his own order: Christ the first fruits, *then at his coming* those who belong to Christ. *Then comes the end*, when he hands over the kingdom to God the Father, *after* he has destroyed every ruler and every authority and power."

Peter's criterion for judgment based on believers' submission to volatile earthly authorities pushes to the edges of New Testament thought.

Hope Defended against Scoffers in 2 Peter

Ancient testamentary literature, presented as an honored elder's farewell address, customarily included a defense of his character and lifework along with a bestowal of blessings and warnings on his descendants.[39] Anticipating his imminent death, the "Peter" of this second letter reminds his people of his faithful ministry and confirms the truth of his "prophetic message" in "ma[king] known to [them] the power and coming [*parousian*] of our Lord Jesus Christ" (2 Pet. 1:16, 19).

The *parousia* highlighted here, however, is a *past* event that Peter personally witnessed: the luminous *transfiguration* of the earthly Jesus "on the holy mountain," where "he received honor and glory from God the Father" (2 Pet. 1:17–18). According to Gospel accounts, Peter proposes building three tents on the mountain, one each for Jesus, Moses, and Elijah, the latter two figures appearing with Jesus in an engulfing cloud (Matt. 17:1–8; Mark 9:2–8; Luke 9:28–36). Though Peter is overwhelmed and doesn't know what to say (Mark 9:6), his tent-building proposal probably reflects his desire to enshrine the epiphany. He may well have been thinking that this stunning event signaled the consummation of God's rule, since a few days before Jesus announced that "there are some standing here who will not taste death until they see that the kingdom has come with power" (9:1).

So this is it, right? The culmination of God's glorious realm. The end of death. No more putting off mortal earthly body tents; time to dwell in eternal heavenly tents (cf. Luke 16:9; 2 Cor. 5:1–5). Not exactly. The transfiguration sets the stage for finalizing God's kingdom but does not finish the drama. The majestic vision dissolves as suddenly as it appeared, leaving Jesus and Peter (with two other disciples) to resume their earthly business. As they descend the mountain, Jesus makes clear that he is still destined "to go through many sufferings" (Mark 9:12); and just before the transfiguration, he confirms his climactic "com[ing] in the glory of his Father with the holy angels" (8:38; cf. 13:26–27; 14:62).[40] In short, Jesus's temporary transfiguration *prefigures* his resurrection, exaltation, and reappearance. Fulfillment is yet to come.

---

39. See Gurtner, *Introducing the Pseudepigrapha*, 165–66; Kolenkow, "Literary Genre"; J. Collins, "Testamentary Literature."

40. No angels attend the transfiguration.

This brings us back to the "Peter" persona of 2 Peter, who knows that the transfiguration is *not* Jesus's final *parousia*. Peter expects to die soon, to "put off [his] tent," as he literally states in 2 Peter 1:14. He must wait, along with those who survive him, "until the day dawns and the morning star rises" (1:19). As Daniel Harrington notes, this day "must allude to the Day of the Lord, which involves the *parousia*, the general resurrection, and the Last Judgment."[41] The "morning star" likely refers to the coming Jesus (see Rev. 2:28; 22:16).

Peter's audience of "exiles," however, are experiencing a severe crisis of confidence in Christ's return, sparked by an internal group of "false prophets" (2 Pet. 2:1), who scoff at the foolhardy hope that Christ will put the world to rights after all this delay—not just since Christ's and the apostles' deaths—but "from the beginning of creation!" (3:4). If wicked behavior and worldly business keep humming along as usual, why expect Christ suddenly to come to the rescue? Why not join the party and get what you can while you can?

Peter mounts his case against these dissonant, distressing scoffers on three grounds: historical precedent, temporal perspective, and moral purpose.

HISTORICAL PRECEDENT

The scoffers have a selective memory to serve their indulgent interests. In their superficial appeal to human history, they have conveniently forgotten two major acts of divine judgment against evildoers: the flood that devastated the violence-filled world in Noah's day and the fire that destroyed the rapacious citizens of Sodom and Gomorrah in Lot's day. Only Noah, Lot, and a few family members were spared (2 Pet. 2:4–10; 3:5–6; cf. Gen. 6:11–13, 18; 19:15–29; 1 Pet. 3:20; Jude 7).

The wicked populations in Noah's and Lot's eras were oblivious to censorious prophets of doom and blithely assumed they could keep operating with impunity. Thus, Peter argues, this business-as-usual mentality, contemptuous of naysayers, is in fact a *historical sign* that divine reckoning is at hand, that the day of the Lord, at once redemptive and retributive, is near. In this belief, Peter mirrors Jesus's view of God's coming kingdom "on the day that the Son of Man is revealed," based on the prototypical days of Noah and Lot (Luke 17:22–30). Peter also invokes the image of the Lord's coming "like a thief" (2 Pet. 3:10) that we've seen in other New Testament writings. Jesus will soon come to secure his faithful suffering people and shatter the scoffers' false security.

41. Harrington, "2 Peter," 257.

Temporal Perspective

It's well and good for Peter to refer to ancient biblical history. But there remains the persisting dilemma of Jesus's *parousia* being delayed since his resurrection and ascension. What is God waiting for? More prolonged suffering for believers, so they will be more grateful when finally rescued? That's a cynical option, and Peter doesn't go there. Instead, he accounts for the extended delay on temporal and moral grounds.

On the temporal side, Peter employs a cognitive strategy to deal with cognitive dissonance. You correct wrong thinking by right thinking—in this case, by right thinking about time: "But do not ignore this one fact, beloved, that with the Lord one day is like a thousand years, and a thousand years are like one day" (2 Pet. 3:8). So, one day equals one thousand years? Seems more like myth than math—more like one of those "cleverly devised myths" of the scoffers (1:16). But Peter argues from a different chronology. He adopts the Creator's eternal cosmic perspective, holding together all history from beginning to end as a dynamic whole compressed into one pregnant moment, with "end" conceived as *telos* (completion, fulfillment), not *terminus* (depletion, curtailment). Though Peter envisions an incendiary apocalyptic agenda in which at "the coming of the day of God . . . the heavens [and earth] will be set ablaze and dissolved," this is not THE END but rather the transition to a new beginning: "In accordance with [God's] promise, we wait for *new heavens and a new earth*, where righteousness is at home" (3:12–13).

And whether we wait a day, a year, or one-thousand-plus years makes no difference to God, as the psalmist whom Peter paraphrases extolled (Ps. 90:4). Not that God is indifferent to human experience. Far from it: "Lord, you have been our dwelling place [or refuge] in all generations . . . from everlasting to everlasting" (90:1–2). Still, we suffer daily and die after seventy or eighty years, if we're lucky (90:9–10), and we naturally wonder "how long" this hard life-and-death cycle will persist (90:13). Just one day of chronic pain can feel like an eternity to us mortals, and a thousand years hardly registers as real.

So what's the point? Are we meant to just wait indefinitely for Jesus to return when God says it's time—a time we cannot hope to fathom (cf. Eccles. 3:9–11)? The psalmist doesn't stay in the theoretical clouds but brings the matter down to earth with timely wisdom for joyful and useful living throughout our days:

> So teach us to count our days
>   that we may gain a wise heart. . . .
> Satisfy us in the morning with your steadfast love,
>   so that we may rejoice and be glad all our days. (Ps. 90:12, 14; cf. v. 15)

Although the writer of 2 Peter doesn't quote this part of Psalm 90, he takes the same practical angle as the psalmist does on full and faithful life here and now, for however short or long God allows. Instead of quibbling about time, Peter exhorts his readers to concentrate on "what sort of persons [you ought] to be in leading lives of holiness and godliness" (2 Pet. 3:11).[42] He even hints that we can "hasten the coming of the day of God" through such virtuous living (3:12).[43] At any rate, God runs the clock; we have more than enough challenge running our lives.

MORAL PERSPECTIVE

The emphasis on model daily living in advance of Jesus's coming establishes a key moral principle. Eschatology, ethics, and evangelism coalesce and go a long way in 2 Peter toward mitigating the temporal problem of the delayed *parousia*. God has a clear reason for extending earthly history. God is not inherently "slow" to move, like a huge ship changing course, but intentionally "patient" to give maximum time for people to "come to repentance" and change their courses before judgment day (3:9). God takes no delight in condemning the wicked but rather desires not only that "you" believers not veer from the right way but that "all" sinners, including scoffers, change their hearts, minds, and lives in the extended time God allots (3:9).

Again, God's being slow to judge does not mean God is soft on sin or disinclined, either by disinterest or by indulgent disposition, to execute justice and righteousness. But the just and righteous God abounds in mercy and compassion (Exod. 34:6–7; Ps. 103:6–8). The heart of God holds these virtues in dynamic tension. As Paul writes in Romans, "We know that God's judgment . . . is in accordance with truth. Do you imagine . . . you will escape the judgment of God? Or do you despise the riches of his kindness and forbearance and patience? Do you not realize that God's kindness is meant to lead you to repentance?" (Rom. 2:2–4).[44]

Though Peter does not quote Paul, he affirms "our beloved brother Paul" and the "wisdom" he conveys "in all his letters," especially concerning "the patience of our Lord as salvation" (2 Pet. 3:15–16). While characteristically both just and merciful, God temporally tilts toward mercy. God punishes as last resort, not first response. Final judgment is surely coming soon (2:9; 3:7) but not as soon as suffering believers might like.

42. See L. Johnson, *Writings of the New Testament*, 443.
43. Cf. Sir. 36:10; G. Green, *Jude and 2 Peter*, 333–34.
44. See Donelson, *I & II Peter*, 275.

In the meantime, believers should keep reaching out to unbelievers, hoping to win them to Christ's true way through their "lives of holiness and godliness" (2 Pet. 3:11). This challenge harks back to 1 Peter's exhorting Christian wives to convert unbelieving husbands via the "the purity and reverence of your lives" (1 Pet. 3:1–2), though it should be noted that 2 Peter does not associate godly living with submission to ungodly patriarchs. As they "wait" (repeated three times in 3:12–14) for Christ's coming, believers must tend to their own characters, "striv[ing] to be found by him at peace, without spot or blemish" (3:14). Such faithful living in the interim may spur others to repentance and redemption, thereby speeding the Lord's return and lessening the numbers of condemned sinners (3:11–12).

Epilogue

Streaming the Good News

Having explored seven challenges that shaped the New Testament writings, we may now ask, "What were these writings shaped into?" Or "How did these writers answer the challenges?" "Shaping" implies a final, finished product, like a honey jar or soup bowl a potter molds out of clay; and "answer" suggest a definitive yes/no, true/false response: "Is this car new or used? Oh, it's used, a 2019 model with 34,000 miles and a small dent in the bumper. It's all here in the CARFAX report."

But that's not how literary works work. It's not how the New Testament works. Yes, we have the finished product of a twenty-seven-volume canon (as finished as textual critics can reconstruct the documents). But the writings are more fluid and open-ended than the notion of a "product" might suggest.

To return to the pottery image, a biblical one in fact, Jeremiah envisioned a potter "working at his wheel. The vessel he was making of clay was spoiled in the potter's hand, and he reworked it into another vessel, as seemed good to him" (Jer. 18:3–4). In this picture, the potter represents God shaping the covenant people of Judah (reminiscent of God forming the first human from the earth in Gen. 2:7). The people, however, become "spoiled" in God's hands, as they do not perfectly yield to God's creative plan. Rather than discarding them, however, and starting over with a new batch, God *re*works, *re*shapes the people "as seemed good to him" (though Jeremiah is not optimistic about their compliance). The "clay"-creations bear the marks of their marring and scarring like the eponymous Israel, who limped from a dislocated hip-and-thigh after his intense wrestling match with God (Gen. 32:22–32), and like the apostle Paul, who struggled in his fragile-yet-flourishing "clay jar" life, "always carrying in the body the death of Jesus, so that the life of Jesus may also be made visible in our bodies" (2 Cor. 4:10). God's dynamic handiwork works *with* earthly materials, cracks and all, to work *out* God's good purpose "as it seems good to him." God does not work magic but rather *manufactures* in ongoing creative processes.

Thus we may imagine the New Testament writings as coscripted by God and Christ-believers, "co-potters" co-processing the impact of the explosive events of Christ's life, death, resurrection, and ascension on the world, past, present, and future. To extend the metaphor, as water is needed to make the clay pliable and purposeful, so the living water of God's Spirit (John 3:5; 7:38–39) lubricates New Testament formation and interpretation. Again, I stress the open-ended forma-tive, interpretive process. Jeremiah's description of God's persistent remolding of the people "as it seemed good to him" finds a notable echo in Acts' assessment of the apostles' decision, codified in an "official" letter, to accept uncircumcised Gentile believers: "It has seemed good to the Holy Spirit and to us" (Acts 15:28).

Acts and other New Testament writings attest to the need for continuing spiri-tual discernment. Several books do not so much end as break off in anticipation of further action and reflection.

- Mark's most likely original "ending" leaves everything hanging with the women, assigned to inform the male apostles of a future reunion with the risen Jesus in Galilee, fleeing in fear from Jesus's empty tomb (Mark 16:8). Though their report clearly gets out and inspires Mark and other Gospel writers, Mark opts not to narrate any post-resurrection rendezvous, as if to invite readers to remain open to fresh, challenging encounters with Christ.

- Acts "ends" by reporting Paul's continued preaching about God's rule in Christ "without hindrance [or unhinderedly, *akōlytōs*]"—literally the last word in Acts—encouraging readers to keep believing and proclaiming Christ even under duress (Acts 28:31). Though Acts was written years after Paul's death, the narrative breaks off with Paul's unhindered mission under house arrest, as if nothing, including death, can truly arrest the gospel of Christ.

- Paul's letters frequently close with future plans. In Romans, for example, he reports, "But now, with no further place for me in these regions, I desire, as I have for many years, to come to you when I go to Spain. For I do hope to see you on my journey and be sent on by you. . . . At present, however, I am going to Jerusalem in a ministry to the saints" (15:23–25). Paul made it to Jerusalem and Rome, with difficulties at every turn, but never made it out of Rome to Spain or anywhere else. Yet Paul's message of Christ, richly expounded in the Roman letter, reached Spain and is still preached there today and across the world.

- Revelation closes the New Testament canon with audacious tension. On one hand, it jealously guards its final authority, issuing vehement curses against anyone who dares add to or subtract "from the words . . . described in this book" (22:18–19). All that Revelation unveils it tightly reseals: an open-and-shut case! Yet at the same time it looks out and ahead to what is to come—more specifically *who* is to come, the dynamic "Lord God, who is and who was and who is to come" (1:8): "The one who testifies to these things says, 'Surely I am coming soon.' Amen. Come, Lord Jesus!" (22:20).

The New Testament writings proclaim Christ not so much as the "be all and end all" as the "*being* all and *ending* all" or, better, the "beginning(s) of the end(s),"[1] beginning again and again—in fits and starts, leaps and bounds—in flow with the God of creative beginnings from "the beginning" (Gen. 1:1). In challenge 1, we noted how all four New Testament Gospels, in distinctive ways, begin their stories of Christ midstream, as it were, in continuity with the beginnings of God's work narrated in the Hebrew Bible/Old Testament.

We may further reprise challenge 1 ("Old and New: The Historical Challenge of Innovation and Evolution") as exemplary of the big picture encompassing all the challenging "big ideas" of the New Testament writings. This corpus was substantially shaped amid tensions that arose between older forms of Jewish biblical tradition and newer developments in Christ. While the writings negotiate these tensions in different ways, they do so out of a broadly shared commitment to *extension* and *evolution*, not extinction and evasion, of that "old-time religion." Jesus's *extending* Torah in the Sermon on the Mount, not abolishing or proposing "antitheses" to it (Matt. 5:17–48), provides a basic pattern followed throughout the New Testament.

Recent studies in cognitive science, neuropsychology, and cosmology shed further light on dealing with tensions between the Testaments and within the New Testament. Increasing attention has been given to "the extended mind."[2] Liberating the mind from strict confinement to "brain-bound" matter, cognitive

---

1. Cf. Moltmann, *In the End*.
2. Paul, *Extended Mind*; Siegel, *Mind*, 10–16, 33–41, 46–48; Clark and Chalmers, "Extended Mind"; Slaby, "Emotions."

researchers have explored more "extensive," complex networks of thought, feeling, and action between the entire sensing body and the external environment,
especially other embodied persons. As Annie Murphy Paul states, "We think with
our bodies, our spaces, and our relationships. . . . Elements of the world outside
may act as mental 'extensions,' allowing us to think in ways our brains could not
manage on their own."[3]

As the mind extends in space, inward and outward, it also extends in time,
backward and forward, through memory and prospection. Remembering is not
simple clerical retrieval but complex, creative re-membering: reconfiguring past
events in varying degrees of precision that affect our present perceptions and
future prospects in a vibrant stream of thought-and-feeling. According to the
neuropsychologist Antonio Damasio, the shape and force of these memory images "depends on how much emotion and feeling were generated by their traversal
in the stream of our mind." The more intensely "refined" the memory, the more
potential it has for coloring and clashing with current reality: "Sometimes the
recollection of the old material is so refined that it even competes with the new
material now being generated."[4] In other words, emotional upheaval and cognitive dissonance extend or "expand" (Damasio's term) cherished older concepts
in new directions.

If anything can be said of the New Testament writers and other reform-minded
Jewish groups like the Pharisees, it is that they were passionately engaged in the
history of God's dealings with Israel and the world from "the beginning," as interpreted in biblical law, prophecy, and other writings. The New Testament authors
never dreamed of jettisoning the "old" faith as they embraced Christ's "new"
revelation. Their only options were to adapt, select, extend, and evolve with and
from the "old." To be sure, theirs was not an inevitable or purely "natural" evolution. Many Pharisees and other Jews extended their spiritual minds in directions
not centered on Jesus Christ; and a few New Testament writings teetered on the
edge of replacing Judaism, even as many subsequent Christians have gone over
the anti-Jewish cliff, canceling their old subscription. But overall, the New Testament reflects thoughtful, respectful, heartfelt evolution of the faiths of Abraham,
Moses, David, Solomon, Isaiah, and others in new ways forged by Christ.[5]

3. Paul, *Extended Mind*, x–xi. More formally, she designates three areas of mind extension: embodied
cognition ("interoception" throughout the body), situated cognition (in the environment), and distrib-
uted cognition (through social relationships).

4. Damasio, *Strange Order*, 93; see the whole chapter "Expanding Minds," 84–98.

5. Debates persist about the nature and extent of intentional anti-Judaism within the New Testament.
See, e.g., Donaldson, *Jews and Anti-Judaism*; Fredriksen and Reinhartz, *Jesus*.

While scientists, philosophers, and theologians continue to debate fine points of evolution, they generally accept that "evolution is a process marked by novelty, creativity, and future; new entities rise up out of the old as elements become more complex and converge."[6] It's all about *movement* or *motion* across time and space. As Barbara Tversky dramatically puts it, "Everything is always in motion. Physicists tell us that if the quivering molecules in your desk moved in sync, the desk would leap from the floor. Even sedentary plants grow and sway and turn toward the sun and open and close. They have to; they would die if they didn't move." Moreover, "Thought, too, is constantly moving, and sometimes hard to catch. Ideas leapfrog over ideas. . . . From the never-ceasing flux around us, we carve entities out of space and out of time: people, places, things, and events. We freeze them, turn them into words and concepts."[7] But these new thoughts melded out of older materials—together with (e)motions that motivate ideas and actions—melt into the stream of the creative universe. "The things that we create (like these words) stay there, in space, changing the thought of people we will never know and can't even imagine."[8]

We may thus picture the New Testament writings as live-streaming networks of the Jesus *movement*, broadcasting an array of thoughts and feelings, convictions and tensions concerning Jesus's dynamic, apocalyptic impact in the world. Remarkably, their witness continues to resound through time and space, affecting and "changing the thought of people"—like us—in ways the New Testament writers could never imagine.

6. Delio, *Unbearable Wholeness*, 18–19.
7. Tversky, *Mind in Motion*, 1.
8. Tversky, *Mind in Motion*, 2.

Bibliography

Allison, Dale C., Jr. *The New Moses: A Matthean Typology*. Eugene, OR: Wipf & Stock, 2013.

Anderson, Gary A. *Charity: The Place of the Poor in the Biblical Tradition*. New Haven: Yale University Press, 2013.

Anderson, Robert T. *The Samaritan Pentateuch: An Introduction to Its Origin, History, and Significance for Biblical Studies*. Atlanta: Society of Biblical Literature, 2012.

Anderson, Robert T., and Terry Giles. *The Keepers: An Introduction to the History and Culture of the Samaritans*. Peabody, MA: Hendrickson, 2002.

Applebaum, Anne. *Twilight of Democracy: The Seductive Lure of Authoritarianism*. New York: Doubleday, 2020.

Aristotle. *De Anima*. Translated with Introduction and Notes by C. D. C Reeve. Indianapolis: Hackett, 2017.

_____. *On Generation and Corruption*. Translated by H. H. Joachim. Internet Classics Archive. http://classics.mit.edu/Aristotle/gener_corr.html.

———. *On Rhetoric: A Theory on Civic Discourse*. Translated by George A. Kennedy. 2nd ed. New York: Oxford University Press, 2007.

Aronson, Elliot, and Carol Tavris. "The Role of Cognitive Dissonance in the Pandemic." *The Atlantic*, July 12, 2020. https://www.theatlantic.com/ideas/archive/2020/07/role -cognitive-dissonance-pandemic/614074/.

Barclay, John M. G. "Crucifixion as Wisdom: Exploring the Ideology of a Disreputable Social Movement." In *The Wisdom and Foolishness of God: First Corinthians 1–2 in Theological Exploration*, edited by Christophe Chalamet and Hans-Christoph Askani, 1–20. Minneapolis: Fortress, 2015.

———. *Paul and the Power of Grace*. Grand Rapids: Eerdmans, 2020.

Barrett, Lisa Feldman. *Seven and a Half Lessons about the Brain*. Boston: Houghton Mifflin Harcourt, 2020.

Barrett, Lisa Feldman, Michael Lewis, and Jeannette M. Haviland-Jones, eds. *Handbook of Emotions*. 4th ed. New York: Guilford, 2018.

Bartlett, David L. "Adoption in the Bible." In *The Child in the Bible*, edited by Marcia J. Bunge, Terence E. Fretheim, and Beverly Roberts Gaventa, 375–98. Grand Rapids: Eerdmans, 2008.

Bateman, Herbert W., ed. *Four Views on the Warning Passages in Hebrews*. Grand Rapids: Kregel, 2007.

Bauckham, Richard. "James and Jesus." In *The Brother of Jesus: James the Just and His Mission*, edited by Bruce Chilton and Jacob Neusner, 100–135. Louisville: Westminster John Knox, 2001.

Bauer, Walter, F. W. Danker, W. F. Arndt, and F. W. Gingrich. *Greek-English Lexicon of the New Testament and Other Early Christian Literature*. 3rd ed. Chicago: University of Chicago Press, 2000.

Beal, Timothy. *The Book of Revelation: A Biography*. Lives of Great Religious Books. Princeton: Princeton University Press, 2018.

Beck, Julie. "The Christmas the Aliens Didn't Come: What a Failed Doomsday Prophecy Taught Psychologists about the Nature of Belief." *The Atlantic*, December 18, 2015. https://www.theatlantic.com/health/archive/2015/12/the-christmas-the-aliens-didnt-come/421122/.

Ben-Ghiat, Ruth. *Strongmen: Mussolini to the Present*. New York: Norton, 2020.

Berger, Peter, and Anton Zijderveld. *In Praise of Doubt: How to Have Convictions without Becoming a Fanatic*. New York: HarperOne, 2009.

Blackwell, Ben C., John K. Goodrich, and Jason Maston, eds. *Paul and the Apocalyptic Imagination*. Minneapolis: Fortress, 2016.

Borg, Marcus J. *Speaking Christian: Why Christian Words Have Lost Their Power and How They Can Be Restored*. New York: HarperOne, 2011.

Bowden, Anna M. V. "Getting Jesus off the Altar: Undoing Atonement Readings in Revelation." *Rev&Exp* 118 (2021): 54–61.

Brown, Raymond E. *The Community of the Beloved Disciple*. New York: Paulist Press, 1979.

Brown, William P. *The Seven Pillars of Creation: The Bible, Science, and the Ecology of Wonder*. New York: Oxford University Press, 2010.

Brueggemann, Walter. *Sabbath as Resistance: Saying No to the Culture of Now*. Rev. ed. Louisville: Westminster John Knox, 2017.

Buber, Martin. *I and Thou*. Translated by Walter Kaufmann. New York: Scribner's Sons, 1970.

Burge, Gary M. *The Anointed Community: The Holy Spirit in the Johannine Tradition*. Grand Rapids: Eerdmans, 1987.

Burke, Trevor J. *Adopted into God's Family: Exploring a Pauline Metaphor*. New Studies in Biblical Theology 22. Downers Grove, IL: IVP Academic, 2006.

Burridge, Richard A. *Four Gospels, One Jesus: A Symbolic Reading*. 3rd ed. Grand Rapids: Eerdmans, 2014.

Camus, Albert. *The Myth of Sisyphus, and Other Essays*. Translated by Justin O'Brien. 1955. Reprint, New York: Vintage International, 1991.

Caputo, John D. *Hoping against Hope: Confessions of a Postmodern Pilgrim*. Minneapolis: Fortress, 2015.

———. *Specters of God: An Anatomy of the Apophatic Imagination*. Bloomington: Indiana University Press, 2022.

———. *The Weakness of God: A Theology of the Event*. Bloomington: Indiana University Press, 2006.

Carey, Greg. *Death, the End of History, and Beyond: Eschatology in the Bible*. Interpretation. Louisville: Westminster John Knox, 2023.

———. *Faithful & True: A Study Guide to the Book of Revelation*. Cleveland: Pilgrim, 2022.

———. *Ultimate Things: An Introduction to Jewish and Christian Apocalyptic Literature*. St. Louis: Chalice, 2005.

Carey, Holly J. "Traditio-Historical Criticism." In *Hearing the New Testament: Strategies for Interpretation*, edited by Joel B. Green, 102–21. 2nd ed. Grand Rapids: Eerdmans, 2010.

Carter, Warren. *Mark*. Wisdom Commentary 42. Collegeville, MN: Liturgical Press, 2019.

———. *Matthew and Empire: Initial Explorations*. Harrisburg, PA: Trinity Press International, 2001.

———. *Seven Events That Shaped the New Testament World*. Grand Rapids: Baker Academic, 2013.

Claassens, L. Juliana M. *Mourner, Mother, Midwife: Reimagining God's Delivering Presence in the Old Testament*. Louisville: Westminster John Knox, 2012.

Clark, Andy, and David Chalmers. "The Extended Mind." *Analysis* 58 (1998): 7–19.

Cobb, John B., Jr. *Salvation: Jesus's Mission and Ours*. Anoka, MN: Process Century, 2020.

Collins, Adela Yarbro. *Paul Transformed: Reception of the Person and Letters of Paul in Antiquity*. The Anchor Yale Bible Reference Library. New Haven: Yale University Press, 2022.

Collins, John J. *The Apocalyptic Imagination: An Introduction to Jewish Apocalyptic Literature*. 3rd ed. Grand Rapids: Eerdmans, 2016.

———. "The Testamentary Literature in Recent Scholarship." In *Early Judaism and Its Modern Interpreters*, edited by Robert A. Kraft and George W. E. Nickelsburg, 268–85. The Bible and Its Modern Interpreters. Atlanta: Scholars Press, 1986.

———. "The Transformation of Aseneth." In *Bodies, Borders, Believers: Ancient Texts and Present Conversations*, edited by Anne Hege Grung, Marianne Bjeland Kartzow, and Anna Rebecca Solevåg, 93–98. Eugene, OR: Pickwick, 2015.

Cone, James H. *The Cross and the Lynching Tree*. Maryknoll, NY: Orbis Books, 2011.

Conzelmann, Hans. *The Theology of St. Luke*. Translated by Geoffrey Buswell. London: SCM, 1960.

Costandi, Moheb. *Neuroplasticity*. Cambridge: MIT Press, 2016.

Crossan, John Dominic, and Jonathan L. Reid. *In Search of Paul: How Jesus's Apostle Opposed Rome's Empire with God's Kingdom*. New York: HarperSanFrancisco, 2004.

Damasio, Antonio. *The Strange Order of Things: Life, Feeling, and the Making of Cultures*. New York: Pantheon, 2018.

Danker, Frederick W., with Kathryn Krug. *The Concise Greek-English Lexicon of the New Testament*. Chicago: University of Chicago Press, 2009.

Darr, Katherine Pfisterer. "The Book of Ezekiel." In *The New Interpreter's Bible*, edited by Leander E. Keck et al., 6:1075–1607. Nashville: Abingdon, 2001.

Davis, Ellen F. *Biblical Prophecy: Perspectives for Christian Theology, Discipleship, and Ministry.* Interpretation. Louisville: Westminster John Knox, 2014.

Delio, Ilia. *Christ in Evolution.* Maryknoll, NY: Orbis Books, 2008.

———. *Making All Things New: Catholicity, Cosmology, Consciousness.* Maryknoll, NY: Orbis Books, 2015.

———. *The Unbearable Wholeness of Being: God, Evolution, and the Power of Love.* Maryknoll, NY: Orbis Books, 2013.

Dermendzhiyskais, Elitsa. "Feeling, In Situ." *Aeon*, October 8, 2021. https://aeon.co/essays/what-if-emotions-arent-universal-but-specific-to-each-culture.

Descartes, René. *The Passions of the Soul.* Translated by Stephen H. Vos. Indianapolis: Hackett, 1989. First published 1649.

deSilva, David A. *Despising Shame: Honor Discourse and Community Maintenance in the Epistle to the Hebrews.* 2nd ed. Studies in Biblical Literature. Atlanta: Society of Biblical Literature, 2008.

———. *The Hope of Glory: Honor Discourse and New Testament Interpretation.* Collegeville, MN: Liturgical Press, 1999.

DeSteno, David. *How God Works: The Science behind the Benefits of Religion.* New York: Simon & Schuster, 2021.

Dodd, C. H. *The Interpretation of the Fourth Gospel.* Cambridge: Cambridge University Press, 1953.

Donaldson, Terence L. *Jews and Anti-Judaism in the New Testament: Decision Points and Divergent Interpretations.* Waco: Baylor University Press, 2010.

Donelson, Lewis R. *I & II Peter and Jude.* NTL. Louisville: Westminster John Knox, 2010.

Donne, John. *Selections of Divine Poems, Sermons, Devotions, and Prayers.* Edited by John Booty. Classics of Western Spirituality. Mahwah, NJ: Paulist Press, 1990.

Downs, David J. "Economics, Taxes, and Tithes." In *The World of the New Testament: Cultural, Social, and Historical Contexts*, edited by Joel B. Green and Lee Martin MacDonald, 156–68. Grand Rapids: Baker Academic, 2013.

———. *The Offering of the Gentiles: Paul's Collection for Jerusalem in Its Chronological, Cultural, and Cultic Contexts.* Grand Rapids: Eerdmans, 2016.

———. "Physical Weakness, Illness and Death in 1 Corinthians 11.30: Deprivation and Overconsumption in Pauline and Early Christianity." *NTS* 65 (2019): 572–88.

Dunn, James D. G. *The Theology of Paul the Apostle.* Grand Rapids: Eerdmans, 1998.

———. *Unity and Diversity in the New Testament: An Inquiry into the Character of Earliest Christianity.* 3rd ed. London: SCM, 2006. First published 1977.

Dyer, Bryan R. "'All of These Died in Faith': Hebrews 11 and Faith in the Face of Death." *CBQ* 83 (2021): 638–54.

———. *Suffering in the Face of Death: The Social Context of the Epistle to the Hebrews.* Library of New Testament Studies 568. London: Bloomsbury T&T Clark, 2017.

Eisenbaum, Pamela. "The Letter to the Hebrews." In *The Jewish Annotated New Testament: New Revised Standard Version*, edited by Amy-Jill Levine and Marc Zvi Brettler, 460–88. 2nd ed. New York: Oxford University Press, 2011.

Eklund, Rebekah. *Practicing Lament*. Cascade Companions. Eugene, OR: Cascade Books, 2021.

Emerson, Ralph Waldo. "Self-Reliance." 1841. Reproduced as a PDF by Peter Doyle, University of Dartmouth. https://math.dartmouth.edu/~doyle/docs/self/self.pdf.

Erdrich, Louise. *The Night Watchman*. New York: HarperCollins, 2020.

———. *The Round House*. New York: HarperCollins, 2012.

Evans, Craig A. "Prophet, Paul as." In *Dictionary of Paul and His Letters*, edited by Gerald F. Hawthorne, Ralph P. Martin, and Daniel G. Reid, 762–65. Downers Grove, IL: InterVarsity, 1993.

Evans, Craig A., and Aaron W. White, eds. *Who Created Christianity? Fresh Approaches to the Relationship between Paul and Jesus*. Carol Stream, IL: Tyndale, 2020.

Feldman, Louis H. *Jew & Gentile in the Ancient World*. Princeton: Princeton University Press, 1993.

Feldman, Louis H., and Meyer Reinhold, eds. *Jewish Life and Thought among Greeks and Romans: Primary Readings*. Minneapolis: Fortress, 1996.

Ferber, Ilit, and Paula Schwebel, eds. *Lament in Jewish Thought: Philosophical, Theological, and Literary Perspectives*. Berlin: de Gruyter, 2014.

Festinger, Leon, Henry W. Reicken, and Stanley Schachter. *When Prophecy Fails: A Social and Psychological Study of a Modern Group That Predicted the Destruction of the World*. Mansfield Centre, CT: Martino, 2009. First published 1956.

Foer, Jonathan Safran. *Extremely Loud and Incredibly Close*. Boston: Houghton Mifflin, 2005.

Fontaine, Johnny J. R., and Klaus R. Scherer. "Emotion Is for Doing: The Action Tendency Component." In *Components of Emotional Meaning: A Sourcebook*, edited by Johnny J. R. Fontaine, Klaus R. Scherer, and Cristina Soriano, 170–85. Series in Affective Science. Oxford: Oxford University Press, 2013.

Foster, Paul. "Vespasian, Nerva, Jesus and the *Fiscus Judaicus*." In *Israel's God and Rebecca's Children*, edited by David B. Capes, April D. DeConick, Helen K. Bond, and Troy Miller, 303–20. Waco: Baylor University Press, 2007.

Fredriksen, Paula. *Paul: The Pagans' Apostle*. New Haven: Yale University Press, 2017.

———. "Paul, the Perfectly Righteous Pharisee." In *The Pharisees*, edited by Joseph Sievers and Amy-Jill Levine, 112–35. Grand Rapids: Eerdmans, 2021.

Fredriksen, Paula, and Adele Reinhartz, eds. *Jesus, Judaism, and Christian Anti-Judaism: Reading the New Testament after the Holocaust*. Louisville: Westminster John Knox, 2002.

Fretheim, Terence E. *God and World in the Old Testament: A Relational Theology of Creation*. Nashville: Abingdon, 2005.

Friesen, Steven J. "Poverty in Pauline Studies: Beyond the So-Called New Consensus." *JSNT* 26 (2004): 323–61.

Frijda, Nico H., and Batja Mesquita. "The Analysis of Emotions: Dimensions of Variation." In *What Develops in Emotional Development?*, edited by Michael F. Mascolo and Sharon Griffin, 273–95. New York: Plenum, 2013.

Gale, Aaron M. "The Gospel according to Matthew." In *The Jewish Annotated New Testament: New Revised Standard Version*, edited by Amy-Jill Levine and Marc Zvi Brettler, 9–66. 2nd ed. New York: Oxford University Press, 2011.

Garland, David E. "The Temple Tax in Matthew 17:24–25 and the Principle of Not Causing Offense." In *Treasures New and Old: Contributions to Matthean Studies*, edited by David R. Bauer and Mark Allan Powell, 69–98. SBL Symposium Series 1. Atlanta: Scholars Press, 1996.

Gaventa, Beverly Roberts. *Our Mother Saint Paul*. Louisville: Westminster John Knox, 2007.

———. *When in Romans: An Invitation to Linger with the Gospel according to Paul*. Grand Rapids: Baker Academic, 2016.

Gench, Frances Taylor. *Encountering God in Tyrannical Texts: Reflections on Paul, Women, and the Authority of Scripture*. Louisville: Westminster John Knox, 2015.

Gitay, Jehoshua. "Kittim." In *HarperCollins Bible Dictionary*, edited by Mark Allan Powell, 522. Revised and updated ed. New York: HarperCollins, 2011.

Glancy, Jennifer A. *Slavery as Moral Problem in the Early Church and Today*. Facets. Minneapolis: Fortress, 2011.

———. *Slavery in Early Christianity*. Minneapolis: Fortress, 2006.

Goldie, Peter. *The Mess Inside: Narrative, Emotion, and the Mind*. Oxford: Oxford University Press, 2012.

———, ed. *The Oxford Handbook of Philosophy of Emotion*. Oxford: Oxford University Press, 2010.

Gombis, Timothy G. "Arguing with Scripture in Galatia: Galatians 3:10–14 as a Series of Ad Hoc Arguments." In *Galatians and Christian Theology: Justification, the Gospel, and Ethics in Paul's Letter*, edited by Mark W. Elliott, Scott J. Hafemann, N. T. Wright, and John Frederick, 82–90. Grand Rapids: Baker Academic, 2014.

———. "The 'Transgressor' and the 'Curse of the Law': The Logic of Paul's Argument in Galatians 2–3." *NTS* 53 (2007): 81–93.

Gorman, Michael J. *Participating in Christ: Explorations in Paul's Theology and Spirituality*. Grand Rapids: Baker Academic, 2019.

Graham, Jesse, Jonathan Haidt, Sena Koleva, Matt Motyl, Ravi Iyer, Sean P. Wojcik, and Peter H. Ditto. "Moral Foundations Theory: The Pragmatic Validity of Moral Pluralism." *Advances in Experimental Social Psychology* 47 (2013): 55–130.

Gray, Patrick. *Godly Fear: The Epistle to the Hebrews and Greco-Roman Critiques of Superstition*. Academia Biblica 16. Atlanta: Society of Biblical Literature, 2003.

———. "The Liar Paradox and the Letter to Titus." *CBQ* 69 (2007): 302–14.

Green, Gene. *Jude and 2 Peter*. Baker Exegetical Commentary on the New Testament. Grand Rapids: Baker Academic, 2008.

Green, Joel B. *Body, Soul, and Human Life: The Nature of Humanity in the Bible*. Studies in Theological Interpretation. Grand Rapids: Baker Academic, 2008.

———. *Conversion in Luke-Acts: Divine Action, Human Cognition, and the People of God.* Grand Rapids: Baker Academic, 2015.

———. "Healthcare Systems in Scripture." In *Dictionary of Scripture and Ethics*, edited by Joel B. Green, 358–60. Grand Rapids: Baker Academic, 2011.

Green, Joel B., and Lee Martin McDonald, eds. *The World of the New Testament: Cultural, Social, and Historical Contexts.* Grand Rapids: Baker Academic, 2013.

Greenberg, Moshe. "Design and Themes of Ezekiel's Program of Restoration." In *Interpreting the Prophets*, edited by James Luther Mays and Paul J. Achtemeier, 215–36. Philadelphia: Fortress, 1987.

Griffin, David Ray, John B. Cobb Jr., Richard A. Falk, and Catherine Keller. *The American Empire and the Commonwealth of God: A Political, Economic, Religious Statement.* Louisville: Westminster John Knox, 2006.

Groody, Daniel G. Introduction to *Gustavo Gutiérrez: Spiritual Writings*, edited by Daniel G. Groody, 21–43. Maryknoll, NY: Orbis Books, 2011.

Gupta, Nijay K. "1 Maccabees and Romans 14:1–15:13." In *Reading Romans in Context: Paul and Second Temple Judaism*, edited by Ben C. Blackwell, John K. Goodrich, and Jason Maston, 151–57. Grand Rapids: Zondervan Academic, 2015.

Gurtner, Daniel M. *Introducing the Pseudepigrapha of Second Temple Judaism: Message, Context, and Significance.* Grand Rapids: Baker Academic, 2020.

Haidt, Jonathan. *The Righteous Mind: Why Good People Are Divided by Politics and Religion.* New York: Vintage, 2012.

Hamid, Mohsin. *The Reluctant Fundamentalist.* Orlando, FL: Harcourt, 2007.

Hanson, K. C. "The Galilean Fishing Economy and the Jesus Tradition." *BTB* 27, no. 3 (1997): 99–111.

Harb, Gertraud. "Matthew 17.24–27 and Its Value for Historical Jesus Research." *Journal for the Study of the Historical Jesus* 8 (2010): 254–74.

Harrington, Daniel J. "2 Peter." In *1 Peter, Jude and 2 Peter*, by Donald P. Senior and Daniel J. Harrington, 227–99. Sacra Pagina 15. Collegeville, MN: Liturgical Press, 2003.

Hartin, Patrick J. *James.* Sacra Pagina 14. Collegeville, MN: Liturgical Press, 2003.

Haubner, Julianna. "11 Novels about 9/11 Worth Reading." *Off the Shelf*, September 11, 2017. https://offtheshelf.com/2017/09/11-novels-911-worth-reading/.

Haught, John F. *Making Sense of Evolution: Darwin, God, and the Drama of Life.* Louisville: Westminster John Knox, 2010.

Heim, Erin M. *Adoption in Galatians and Romans: Contemporary Metaphor Theories and the Huiothesia Metaphors.* Biblical Interpretation 153. Leiden: Brill, 2017.

———. "In Him and through Him: Adoption and Christocentric Anthropology." In *Christ and the Created Order: Perspectives from Theology, Philosophy, and Science*, edited by Andrew B. Torrance and Thomas H. McCall, 129–49. Grand Rapids: Zondervan Academic, 2018.

———. "The Inward Groaning of Adoption (Rom. 8:12–25): Recovering the Pauline Adoption Metaphor for Mothers in the Adoption Triad." In *Making Sense of Motherhood:*

Biblical and Theological Perspectives, edited by Beth M. Stovell, 65–80. Eugene, OR: Wipf & Stock, 2016.

Hicks, Richard J. "Moral Progress in Philippians: Epaphroditus' 'Near-Death Weakness' in Paul's Rhetorical Strategy." *Zeitschrift für die neutestamentliche Wissenschaft* 107 (2016): 232–65.

Hill, Craig C. *In God's Time: The Bible and the Future*. Grand Rapids: Eerdmans, 2002.

Hock, Ronald F. *The Social Context of Paul's Ministry: Tentmaking and Apostleship*. Philadelphia: Fortress, 1980.

Hockey, Katherine M. *The Role of Emotion in 1 Peter*. Society for New Testament Studies Monograph Series 173. Cambridge: Cambridge University Press, 2019.

Horrell, David G. *Solidarity and Difference: A Contemporary Reading of Paul's Ethics*. London: Bloomsbury T&T Clark, 2016.

Horrell, David G., Cherryl Hunt, and Christopher Southgate. *Greening Paul: Reading the Apostle in a Time of Ecological Crisis*. Waco: Baylor University Press, 2010.

Horsley, Richard A. *Jesus and the Spiral of Violence: Popular Jewish Resistance in Roman Palestine*. New York: Harper & Row, 1987.

Horsley, Richard A., and John S. Hanson. *Bandits, Prophets, and Messiahs: Popular Movements at the Time of Jesus*. New York: Harper & Row, 1985.

Jewett, Robert. *Romans: A Commentary*. Hermeneia. Minneapolis: Fortress, 2006.

Johnson, Elizabeth A. *Creation and the Cross: The Mercy of God for a Planet in Peril*. Maryknoll, NY: Orbis Books, 2018.

Johnson, Luke Timothy. *Constructing Paul*. Vol. 1 of *The Canonical Paul*. Grand Rapids: Eerdmans, 2020.

———. *Hebrews: A Commentary*. NTL. Louisville: Westminster John Knox, 2006.

———. *The Letter of James: A New Translation with Introduction and Commentary*. Anchor Bible 37A. New York: Doubleday, 1995.

———. *The New Testament: A Very Short Introduction*. New York: Oxford University Press, 2010.

———. *The Writings of the New Testament*. 3rd ed. Minneapolis: Fortress, 2010.

Josephus, Flavius. "Against Apion." In *The New Complete Works of Josephus*. Translated by William Whiston with commentary by Paul L. Maier. Revised and expanded ed., 937–81. Grand Rapids: Kregel, 1999.

———. *The New Complete Works of Josephus*. Translated by William Whiston with commentary by Paul L. Maier. Revised and expanded ed. Grand Rapids: Kregel, 1999.

Kartveit, Magnar. *The Origin of the Samaritans*. Supplements to Vetus Testamentum 128. Leiden: Brill, 2009.

Kasser, Rodolphe, Marvin Meyer, and Gregor Wurst, eds. *The Gospel of Judas*. Washington, DC: National Geographic, 2006.

Keener, Craig S. *Acts: An Exegetical Commentary*. Vol. 2, *3:1–14:28*. Grand Rapids: Baker Academic, 2013.

Keller, Catherine. *Facing Apocalypse: Climate, Democracy, and Other Last Chances*. Maryknoll, NY: Orbis Books, 2021.

Keltner, Dacher. *The Power Paradox: How We Gain and Lose Influence*. New York: Penguin Books, 2016.

Kloppenborg, John S. *Christ's Associations: Connecting and Belonging in the Ancient City*. New Haven: Yale University Press, 2019.

Koester, Craig R. *Symbolism in the Fourth Gospel: Meaning, Mystery, Community*. 2nd ed. Minneapolis: Fortress, 2003.

Kolenkow, Anitra Bingham. "The Literary Genre 'Testament.'" In *Early Judaism and Its Modern Interpreters*, edited by Robert A. Kraft and George W. E. Nickelsburg, 259–67. The Bible and Its Modern Interpreters. Atlanta: Scholars Press, 1986.

Lenchak, Timothy A. "The Exaltation of the Cross." *Bible Today* 57 (2019): 307–13.

Levenson, Jon D. *Resurrection and the Restoration of Israel: The Ultimate Victory of the God of Life*. New Haven: Yale University Press, 2006.

Levine, Amy-Jill. "Gospel of Matthew." In *Women's Bible Commentary*, edited by Carol A. Newsom, Sharon H. Ringe, and Jacqueline E. Lapsley, 465–77. 3rd ed. Louisville: Westminster John Knox, 2012.

———. *Sermon on the Mount: A Beginner's Guide to the Kingdom of Heaven*. Nashville: Abingdon, 2020.

Levison, Jack. *An Unconventional God: The Spirit according to Jesus*. Grand Rapids: Baker Academic, 2020.

Lewis, Nicola Denzey. "Roman Imprisonment." Bible Odyssey. https://www.bibleodyssey.org/ask-a-scholar/roman-imprisonment/.

Lightfoot, J. B. *Saint Paul's Epistles to the Colossians and to Philemon*. Rev. ed. Zondervan Commentary. Grand Rapids: Zondervan, 1959. First published 1879.

Lincoln, Abraham. "House Divided." June 16, 1858. Illinois Republican State Convention, Springfield, IL. Abraham Lincoln Online: Speeches and Writings. https://www.abraham lincolnonline.org/lincoln/speeches/house.htm.

———. "Second Inaugural Address." March 4, 1865. Website of the Lincoln Memorial, National Park Service, US Department of the Interior. https://www.nps.gov/linc/learn /historyculture/lincoln-second-inaugural.htm.

Lowe, Robert, and Tom Ziemke. "The Feeling of Action Tendencies: On the Emotional Regulation of Goal-Directed Behavior." *Frontiers in Psychology*, December 27, 2011. https://www.frontiersin.org/articles/10.3389/fpsyg.2011.00346/full.

Marchal, Joseph A. "Slaves as Wo/men and Unmen: Reflecting upon Euodia, Syntyche, and Epaphroditus in Philippi." In *The People beside Paul: The Philippian Assembly and History from Below*, edited by Joseph A. Marchal, 141–76. Early Christianity and Its Literature 17. Atlanta: SBL Press, 2015.

Martin, Dale B. *Slavery as Salvation: The Metaphor of Slavery in Pauline Christianity*. New Haven: Yale University Press, 1990.

McCullough, David. *John Adams*. New York: Touchstone, 2002.

Meier, John P. "Antioch." In *Antioch & Rome: New Testament Cradles of Catholic Christianity*, by Raymond E. Brown and John P. Meier, 11–72. London: Geoffrey Chapman, 1983.

Mermelstein, Ari. *Power and Emotion in Ancient Judaism: Community and Identity in Formation*. Cambridge: Cambridge University Press, 2021.

Middleton, Paul. *The Violence of the Lamb: Martyrs as Agents of Judgment in the Book of Revelation*. London: Bloomsbury T&T Clark, 2018.

Mitchell, Margaret M. "Peter's 'Hypocrisy' and Paul's: Two 'Hypocrites' at the Foundation of Earliest Christianity." *NTS* 58 (2012): 213–34.

Moffitt, David K. *Rethinking the Atonement: New Perspectives on Jesus's Death, Resurrection, and Ascension*. Grand Rapids: Baker Academic, 2022.

Moltmann, Jürgen. *The Crucified God: The Cross of Christ as the Foundation and Criticism of Christian Theology*. Translated by R. A. Wilson, John Bowden, and Margaret Kohl. Minneapolis: Fortress, 1993.

———. *In the End—the Beginning: The Life of Hope*. Translated by Margaret Kohl. Minneapolis: Fortress, 2004.

Moors, Agnes. "Flavors of Appraisal Theories of Emotion." *Emotion Review* 6 (2014): 303–7.

Moors, Agnes, Phoebe C. Ellsworth, Klaus R. Scherer, and Nico H. Frijda. "Appraisal Theories of Emotions: State of the Art and Future Development." *Emotion Review* 5 (2013): 119–24.

Morray-Jones, C. R. A. "Paradise Revisited (2 Cor. 12:1–12): The Jewish Mystical Background of Paul's Apostolate. Part 1: The Jewish Sources." *HTR* 86 (1993): 177–217.

———. "Paradise Revisited (2 Cor. 12:1–12): The Jewish Mystical Background of Paul's Apostolate. Part 2: Paul's Heavenly Ascent and Its Significance." *HTR* 86 (1993): 265–92.

Myers, David G. *The Pursuit of Happiness*. New York: William Morrow, 1992.

Myers, David G., and Malcolm A. Jeeves. *Psychology through the Eyes of Faith*. 2nd ed. New York: HarperCollins, 2003.

Nickelsburg, George W. E., and James C. VanderKam. *1 Enoch: A New Translation*. Minneapolis: Fortress, 2004.

Noam, Vered. "Pharisaic Halakah as Emerging from 4QMMT." In *The Pharisees*, edited by Joseph Sievers and Amy-Jill Levine, 55–79. Grand Rapids: Eerdmans, 2021.

Novakovic, Lidija. "Jews and Samaritans." In *The World of the New Testament: Cultural, Social, and Historical Contexts*, edited by Joel B. Green and Lee Martin McDonald, 207–15. Grand Rapids: Baker Academic, 2013.

Nussbaum, Martha C. *Upheavals of Thought: The Intelligence of Emotions*. Cambridge: Cambridge University Press, 2001.

Nye, Joseph S., Jr. *Soft Power: The Means to Success in World Politics*. New York: PublicAffairs, 2004.

Oliver, Isaac W. "Simon Peter Meets Simon the Tanner: The Ritual Insignificance of Tanning in Ancient Judaism." *NTS* 59 (2013): 50–60.

Painter, John. *1, 2, and 3 John*. Sacra Pagina 18. Collegeville, MN: Liturgical Press, 2002.

Palmer, Parker J. *Healing the Heart of Democracy: The Courage to Create a Politics Worthy of the Human Spirit*. San Francisco: Jossey-Bass, 2011.

Paul, Annie Murphy. *The Extended Mind: The Power of Thinking outside the Brain*. Boston: Houghton Mifflin Harcourt, 2021.

Pausanias. *Description of Greece*. Translated by W. H. S. Jones and H. A. Ormerod. Cambridge, MA: Harvard University Press, 1918.

PBS. "God in the White House." *American Experience*. https://www.pbs.org/wgbh/american experience/features/godinamerica-white-house/.

Pennebaker, James W. "Putting Stress into Words: Health, Linguistic, and Therapeutic Implications." *Behaviour Research and Therapy* 31 (1993): 539–48.

Pennebaker, James W., and Joshua M. Smyth. *Opening Up by Writing It Down: How Expressive Writing Improves Health and Eases Emotional Pain*. 3rd ed. New York: Guilford, 2016.

Peppard, Michael. *The Son of God in the Roman World: Divine Sonship in Its Social and Political Context*. New York: Oxford University Press, 2011.

Perkins, Pheme. "The Letter to the Ephesians." In *The New Interpreter's Bible*, edited by Leander E. Keck et al., 11:349–466. Nashville: Abingdon, 2000.

Pervo, Richard I. *Dating Acts: Between the Evangelists and the Apologists*. Santa Ana, CA: Polebridge, 2006.

Plamper, Jan. *The History of Emotions: An Introduction*. Translated by Keith Tribe. Emotions in History. Oxford: Oxford University Press, 2015.

Plato. *The "Republic" of Plato*. Translated by Allan Bloom. 2nd ed. New York: Basic Books, 1991.

Plutchik, Robert. "The Nature of Emotions." *American Scientist* 89 (2001): 344–50.

Powell, Mark Allan. *Introducing the New Testament: A Historical, Literary, and Theological Survey*. 2nd ed. Grand Rapids: Baker Academic, 2018.

Pregeant, Russell. *For the Healing of the Nations: A Biblical Vision*. Eugene, OR: Cascade Books, 2016.

Prinzing, Michael M. "Religion Gives Life Meaning: Can Anything Else Take Its Place?" *Psyche*, April 27, 2022. https://psyche.co/ideas/religion-gives-life-meaning-can-anything -else-take-its-place.

Pummer, Reinhard. *The Samaritans: A Profile*. Grand Rapids: Eerdmans, 2016.

———. "Was There an Altar or a Temple in the Sacred Precinct on Mt. Gerizim?" *Journal for the Study of Judaism* 47 (2016): 1–21.

Reardon, Timothy W. "'Hanging on a Tree': Deuteronomy 21.22 and the Rhetoric of Jesus' Crucifixion in Acts 5.12–42." *JSNT* 37 (2015): 407–31.

Reddy, William M. *The Navigation of Feeling: A Framework for the History of Emotions*. Cambridge: Cambridge University Press, 2001.

Reeder, Caryn A. *The Samaritan Woman's Story: Reconsidering John 4 after #ChurchToo*. Downers Grove, IL: IVP Academic, 2022.

Rhee, Helen. *Illness, Pain, and Health Care in Early Christianity*. Grand Rapids: Eerdmans, 2022.

Rossing, Barbara R. *The Rapture Exposed: The Message of Hope in the Book of Revelation*. New York: Basic Books, 2004.

Russell, James A. "Core Affect and the Psychological Construction of Emotion." *Psychological Review* 110 (2003): 145–72.

Sacks, Jonathan. *The Dignity of Difference: How to Avoid the Clash of Civilizations*. London: Continuum, 2002.

Sainsbury, R. M. *Paradoxes*. 3rd ed. Cambridge: Cambridge University Press, 2009.

Sampley, J. Paul. "The Second Letter to the Corinthians: Introduction, Commentary, and Reflections." In *The New Interpreter's Bible*, edited by Leander E. Keck et al., 11:3–180. Nashville: Abingdon, 2000.

Sawicki, Marianne. *Crossing Galilee: Architectures of Contact in the Occupied Land of Jesus*. Harrisburg, PA: Trinity Press International, 2000.

Schellenberg, Ryan S. "The Rest of Paul's Imprisonments." *Journal of Theological Studies* 69 (2018): 533–72.

Scott, J. M. "Adoption, Sonship." In *Dictionary of Paul and His Letters*, edited by Gerald F. Hawthorne, Ralph P. Martin, and Daniel G. Reid, 15–18. Downers Grove, IL: InterVarsity, 1993.

Segal, Alan F. *Paul the Convert: The Apostolate and Apostasy of Saul the Pharisee*. New Haven: Yale University Press, 1990.

———. *Rebecca's Children: Judaism and Christianity in the Roman World*. Cambridge, MA: Harvard University Press, 1986.

Senior, Donald P. "1 Peter." In *1 Peter, Jude and 2 Peter*, by Donald P. Senior and Daniel J. Harrington, 1–158. Sacra Pagina 15. Collegeville, MN: Liturgical Press, 2003.

Serri, Mirella. "Dear Trump, Better to Live One Day as a Sheep Than a Hundred as Mussolini." *Huffington Post*, March 1, 2016. https://www.huffpost.com/entry/dear-trump-better-to-live_b_9355864.

Shutt, R. J. H. "Letter of Aristeas." In *The Old Testament Pseudepigrapha*, vol. 2, edited by James H. Charlesworth, 7–34. London: Darton, Longman & Todd, 1985.

Siegel, Daniel J. *Mind: A Journey to the Heart of Being Human*. New York: Norton, 2017.

Silva, Moisés. *Biblical Words and Their Meaning: An Introduction to Lexical Semantics*. Rev. and exp. ed. Grand Rapids: Zondervan, 1994.

Skinner, Matthew L. "Prison." In *The New Interpreter's Dictionary of the Bible*, edited by Katherine Doob Sakenfeld et al., 4:615. Nashville: Abingdon, 2009.

Slaby, Jan. "Emotions and the Extended Mind." In *Collective Emotions: Perspectives from Psychology, Philosophy, and Sociology*, edited by Christian von Scheve and Mikko Salmela, 32–46. Oxford: Oxford University Press, 2014.

Spaeth, Barbara Stanley. "Imperial Cult in Roman Corinth: A Response to Karl Galinsky's 'The Cult of the Roman Emperor: Uniter or Divider?'" In *Rome and Religion: A*

Cross-Disciplinary Dialogue on the Imperial Cult, edited by Jeffrey Brodd and Jonathan L. Reed, 61–81. Writings from the Greco-Roman World Supplement Series 5. Atlanta: Society of Biblical Literature, 2011.

Spencer, F. Scott. "Beyond Trench's Study of Synonyms: Distinguishing New Testament Synonyms for 'Patience.'" *Expository Times* 99 (1988): 140–44.

———. *Dancing Girls, "Loose" Ladies, and Women of "the Cloth": The Women in Jesus' Life.* New York: Continuum, 2004.

———. "The Ethiopian Eunuch and His Bible: A Social-Science Analysis." *BTB* 22 (1992): 155–65.

———. "Feminist Criticism." In *Hearing the New Testament: Strategies for Interpretation*, edited by Joel B. Green, 289–325. 2nd ed. Grand Rapids: Eerdmans, 2010.

———. *The Gospel of Luke and Acts of the Apostles.* Interpreting Biblical Texts. Nashville: Abingdon, 2008.

———. *Journeying through Acts: A Literary-Cultural Reading.* Peabody, MA: Hendrickson, 2004.

———. *Luke.* Two Horizons New Testament Commentaries. Grand Rapids: Eerdmans, 2019.

———. "Metaphor, Mystery, and the Salvation of Israel in Romans 9–11: Paul's Appeal to Humility and Doxology." *Rev&Exp* 103 (2006): 113–38.

———. *Passions of the Christ: The Emotional Life of Jesus.* Grand Rapids: Baker Academic, 2021.

———. *Reading Mark: A Literary and Theological Commentary.* Reading the New Testament, 2nd series. Macon, GA: Smyth & Helwys, 2023.

———. *Salty Wives, Spirited Mothers, and Savvy Widows: Capable Women of Purpose and Persistence in Luke's Gospel.* Grand Rapids: Eerdmans, 2012.

———. "Scripture, Hermeneutics, and Matthew's Jesus." *Interpretation* 64 (2010): 368–78.

———. "Song of Songs as Political Satire and Emotional Refuge: Subverting Solomon's Gilded Regime." *Journal for the Study of the Old Testament* 44 (2020): 667–92.

———. *What Did Jesus Do? Gospel Profiles of Jesus' Personal Conduct.* Harrisburg, PA: Trinity Press International, 2003.

Stendahl, Krister. "The Apostle Paul and the Introspective Conscience of the West." *HTR* 56 (1963): 199–215.

Stenschke, Christoph. "Obstacles on All Sides: Paul's Collection for the Saints in Jerusalem. Part 1." *EuroJTh* 24 (2015): 19–32.

———. "Obstacles on All Sides: Paul's Collection for the Saints in Jerusalem. Part 2." *EuroJTh* 25 (2016): 6–17.

Stevenson, Kalina Rose. *The Vision of Transformation: The Territorial Rhetoric of Ezekiel 40–48.* Society of Biblical Literature Dissertation Series 154. Atlanta: Scholars Press, 1996.

Sumney, Jerry L. *Colossians: A Commentary.* NTL. Louisville: Westminster John Knox, 2008.

Tannehill, Robert C. *The Narrative Unity of Luke-Acts: A Literary Interpretation.* Vol. 2 of *The Acts of the Apostles.* Minneapolis: Fortress, 1990.

Tavris, Carol, and Elliot Aronson. *Mistakes Were Made (but Not by Me): Why We Justify Foolish Beliefs, Bad Decisions, and Hurtful Acts.* Rev. and exp. ed. Boston: Mariner, 2020.

Thiessen, Matthew. *A Jewish Paul: The Messiah's Herald to the Gentiles*. Grand Rapids: Baker Academic, 2023.

Tillich, Paul. *The Courage to Be*. 2nd ed. New Haven: Yale University Press, 2000. First published 1952.

Towles, Amor. *The Lincoln Highway*. New York: Viking, 2021.

Tversky, Barbara. *Mind in Motion: How Action Shapes Thought*. New York: Basic Books, 2019.

UNESCO. "Mount Gerizim and the Samaritans." https://whc.unesco.org/en/tentativelists /5706/.

Vermes, Geza. *The Complete Dead Sea Scrolls in English*. 7th ed. London: Penguin Books, 2011.

Volf, Miroslav. *Exclusion and Embrace: A Theological Exploration of Identity, Otherness, and Reconciliation*. Nashville: Abingdon, 1996.

Wall, Robert W. "Simon 'Son' of Jonah: The Conversion of Peter in the Context of Canon." *JSNT* 29 (1987): 79–90.

Wallis, Jim. *God's Politics: Why the Right Gets It Wrong and the Left Doesn't Get It*. New York: HarperCollins, 2005.

Weil, Simone. *Gravity and Grace*. Translated by Arthur Wills. Lincoln: University of Nebraska Press, 1997. First published 1952.

Welborn, L. L. *Paul, the Fool of Christ: A Study of 1 Corinthians 1–4 in the Comic-Philosophic Tradition*. London: Bloomsbury Academic, 2005.

———. *Paul's Summons to Messianic Life: Political Theology and the Coming Awakening*. Insurrections. New York: Columbia University Press, 2015.

Wenham, David. *Paul: Follower of Jesus or Founder of Christianity?* Grand Rapids: Eerdmans, 1995.

Wiggins, Grant, and Jay McTighe. *Understanding by Design*. 2nd ed. Alexandria, VA: Association for Supervision and Curriculum Development, 2005.

Willson, Mary A. "'Cursed Is Everyone Who Is Hanged on a Tree': Paul's Citation of Deut. 21:23 in Gal. 3:13." *Trinity Journal* 36 (2015): 217–40.

Wilson, Brittany. *The Embodied God: Seeing the Divine in Luke-Acts and the Early Church*. New York: Oxford University Press, 2021.

———. *Unmanly Men: Reconfigurations of Masculinity in Luke-Acts*. Oxford: Oxford University Press, 2015.

World Trade Organization. "The General Agreement on Tariffs and Trade (GATT 1947)." https://www.wto.org/english/docs_e/legal_e/gatt47_01_e.htm.

Wright, N. T. *Into the Heart of Romans: A Deep Dive into Paul's Greatest Letter*. Grand Rapids: Zondervan Academic, 2023.

Zangenberg, Jürgen. Review of *The Keepers: An Introduction to the History and Culture of the Samaritans*, by Robert T. Anderson and Terry Giles. *Review of Biblical Literature* 6 (2004): 357–60.

Zerilli, John. *The Adaptable Mind: What Neuroplasticity and Neural Reuse Tell Us about Language and Cognition*. New York: Oxford University Press, 2021.

Scripture and Ancient Writings Index

Subject Index

214